SMART
CITIES

THAT WORK FOR EVERYONE

SMART CITIES

THAT WORK FOR EVERYONE

7 Keys to Education & Employment

TOM VANDER ARK with **MARY RYERSE**

GETTING SMART
Think. Learn. Innovate.

Published by **Getting Smart**
1600B SW Dash Point Rd #311
Federal Way, WA 98023
www.gettingsmart.com

Getting Smart is an imprint of

 Eifrig Publishing ʟʟᴄ
PO Box 66, Lemont, PA 16851, USA
Knobelsdorffstr. 44, 14059 Berlin, Germany
www.eifrigpublishing.com

For information regarding permissions, write to:
editor@gettingsmart.com

Library of Congress Cataloging-in-Publication Data

Vander Ark, Tom
    Smart Cities that Work for Everyone / by Tom Vander Ark.
        p.   cm.

Paperback: ISBN 978-1-63233-034-5
Ebook: ISBN 978-1-63233-033-8

        1. Education 2. Schools & Teaching
        I. Vander Ark, Tom, II. Title.

19 18 17 16 2015
5 4 3 2 1

Printed on acid-free paper. ∞

TABLE OF CONTENTS

Foreword:
Kevin Johnson, Mayor of Sacramento

I grew up in the low-income community of Oak Park in Sacramento, California, where I attended public schools that did not prepare me for the rigors of college. Fortunately, I was a talented athlete, and basketball was my ticket out of poverty. Unfortunately, when I arrived at college on scholarship I was ill-prepared. I needed remediation, and, frankly, was confused about how I could be a solid student after my time in the K-12 system.

That experience infuriated me and drove me to begin work to ensure that no child from my neighborhood ever had that experience. In 1989, I started an after-school program called St. HOPE Academy, which sought to revitalize the community through education, economic development, the arts and civic leadership. In 2002, we went further when my high school alma mater, Sacramento High School, was threatened with state takeover for academic failure. We embarked on an effort to restructure the school as a charter school.

I met Tom Vander Ark during the Sac High conversion process—which turned out to be more challenging than either of us had anticipated. We both understood the importance of good schools to the health of cities. But we underestimated the tremendous pushback that we'd get from people who wanted to maintain the status quo. Today, St. HOPE operates a pre-Kindergarten through 12th grade public school system in Sacramento that serves more than 1,700 students. We are proud to say that our schools are among the highest performing in the city.

Smart Cities

My vision since being elected mayor of Sacramento in 2008 has been to make Sacramento "a city that works for everyone." To that end, my team has mobilized volunteers, improved public art, attacked homelessness, slowed gang violence and encouraged the city to Think Big with regard to economic development. We launched Stand UP to promote education innovation and Sacramento READS! to boost literacy. We collaborate with the school district to align city services to maximize resources to support public education.

As outlined in the chapter on leadership, education and civic leaders should work together to build a portfolio of compelling schools and programs. School report cards should provide parents and families with information on education options. As outlined in the chapter on talent development, cities should create partnerships to develop great teachers and leaders.

I've been pleased to learn that many mayors share my passion for education and understand its importance to the future of their city. The United States Conference of Mayors (USCM), where I serve as president, has established as a national goal that every student should graduate from high school ready for college and career, regardless of income, race, ethnic or language background, or disability status. This college and career readiness is to be achieved in part by expanding linked learning approaches, including college preparation, career and technical education, and work-based learning.

At the 2014 UCSM annual conference, U.S. mayors passed resolutions aligned with the recommendations in this book, including:

- Equitable access to quality early learning;
- Investing in youth jobs and career and financial education;
- Creating cities of learning, where students earn digital badges to connect in- and out-of-school learning;

- Supporting the implementation of Common Core State Standards (CCSS) with rigorous and comparable assessments;
- Increasing the talent and diversity of the teaching profession;
- Supporting the College Scorecard and processes that support assessing college ratings, affordability and related career implications;
- Strengthening career pathways, expanding apprenticeships and providing access to good middle class jobs; and
- Closing the skills gap to reduce unemployment and ensure employees have skills necessary to work in high-demand fields.

Alongside mayors, faith leaders, civil rights advocates and business executives all have a role to play to level the playing field and extend opportunity to all children. If we expect our educators to create a demanding but supportive environment for students, we need to create the same sort of high-demand, high-support environment for education leaders.

It's clear—you can't have a great city without great schools. If you want to reduce crime and poverty, you need a good education system—it's the great equalizer, it's the passport, it's the civil rights issue of our time.

Smart Cities

Foreword:
Adrian Fenty, Former Mayor of Washington, D.C.

In the *The Race between Education and Technology*, Claudia Goldin and Lawrence Katz argued that "rising educational attainment is the number one driver of prosperity and declining inequality—and U.S. attainment stalled 30 years ago. Other nations have raced by us, often with newer and better education systems. High skills or low wages have become the reality." They concluded that our future success depends on a profound breakthrough in educating our kids.

When I was elected mayor of the District of Columbia in 2007, we had in mind the "profound breakthrough" that Goldin and Katz described. Test scores in the District were among the lowest in the country. On my first day in office, we introduced legislation to take control of our public schools. It was a bold idea and part of a hands-on approach to city government. Chancellor Michelle Rhee quickly implemented new talent development strategies and set to work on building a performance-oriented culture. The changes caused controversy, but they quickly boosted academic results.

In this global economy, talent development is job one for mayors. It starts with quality early learning, it includes great K-12 schools—the feeder system of a city—and adult learning and higher education linked to emerging job clusters.

In addition to the progress we made in education, my administration also built new parks, opened low-income housing, and made the District a safer place to live. New retail developments brought new jobs. It is this sort of "full-court press" that is necessary to revitalize our cities and boost education-based mobility.

For a mayor, talent development also includes creating leadership opportunities for locals and attracting super-smart, innovative people from all over—people who see changing the world as a life mission. City government is a vital service, but it also can be an exciting and challenging working environment.

In this new economy, cities must be pro-innovation and pro-people. As Tom points out in this book, cities can do both by supporting job creation and by making learning a priority. Everyone deserves a supported on-ramp to the innovation economy. That means equitable early learning, great K-12 options, affordable and relevant job training, and vibrant universities.

As a venture investor and business adviser, I appreciate the role of startups and growth companies more than ever. Not every city can and should be Silicon Valley, but every city can leverage local assets and create a vital job formation climate.

Great cities work for everyone. As noted in this book, great cities take sustained leadership, impact-focused partnerships, and aligned investments. What may be most important in the long run is that great cities will feature great learning opportunities. Great cities help everyone learn.

Foreword:
Michele Cahill, Carnegie Corporation

Educators have heard the good news this year that the United States has for the first time reached a high school graduation rate of 80 percent, with gains in large urban districts and among African American and Latino students as significant contributing factors. Reactions to this achievement have been mixed, ranging from celebration to cautious optimism to dismissal, the latter due to recognition that graduation does not equal college readiness, particularly for low-income students. At a time when earnings are tracking so closely with educational achievement and income inequality is growing, our young people will depend more than ever on schools to prepare them with the meaningful knowledge and skills needed for success in postsecondary education and careers. Without effective high schools, the social contract with young people that lies at the heart of the American dream—invest in yourself, work hard and learn, and you will have opportunities for rewarding work and meaningful choices about your future—is clearly at risk. While there are broader, non-education factors involved in our country's high rates of child poverty and growing inequality that need to be addressed, the stakes are high and the need is urgent for redesigning our high schools. We need to ask, as rigorously as we can, what it will take to get to 90 percent graduation rates *with college readiness* in the coming decade.

Fortunately, we have existing proof points that it is indeed possible to provide adolescents—even those who enter high school substantially behind—with an academically challenging curriculum and accelerated learning that enable them to catch up, get on track and graduate ready to succeed in postsecondary education. Greg Duncan and Richard Murnane write about

"High Schools That Improve Life Chances" in their recent book, _Restoring Opportunity: The Crisis of Inequality and the Challenge for American Education_, which profiles the New York City Small Schools of Choice initiative and its evaluation results. The evidence they cite is highly encouraging, especially now that researchers from MIT and Duke have confirmed the original findings of the social policy research organization MDRC and are identifying positive outcomes in students' first years of college.

Looking to implications for the country, the question is, "What will it take to do this at scale?" As someone involved in the New York City Small Schools of Choice initiative work and in high school reform more generally, and with more than forty years of experience in K-12 and higher education, youth development, and the nonprofit, government and philanthropy sectors behind me, I have come to see that an _ecosystem for learning_ is essential; moreover, design thinking is essential for creating this ecosystem and for enabling it to work at scale. An ecosystem draws in energy and contributions from a broad base of leadership, including educators, advocates, policy makers, philanthropy, government and civic voices. To be effective, their efforts must be rooted in common design principles that guide them in creating good secondary schools that significantly improve life chances.

At the heart of an ecosystem for learning is an ability to draw upon the assets of an entire city or community to support students as they grapple with the two primary tasks of adolescence: building competencies and forming their identities. In New York City, this involved a competitive design process rooted in common principles informed by research about teaching, learning, the organization of schools, and youth development and resiliency. Educators who proposed schools had to engage in a rigorous planning and approval process, and their plans had to demonstrate the capacity to put in place core elements: strong and capable school leadership; a school culture that promoted positive youth development through caring relationships, high expectations for all students, and student voice and contributions; high-quality teaching across disciplines; accountability for all students; an academically strong curriculum; and parent and community engagement. Only teams that met these criteria were approved to open schools.

Where does the ecosystem come in? To meet these challenging criteria, we needed to redefine "school" as a porous organization and redefine "partnership" as a core design element, not an add-on. When partnership is a core element of school design, students have opportunities for relationships with adults and experiences that literally expand the world that is well-known to them through connections with cultural organizations, professional and business settings, science and technical organizations, or community services. Students have opportunities to take on new roles and try out identities that can motivate them and build confidence and effort. Partnerships that are designed as core to schooling also can expand and deepen curriculum through themes, Project-Based Learning, internships, student research and expeditions.

Design thinking gives real roles to partner organizations in a learning ecosystem. New approaches are pushing the boundaries, as digital and blended learning open up new opportunities for educators to think creatively about how to credit student work accomplished outside a traditional classroom in an expanded learning time framework. From an equity perspective, building an ecosystem that affords access to learning opportunities that extend and enrich academics is highly promising, as economically advantaged families are dramatically increasing their investments in student talent-building activities and experiences in out-of-school time.

Moving this agenda in a time of tight budgets and high standards is challenging. Yet it can be a powerful strategy for increasing student engagement and effort, for supporting teachers in meeting college-ready standards, and, most of all, for tapping the extra capacity we will need to get to college readiness at scale].

 Michele Cahill on Smart Cities

Smart Cities

Preface

Cities, some would argue, are the world's greatest inventions, bringing productivity and opportunity to billions. But for many, cities are a hellhole of poverty and violence offering no visible way out. While sociologists have studied cities for years, a new generation of technologists, systems thinkers, and sustainability advocates is taking a fresh look at living together in close proximity. There are a number of interesting new hypotheses about how cities should evolve to be more livable and sustainable, including efforts to build density, speed transport, reduce consumption, boost employment and raise wages. In the long run, what will matter most is learning.

Now that anyone can learn almost anything anywhere there is a broadband connection, digital tools and networks are changing our assumptions about human development and changing the opportunity set for individuals and communities. As the subtitle of my book *Getting Smart* suggested, personal digital learning is changing the world.

With the shift from print to digital well underway, it was becoming obvious that new tools and new school models were being developed and adopted in some places much more quickly than others. The Smart Cities project was launched to investigate the civic formula required to dramatically boost learning outcomes and employability and, as Mayor Johnson suggested, create cities that work for everyone.

This project set out to explore questions in these five areas:

- Where do innovations in learning occur? What are the drivers of innovation? How and why are innovations incorporated by formal systems of education? How do innovations in learning spread? What role do incentives and barriers play?

- Why is K-12 education in America susceptible to superficial fads but resistant to best practice sharing and fundamental innovations?
- Why are some cities improving learning opportunities and outcomes and some are not? What should learning and civic leaders do to rapidly boost learning and employment opportunities and outcomes?
- What role does state and federal policy play in encouraging or blocking improvement and innovation?
- Can the learning sector be a job creator? Does every city need an incubator and education technology (EdTech) fund or will these capabilities naturally cluster? What should every city do now?

With this ambitious list of questions in mind, the crowdsourced Smart Cities blog series was launched in 2012 to catalog the innovations in learning in America's great cities. Hundreds of people contributed this this broad but rather informal investigation. In the spring of 2014, more than 60 thought leaders were invited to contribute to this book project.

My preparation for this project included five years as an executive for a public company, five years as a public school superintendent, seven years as an instructor in finance, strategy, and leadership in two MBA programs, six years as a partner in the leading education venture fund, and philanthropic sponsorship of 1,200 new schools, 400 nonprofit organizations, and school improvement efforts in three dozen very challenging urban environments. The Getting Smart team has, in the last few years, published 33 papers, several books, and more than 5,000 blogs on related topics. The point of this immodesty is that the subject of innovations in learning is a long-time interest, and the conclusions derived through this widespread but informal process are well grounded in success and failure on a large scale in several sectors. A clear, although not simple, premise emerged as seven keys to smart cities.

Premise. As the majority of the world's population becomes urban, cities must become centers of learning for young and old. Every person, organization and region needs to get smart— to skill up, learn more and build new capacities faster and cheaper than ever. In the long run, education is *the* economic development agenda.

Innovative new tools and schools are making it possible for individuals, organizations and cities to boost learning outcomes. Most learning innovations occur in what this book will call "ecosystems"—and these unique environments begin with a handful of people with an innovation mindset. This combination of persistence, entrepreneurship and a collaborative focus on impact can be taught in every classroom and encouraged in every city.

Following forewords from two remarkable city leaders and one lifelong advocate for youth development, and then introductions to the concepts of smart cities and next generation learning, this book focuses on the seven keys to education and employment: Innovation Mindset, Sustained Leadership, Talent Development, Collective Impact, Aligned Investment, New Tools and Schools, and Advocacy and Policy.

This book is intended to serve as an outline for regional action and investment, a guide for philanthropic and venture investment, a blueprint for civic entrepreneurs and Edupreneurs, and a signal to educators of where the sector is headed.

Using this book. To help readers navigate the chapters and make the most of the information, there are chapter signposts to help denote certain features:

Education Vignettes appear at the beginning of each chapter and feature a person or school making a difference toward each of the seven smart cities keys.

Blog Boxes appear throughout the book and contain blog excerpts connected to the focus of the chapter.

Video Hangout Links appear in each chapter and include one or more video recordings of a discussion between the author and contributors.

Chapter Summaries appear at the end of each chapter, denoted with the related key's badge, and present main points.

The intent of this book is to provide a framework for action and tools for implementation. To that end, the following supplemental resources are referenced in the book and can be accessed through the Appendices:

- **Contributor Blog Posts.** This book features over 55 contributors, most of whom submitted a blog that, in addition to being excerpted in this book in the form of a quote or a "blog box," was featured on GettingSmart. com. Links to the complete blogs, along with contributor bios, are featured in Appendix A.

- **Video Hangout Recordings.** To bring the content within each key to life, some of the contributors were interviewed via Google Hangout. Links to the 10 to 12 minute recordings of these interviews are noted by icon in the book and also listed alongside the relevant author bio.

- **City Blog Posts.** Blogs highlighting promising education, EdTech, partnership, investment and innovation practices have been written and updated for 25 cities. These are listed in Appendix B and accessed via GettingSmart.com.

- **Entity URLs.** A summary of URLs for the websites of organizations referenced in this book is included in Appendix C.

- **Asset Mapping Template.** A blank template to facilitate local asset mapping regarding the seven keys to smart cities has been provided in Appendix D.

- **Additional Resources.** Additional information and useful tools have been provided in Appendix E.

Acknowledgements

More than five dozen thought leaders wrote blogs in the Smart Cities series; excerpts of most of them appear in text boxes in each chapter. They are all listed in Appendix A with links to their full published posts. While we appreciate these valuable blogs, each of these leaders has made *quality learning at scale* their life mission and passion—and it is their lifetime contribution for which we are most grateful.

Among these thought leaders, particular thanks go to Michele Cahill and Leah Hamilton. We've collaborated for 15 years on America's thorniest education challenges, and I deeply appreciate their attention to poverty and youth development. A grant from Carnegie Corporation made this book possible.

Project manager and editor Mary Ryerse assembled the giant Google Doc that became this book. She hosted dozens of Google Hangouts and edited dozens of blog posts. She lived through rewrites and reorgs and prompted more than a few herself. She learned a lot about publishing and taught many lessons on managing. Passionate about the topic, pleasant in adversity, a better partner for this adventure I could not have found.

My colleagues at Getting Smart have been helpful and patient in this effort, particularly my writing partner Carri Schneider— we've written 3 dozen papers together describing the future of learning and many of them are referenced in this book. Karen, Caroline and Katie, my wife and daughters, are great partners on this mission to accelerate innovations in learning. Their support during a two-year personal learning exploration of cities made this project possible. Thank you Kambra Bolch for copyediting, Kelley Tanner for design, and Penelope Eifrig and Laura Nadler for publishing support.

Smart Cities

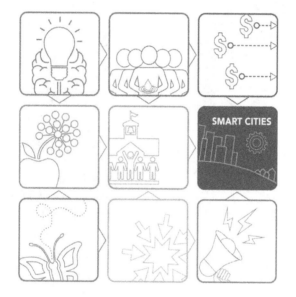

Cities That Work for Everyone

Teacher Innovator:
Andrew Coy

Teacher Andrew Coy left what was supposed to be the most innovative high school in Baltimore frustrated with the pace of change and the inability to create current and compelling learning experiences. With persistence, he gained control of a recreation center abandoned by the city and created the Digital Harbor Foundation. The rec-center-turned-tech-center hosts before, during and after school learning experiences. With the chamber of commerce, county, investors and other Edupreneurs, Andrew sparked a new conversation and created the initiative EdTech.MD to promote innovations in learning, support convening, and grow human and financial capital. This wave of Baltimore entrepreneurship builds on 20 years of national EdTech leadership from companies including Connections Education and Sylvan Learning, as well as investors like New Markets Venture Partners, but until recently there were limited links to local schools and teachers. The explosion of EdTech apps, investments and events in this decade is finally making the connection with teachers. In June 2014, only 18 months after opening, Coy and Digital Harbor Foundation launched a national technical assistance center to help other communities replicate the nonprofit's innovative maker programs.

"America is a country that is now utterly divided when it comes to its society, its economy, its politics," said David Simon, creator of the HBO hit series The Wire. "There are definitely two Americas. I live in one, on one block in Baltimore that is part of the viable America, the America that is connected to its own economy, where there is a plausible future for the people born into it. About 20 blocks away is another America entirely." Simon said capitalism has lost sight of its social compact.[1]

Like every American city, Baltimore works remarkably well for some and is home to generational poverty for others— often, as Simon said, in close proximity. In a world where everything that can be automated will be, where creativity and productivity are rewarded, the American divide is between two groups with different skills, mindsets and resources. Andrew Coy is bridging the gap between African American young people growing up in poverty and Baltimore's mostly white entrepreneurs and investors by providing tools and experiences that help young people prepare to participate in the innovation economy.

"The most important pillar behind innovation and opportunity—education—will see tremendous positive change in the coming decades," said Eric Schmidt and Jared Cohen, "as rising connectivity reshapes traditional routines and offers new paths for learning."[2] Coy's iconoclastic shift from a traditional education role to an entrepreneurial role in a new organization signals the development of a new opportunity set represented by the shift from print to digital, from annual to instant feedback, and from fixed facilities and schedules to flexible and mobile learning. The premise, expressed perfectly by Coy, is that "[e]ducation is the single most important investment any community of any size can make in its future."[3]

Why Cities?

More than half the world's population currently lives in cities, and more than 60 percent will by 2030.[4] Urbanization of the planet demands that we learn more about making cities work for everyone. People all over the world are leaving farmland and flocking to cities where they see more opportunity and a stronger safety net. "Cities attract poor people with a promise of a better life," said Harvard economics professor Ed Glaeser. In _Triumph of the City: How Our Greatest Invention Makes Us Richer, Smarter, Greener, Healthier, and Happier_, Glaeser makes a compelling case that the city is humanity's greatest creation and our best hope for the future.

"The successful cities of the 21st century are marked by three things, smart people, small firms and connections to the outside world," Glaeser told CNN's Fareed Zakaria.[5] He continued, "Smart people are able to use the density, to learn from one another and, of course, connections to the outside world are what cities are all about."

While state policy creates context, it is counties, cities and school districts that determine the learning options available to families. They also provide or influence access to youth and family services, another important component of a healthy learning ecosystem. "We're the level of government closest to the majority of the world's people," said former New York City Mayor Michael Bloomberg, continuing, "While nations talk, but too often drag their heels—cities act."[6]

The term *smart cities* has come to refer to effective tools and practices for livable cities. As their website states, the Smart Cities Council envisions "a world where digital technology and intelligent design have been harnessed to create smart, sustainable cities with high-quality living and high-quality jobs." Their work promotes livability, workability and sustainability; this book will show that learnability should be added to the equation. In the long run, the capacity to prepare a large percentage of the population for the idea economy will be the most important economic metric—and it is likely to correlate to social progress and happiness.

The secret to cities: skill-up and startup. Cities are employ-ment and retail hubs and distinct media markets. They may share retail chains and radio formats with other cities, but many have a distinctive vibe. With a few data points and site visits, it is often possible to sense positive momentum—job growth, expanding amenities and a vibrant cultural scene—or decline.

A dozen years ago Richard Florida suggested in *The Rise of the Creative Class* that the clustering of highly capable people in amenity-rich, tolerant cities would benefit all inhabitants of cities generally through a trickle-down effect. It was a fresh look at economic development that continues to influence the urban dialogue. Fitting Florida's hypothesis, most venture funding and new technology come from the Bay Area or New York. But critics note that efforts to create "cool" districts appealing to urbanites fail to benefit a wider circle or stem inequities.[7] Even when benefits are felt, they tend to be limited to economic growth without social progress. Despite what Florida's critics argue, however, some cities experience network effects, a web of variables contributing in positive ways toward progress and opportunity, while other cities see a negative spiral. There may be something to Florida's formula after all—Coy's creative spark suggests that a "clustering of highly capable people" can change the options and attitudes in a city.

Going forward, the capacity to support skill-up and startups will be key to economic development. Every city in the world shares the need to make rapid, broad-based improvement in employment-related skills. That should make education—from early learning to job training—a top regional priority. And rather than chasing big new factories with exorbitant incentives, most cities will fare better by attending to the climate for small and medium enterprise. Underscoring this point while speaking on July 14, 2014, at the National Governors Association meeting, Stephen Rohleder, North America Chief Executive at Accenture urged, "It is important to aggregate the needs of small and medium sized business because in most communities that's where the jobs are coming."

Why Learning Matters to Cities

Despite three generations of dominance in global trade and breathtaking wealth creation for the business elite, social progress has slowed in America. Life, health and opportunity are better for the average person in many other countries, which is the tough truth told by the "Social Progress Index 2014 Report." "Economic growth without social progress results in lack of inclusion, discontent, and social unrest," according to the report co-authored by Harvard economist and business adviser Michael Porter. The report recommends "twin scorecards of success" where "social progress sits alongside economic prosperity."[8] The U.S. ranks second on GDP per capita but is 16th on the Social Progress list with a score bolstered by access to advanced education but penalized by poor health outcomes (70th despite spending more than any country), weak access to basic knowledge (39th place on factors including high school enrollment and adult literacy), and surprisingly weak access to information and communication (23rd on indicators including cell phone subscriptions).[9] The report underscores the importance of a social contract that ensures shelter and nutrition, as well as access to health services and quality education.

"An economy's ability to grow over time—its ability to innovate and raise both productivity and real incomes—is strongly tied to the quality of education provided to the vast majority of workers," said Stanford economist Eric Hanushek. "Skills and intellectual capital are increasingly important in a modern economy, and schools play a central role in the development of valuable skills."[10]

Hanushek further asserts that it is not simply attainment levels that matter, saying, "[H]igher levels of cognitive skill appear to play a major role in explaining international differences in economic growth."[11] He calculates that "a highly skilled workforce can raise economic growth by about two-thirds of a percentage point every year."[12] And that demands a concentration on both opportunities for the "best and brightest" and make sure that "no child is left behind."[13]

Recognized education leaders like Houston Independent School District Superintendent Terry Grier realize that the talent development flows both ways—schools must prepare young people to participate in the economy and talented teachers make that happen. "Houston ISD ... partners with local employers, businesses, and industries—medicine, energy, computer technology, space, arts and humanities, Tier One educational and research institutions—in a reinvention of elementary through secondary education that blends academic rigor with preparation for higher education and career."[14] Grier continues by stressing that "our 21st century campuses are only as good as the principals who lead them and the teachers who create magic in each classroom." Over the last five years HISD embraced a sophisticated talent development strategy and school improvement strategies gleaned from the best networks and updated to include technology enhanced learning. Houston won the 2013 Broad Prize, a recognition of the large urban school district that has made the greatest improvement in student achievement in recent years. The unexpected resurgence of oil and gas boosted the Houston economy, but it will be quality education that sustains it.

Findings. The two-year Smart Cities investigation observed islands of improvement (*e.g.*, traditional schools executing at a high level) and innovation (*e.g.*, new learning formats producing strong results) in cities large and small nationwide, and there was always evidence of effective and sustained leadership, collaborative partnerships and focused investment.

The Smart Cities posts also cataloged the rapid development of new learning tools—platforms, applications, devices—funded by a flood of grants and venture investment. There was little correlation between cities improving learning outcomes and cities where new tools were developed. Startups producing new EdTech tools are almost exclusively located in technology hubs including the Bay Area, New York and Chicago, where they have access to talent and investment. Insulation and resilience of educational institutions made proximity to technology innovation a weak predictor of innovations in learning. For example, among a thousand of the world's most innovative companies, Bay Area schools, with few exceptions, remain very traditional. In education, "a good idea won't walk across the street."

However, there are signs of new connections yielding a strong hypothesis: cities that nourish new tools and new learning models, that connect teachers and technology, will provide better learning opportunities and more productive economies. The emerging EdTech ecosystems in New Orleans exhibit a productive link between technology development and school development. In New York and Chicago, short cycle trials are creating links between teachers and tools.[15] Incubators (usually nonprofit support organizations) and accelerators (incubators with venture aims and seed funding) are popping up around the country, providing support to EdTech startups and making connections with local schools.

Next generation learning environments and new connections between Edupreneurs and teachers are beginning to influence policy and investment. "Looking ahead, innovative models are poised to pave the way for additional, dramatic policy shifts," said policy advocate and school entrepreneur Joe Ableidinger.[16] He sees testing, student progress and educator evaluation becoming "more malleable policy issues as the implementation of new models continues to demonstrate promising, workable alternatives." In other words, schools that work better for students and teachers serve as proof points for updated policies.

Vibrant cities have a portfolio of quality educational options. For the last two decades, that simply meant good local schools, but the learning revolution is expanding the opportunity set every month. We are living through a shift from education as a place down the street to learning as bundle of personal digital services that are engaging, customized, mobile and flexible. For most young people, there will be a place called school, but learning will not be limited to what is offered there. Young and old will increasingly learn based on interest and need, when and how they want, for free or inexpensively; they will have learning partners that queue opportunities in productive modalities; they will utilize their learning for the common good through civic engagement; they will demonstrate and signal learning with certificates, artifacts and references. Vibrant cities will lead with learning.

The Challenges of Reform

Though it is clear that learning matters to cities, the path to reform may not be so clear. Diana Lam's story typifies the urban oscillations of the last two decades. After bringing a turnaround to schools in San Antonio, the political tables turned on her and she took her passion for change to the Providence Schools in 1998. In her second year, her promising plan earned Providence the first big district grant from a national foundation. Three years later, both test scores and tempers were elevated; Lam left Providence and joined Joel Klein as the top educator in New York City.[17] After a controversy-filled 18 months, she was out in New York. Lam's career has paralleled the political cycles that have brought reform and reversion to cities like Providence.

And even when reform does happen, it may not take root, at least close to home. When Lam arrived in Providence, Dennis Littky and Elliot Washor were working with the sophomore class at The Metropolitan Regional Career and Technical Center, informally referred to as "the MET," the first student-centered high school in the Big Picture Learning network. The MET opened in the lower level of the Rhode Island Department of Education (RIDE) with permission from farsighted state chief of education Peter McWalters. Instead of traditional classes, the innovative model high school focused on internships and projects. Big Picture won a big Gates Foundation grant to replicate the model. In doing so, Littky and Washor influenced educators worldwide—but few close to home. Like High Tech High in San Diego, the MET is more widely appreciated internationally than locally, more evidence that in education, good ideas "won't walk across the street."

Providence schools continue to struggle with a traditional, bureaucratically imposed agenda and remain largely hostile to outside options. But their teachers and students are finding and deploying new tools. Nonprofit leaders have introduced new learning models, and there is growing excitement across the state about the opportunity to improve student learning and working conditions for teachers.

Lessons of reform. For 20 years, education has been driven by standards-based reform. The focus on test-driven accountability resulted in a much-needed focus on data but in a narrow way that was often disconnected from powerful learning experiences. Standards-based reforms created an awareness of the value of great teachers and underscored the importance of an ecosystem that recruited, trained and supported great teachers and leaders. But standards-based reforms largely failed to produce the intended dramatic improvement.

New school development, particularly in strong networks, was the most important development of the last decade in K-12 education in the U.S. New school development efforts typically include regional charter management organizations and national school networks. Where combined with a talent development ecosystem, new school development led to improved achievement in Boston, Los Angeles, New York, Washington, D.C., and other big cities.[18] Thousands of new high schools created over the last 15 years contributed to a significant improvement in graduation rates.[19] But almost all of these schools were optimized versions of the old age-cohort slog through print content. Teachers in these new schools often worked very hard to win better results, but there are inherent limits to the old model.

Talent matters, another lesson of reform, was Wendy Kopp's insight two decades ago. She began recruiting graduates from top universities, built a quick summer preparation program, and placed Teach for America teachers in high-need schools. Leadership matters is another reform lesson, as well as the mantra of New Leaders, a nonprofit formed in 2000 by Jon Schnur to prepare school leaders. Others recognizing the importance of leadership include the Broad Academy, which began training system leaders in 2002. In 2003, social entrepreneur Scott Morgan founded Education Pioneers to recruit professionals to work in school district offices.

School development and talent development were the improvement formula for the last 20 years. They optimized the 100-year-old model of education, but they did not fundamentally change the learner experience in most cases. What will mark the next two decades is a dramatic change in the learner experience—what is described in the next chapter as next generation learning.

Welcome to the revolution. In the meantime, a worldwide revolution in learning took place—with Wikipedia and the World Wide Web, suddenly anyone could learn anything, anywhere.[20] Access to free and open learning content became nearly ubiquitous, formal and informal online learning began breaking down barriers of time and location, and less expensive learning formats began extending access to higher education. The mobile inflection of 2010 was launched by the introduction of affordable tablets and an explosion of learning applications adopted by teachers, students and parents. The opportunity set was not lost on investors—venture investment in learning tools went from almost nothing to half a billion a year.[21] The viral infection of learning (and entertainment) capacity has impacted economies, institutions and individuals in ways we are just beginning to understand.

New tools, for people ready to put them to use, proved transformative. Connected teachers in new and traditional schools alike began sharing tools, resources and strategies with colleagues nationwide. Massively Open Online Courses (MOOCs) now provide free access to some of the best professors in the world, but they primarily benefit the prepared. Broadly speaking, it is the intersection of new tools and new schools that holds the most promise for expanding access and boosting achievement. And the potential offered by these new technology tools for every learner to have some "control over time, place, path, and/or pace," as the Christensen Institute says, is a historic opportunity.[22]

Teachers, and great teaching, matter more than ever. For most of us, learning is relational—culture and context matter. Expectations expressed through sustained relationships are those that matter. For young people, the opportunity to be around adults they can imagine becoming (to paraphrase Deborah Meier) is invaluable. New tools create the opportunity for new school models that extend the reach of great teachers.[23]

All of the top school networks and most school districts have come to realize the limitations of the old model and the potential of blending the best of online learning with teacher-led instruction. National new school design competitions like Next Generation Learning Challenges and local innovation incubators like 4.0 Schools in New Orleans underscore the opportunity at the intersection of organizational design thinking and technology development. School networks and districts are connecting education reform and a recent flood of venture capital funding.[24] Leading national education foundations have turned their attention to next generation learning opportunities. The opportunity to learn in America is rapidly improving.

Why Innovation Matters

In the same way that poverty tends to be clustered in neighborhoods where conditions and opportunities are spiraling down, innovation most frequently occurs in areas where conditions create an innovation updraft, or positive network effects. Florida's book _Who's Your City_ presents data showing that, while population and economic activity may be geographically spiky, "[I]t is innovation—the engine of economic growth—that is most concentrated [to certain regions]. It's here that the playing field is least level. Innovation centers, as measured by patents granted worldwide, demonstrate the clustering effect."[25]

Innovation and education build upon each other. While it may be more commonly understood that strong education systems foster innovation, and that innovation generates economic growth, it has now also been shown that innovation is good for learning. In fact, countries with greater levels of innovation see increases in certain educational outcomes, including higher math performance, more equitable achievement, and more satisfied teachers.[26]

EdTech—innovation in learning tools—is one of the most important change forces for good, potentially rivaling cleantech, biotech and the spread of democracy for the potential to promote peace and prosperity on planet Earth. But we do not know much about how these innovations are created and spread—what social scientists call innovation diffusion. Developing new ways to scale quality will be as important as new approaches to learning.

Learning is a complicated mixture of influences of formal institutions and informal experiences. Very simply, learning is a function of the public delivery system, family and cultural transmission, and self-directed activities.

Learning = public delivery + tribal delivery + self-directed

Coming innovations will improve outcomes of each component of this equation. Public delivery systems are incorporating new tools into blended learning environments. Parents and students are using new learning applications. Learners are increasingly self-blending and assembling their own transcripts.

In the United States, the tribal delivery of learning spans a broad distribution of cultural expectations and supports—from Tiger Moms to absentee parents— and may be even broader than the quality of public education. Based on a modest amount of travel, it appears that in Asia, India and many developing countries there is more uniform support for education from the bottom to the top of the socioeconomic pyramid. Perhaps new engagement and community development strategies (discussed in the chapter on new tools and schools) will help break the cycle of generational poverty, extend learning opportunities, and support better decision making.

The idea of self-directed learning is represented by the idea that anyone can learn almost anything anywhere there is a broadband connection. It turns out that uncurated content works only for a motivated few and, for most, access to the idea economy requires more. Lynda Weinman, founder of Lynda.com, says new technology is advancing from the library model with new ways to find and consume learning content with better discoverability, personalization and curation.[27] In the same way museums carefully select content, new technology using comprehensive profiles and predictive algorithms create customized playlists for learners.

The digital learning revolution is reshaping the postsecondary landscape. Almost half of U.S. students take some of their courses online, and many students bundle credits from multiple institutions. A growing percentage of high school students are graduating with college credit. New options are providing lower-cost, faster degree pathways. In dynamic job clusters, new market signaling strategies are replacing degrees as entrance and advancement requirements.

Since the mobile inflection of 2010, there has been an explosion of informal learning opportunities. Almost three billion people have some Internet connectivity.[28] One of seven billion of the world's population has a smart phone.[29] That creates a large and rapidly growing market for learning applications and services. It also builds in a big market for higher education providers paying attention to global demand.

Why Schools Struggle to Innovate

But if all of these new tools, technology and schools are available, why is it that our schools are still struggling? "All established organizations struggle with disruptive innovation or innovations that fundamentally challenge their status quo," said Michael Horn, cofounder of non-profit think tank Clayton Christensen Institute for Disruptive Innovation.[30] "These struggles aren't unique to education. Businesses struggle consistently with the innovator's dilemma—the ability to prioritize disruptive innovations that would cannibalize their existing business," adding that organizations usually lock in on a business model consisting of four elements, including value proposition, resources, processes and revenue formula. "These four components help define an organization's capabilities but also—and perhaps most importantly—what it is not capable of doing," said Horn.[31]

Michael B. Horn:
Why Public Schools Struggle to Innovate

Why do public schools struggle to innovate? It's not because they are public per se. Private and independent schools struggle with certain kinds of innovation, too. Traditional public school districts also have five added challenges to innovating.

1. **Changes in leadership.** Because district and political leadership can shift often, pursuing, refining and staying the course with an innovation that will take some time to implement, let alone perfect, can be difficult. This leads to a "this too shall pass" mentality.

2. **Little autonomy.** In many cases, for political reasons school districts are unable to create a new and autonomous business model, but research shows that doing this is often critical to solving the innovator's dilemma.

3. **Little nonconsumption of schooling.** Nearly everyone has access to what appears to be a free schooling option—there is less room to innovate.

4. **Critical role.** Historically communities have been unwilling to let schools fail because of how important their role is from a social perspective in the community. Parents and communities have not been risk tolerant.

5. **Varied stakeholders.** Public school districts serve an unusually high number of stakeholders with different jobs to be done in an intricately interdependent system. This makes it difficult for new innovations to be accepted without significant modification to meet the diverse needs of such a complicated ecosystem.

By the same token, public school districts do have a couple of advantages in innovating that businesses do not. Political mandates or movements that are sticky and last can cause public schools to change or focus on certain kinds of innovation in ways that businesses struggle with. With new funding streams in particular, schools will chase willingly new ideas, as their customers—society and the government—are giving them clear incentives to do just that.

This is part of the reason that despite the constraints of existing organizations, over the longer haul, public schools have historically been surprisingly good at adapting to new societal needs. That ability to adapt is becoming increasingly challenged, however, as more and more needs are layered on to what is already a heavy load for schools to carry.[32]

In addition to factors Horn identified, there are eight reasons that elementary through postsecondary education struggles to innovate.

Strong constraints. State and federal policy create a pretty confined space: standards influence aims, tests monopolize time, and funding is input-based and programmatic. Local contracts are often ensconced in board policies and state laws creating a Gordian knot of constraints that requires several waivers or changes before doing anything different. Some districts are pushing more budget and accountability to school principals, but few of them have any experience in organizational design, or what Rick Hess calls cage-busting leadership.[33]

Weak incentives. There are relatively weak performance incentives in education. Some recently implemented evaluation and accountability systems have ratcheted up stakes but usually around narrowly defined and crudely measured outcomes. In highly competitive sectors, performance incentives often lead to product and service innovations. There are weak scaling incentives for nonprofits and government agencies—more customers may simply mean more headaches. The lack of scale incentives like performance pay and equity means it is harder to attract talent and encourage growth. Schools have little capacity or incentive to make productivity-improving capital investments and, as a result, there are few efficiency innovations.

Little research and development (R&D). Compared to other sectors, there is far less spent on education research and development. The U.S. invests only 0.2 percent of its education budget on R&D versus the top tech companies that routinely spend more than 10 percent.[34] Despite the impact potential, there is far less spent on learning sciences than other areas of fundamental research. Much of the research undertaken in higher education is focused in arcane subjects driven by doctoral committees rather than any attempt to prioritize by potential impact.

While education is 8.5 percent of GDP, in 2011 it was only 0.3 percent of U.S. capital markets and 1.2 percent of venture capital funding.[35] The situation is improving. Venture investment in K-12 education technology totaled $452 million in 2013.[36]

Low sharing. Education has a way of isolating teachers and turning them into individual practitioners. The lack of support and direction leads to an insular culture that reduces outside influences, as well as structures that reduce permeation. The growth of personal learning communities is beginning to break down isolation.

Little capacity. There is very little change capacity in schools, districts or state offices. It is tough to balance improvement and innovation simultaneously. Schools simply were not designed to innovate. To the extent that they reflect intentionality, public delivery systems support equity and continuity. But the shift to digital and competency-based learning requires a lot of innovation and change capacity.

High complexity. Supporting the development of diverse young people is complex work. Learning, especially for children, is and will remain a distinctly a relationship-based enterprise, so organizational design and development will remain more important than education technology, though most breakthroughs will combine both.

Local control. A highly decentralized system of local control and weak improvement incentives dampens innovation diffusion. Highly effective school models are ignored, productive tools go unused, and community assets are underutilized. "While education struggles to innovate, our kids can't wait," said Abby Andrietsch.[37] "We want meaningful system-wide change, but our kids just can't wait for top-down, systemic reform." Andrietsch, a tireless advocate for kids, directs Schools That Can Milwaukee, which set a goal of creating high-performing schools serving more than 20,000 students. On barriers, she notes, "Well-meaning policy efforts are too often mired in political gamesmanship and reduced to little more than incremental improvements." Meanwhile, students suffer the effects of failing schools. "Their lives can't be put on hold while adults sort things out." Andrietsch adds, "Instead, we must work person-by-person and school-by-school, ensuring exceptional quality across all sectors—traditional district, public charter and private voucher."

Mindset. Andrietsch argues not only for a more responsive form of local governance, but for a whatever-it-takes mindset—as opposed to the compliance mindset demanded by local, state and federal education policy. This compliance mindset (what 50 years ago Jane Jacobs called the Guardian Syndrome stressing obedience, loyalty and tradition[38]) may be the biggest barrier to innovation—and it runs headlong into the current context of American cities. "Schools now find themselves struggling to play catch-up as the economy continues to morph with dizzying speed and unpredictability," said college and career readiness expert David Conley. "Success in the economy and society of the future will be much more a function not simply of what people have learned but of what they are capable of learning."[39] Conley adds that creating lifelong learners will become an increasingly critical and compelling goal of education.

If educators are to prepare young people for the innovation economy, they will need an innovation mindset. "To drive lifelong learning and the success of students early on, we must foster an environment where students learn at their own pace in an encouraging environment that cultivates a deep conceptual understanding of subject matter," said Jessie Woolley-Wilson, DreamBox Learning President and CEO.[40] "When students develop a deep understanding of concepts, they can apply and transfer that learning to new situations and experience success again and again." Jessie calls this critical thinking and adaptability "nimble intelligence." Creating the learning opportunities that develop mental agility in young people begins with ecosystems that encourage educators to be innovators rather than compliance monitors.

7 Keys to Smart Cities

Every day presents a choice—for students, entrepreneurs and civic leaders—to focus on barriers or opportunities. Entrepreneurial ecosystems like the San Francisco Bay Area are infused with an innovation mindset. There are visible benefits and adequate supports for new ventures and a density of risk taking that makes entrepreneurial pathways seem common rather than unusual. The seven keys to smart cities presented in this book can guide leaders in the creation and enhancement of their own smart cities for education and employment.

The first key to better learning opportunities and a vibrant city is an *innovation mindset*, which starts with classrooms that challenge students, provide instructive feedback with failure, and recognize determination as well as achievement. That suggests that young people, like students in Coy's tech center, should have opportunities during and after school to tinker, code, explore and create; they should produce, publish, present and track it all in a portfolio.

Dramatic improvement in urban employability requires *sustained and effective leadership*—the second key. An aggressive improvement and innovation agenda requires a reservoir of political capital earned through years of open dialogue, trustworthy leadership and inspired action. Learning options infused with an innovation mindset require a new bargain with educators focused on outcomes and opportunities more than inputs and rules.

As evidenced by every city making progress on educational outcomes, developing great teachers, leaders and Edupreneurs is critical. *Talent development* is key three.

Partnerships and engagement are crucial to advancing an education and employment agenda; at scale, these *aligned collective impact strategies* are key four.

Smart Cities

This smart cities agenda requires increased and coordinated investment. *Aligning public and private investment* is key five. This includes short-term capital expenditures to encourage the shift to next generation learning and a longer term shift to public education funding from early learning to job training that reflects challenges, is focused on outcomes and creates incentives for innovation.

Supporting the development and adoption of *new tools and next gen learning environments* is key six. Innovation is sustained by *advocacy and policy*, key seven.

Individuals, organizations and communities all share the need to learn and build new capacities faster and cheaper than ever. Innovative new tools and learning opportunities—formal and informal—are making that possible everywhere. Leaders committed to cities that work for everyone expand their impact by developing talent and through partnerships, aligned investments and supportive policies.

7 Keys to Education and Employment

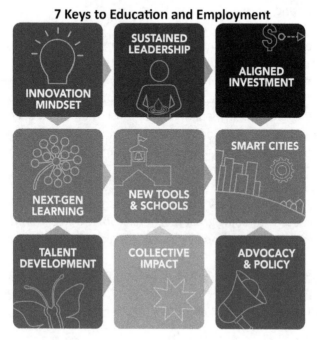

Chapter Summary

- Cities need to skill up fast to boost job formation, employment, economic development and civic participation.

- Smart cities are marked by smart people, small firms and connections to the outside world.

- Next gen learning has the potential to boost college and career readiness and employability.

- Creating better learning opportunities—and smart cities—requires an innovation mindset, sustained leadership, talent development, collective impact, aligned investment, new tools and schools and policy and advocacy.

Why Next Gen Learning is a Game Changer

 Finding Her Voice:
Eliana Bentley

"I have never worked so hard," said then-sixth grader Eliana Bentley about the play she wrote and directed to demonstrate her understanding of life in ancient Rome. "I really did put all my heart into it."

Eliana is a bright and determined student recovering from years of undiagnosed celiac disease, which caused severe challenges in her visual processing and auditory memory. Her mother noted that despite still feeling sick and tired much of the time, Eliana has thrived thanks to High Tech Middle Chula Vista's (HTMCV) hands-on personalized learning environment. She was able to learn in the modality that worked best for her and received targeted support from teachers. "She had been so discouraged by her previous experience that she had given up and formed a self-image of being an incapable outcast," her mother noted, adding that Eliana now has an exponentially increasing desire to learn and participate in school since coming to HTMCV. As HTMCV humanities teacher Andrea Morton puts it, by being encouraged to tap into her inherent abilities, Eliana now leads her class as a writer and knows she has a powerful voice the world wants to hear.[41]

Eliana's experience embodies the key aspects of next gen learning, which combines blended and competency-based approaches to create personalized, appropriately challenging, engaging and supportive learning environments. Next gen learning is a key to creating cities that work for everyone.

The formal education system is being enveloped by new learning technologies and strategies that make the shift to next gen learning inevitable rather than optional. Unlike the top-down, policy-driven reforms attempted over the last 20 years, the shift to personal digital learning is fundamental, not cosmetic. While governance oscillations will speed or slow system responses to external factors, it is clear that we are living through a learning revolution—an opportunity for schools—and cities—to improve learning outcomes faster than ever. This chapter presents a summary of the state of next gen learning, profiling the organic change occurring and some of the individuals and organizations creating it, how the weaknesses in today's school structure create opportunity for reform in both schools and cities, and a blueprint for the collaborative ecosystem that can be created by education and civic leaders building smart cities.

Innovation is a key element to building the ecosystem required to make next gen learning a game change. According to an Organisation for Economic Co-operation and Development (OECD) report, "Innovation in the public sector in general, and in education in particular, could be a major driver for significant welfare gains." The report, titled "Measuring Innovation in Education: A New Perspective," continued by suggesting that innovation can "improve learning outcomes and the quality of education provided; enhance equity; improve efficiency; and remain relevant to a changing economy."[42]

Sparking a Revolution
Despite a learner-centered context, flagship schools and thoughtful state leadership, Providence schools struggle with a traditional reform agenda and are largely resistant to change. The failure of top-down reforms and limitations of traditional education governance are evident in Providence—but so is the promise of organic, from the edges, outside-in innovation. What is new in the last two years is an interest in incorporating blended learning strategies that combine the best of face-to-face instruction with learning online. Teachers are using new tools to engage students and extend learning. Behind the organic movement are individual teacher-leaders like Shawn Rubin who are finding their voice and making a difference. Rubin is the Director of Blended Learning at the Highlander Institute where he manages technology

integration, consulting and professional development programs. He has helped spur surprising energy across Rhode Island.

 Shawn Rubin:
Providence Picking Up The Pace

There are many signs of forward momentum in the last year in Providence:

- EdUnderground, a hands-on laboratory for early-adopter teachers in which they can discover, explore, create and experiment with technology integration strategies, blended learning models and other innovative tactics using hardware, software and maker products;
- EdTechRI, a monthly EdTech Meetup organized by teachers and intended to be a way of getting teachers and products to come together around feedback and beta testing. The group engages more than 300 EdTech creators that exist between New York and Boston, most of which struggle to find real teachers to test and engage with their products;
- An annual Blended Learning Conference every spring supports schools looking for opportunities to connect around this work;
- EdChatRI, one of the leading edu-Twitter chats that pulls educators from across the country every Sunday night. It was founded by two early-adopter principals, Don Miller and Alan Tenreiro, from two different districts in the state;
- Providence Career and Technical Academy, using blended learning to help meld their career and technical courses with their academic courses;
- A grant from the Rhode Island Foundation making Highlander Charter School a blended learning lab school.

The real power of what we have going on in RI is that it's all grass-roots and driven from the educator side of things. We don't yet have a strong startup community here, but our educators love to collaborate around new ideas and test and tinker in any corner of the state that they can.

The Institute's work in Providence has spilled over into a statewide initiative to scale blended learning to all 57 districts and Local Education Agencies (LEAs) in Rhode Island. The project is called Fuse RI and is being supported by The Learning Accelerator, a non-profit organization dedicated to accelerating the implementation of high quality blended learning in schools across America. Through Fuse RI, the Highlander Institute will spend the next three years making Rhode Island the first fully blended learning state.[43]

At the May 2014 blended learning conference co-hosted with Rhode Island Department of Education (RIDE), keynote speaker Richard Culatta from the U.S. Department of Education's Office of Education Technology started his speech by saying, "If every state had a Highlander Institute things would be very different in this country." As Culatta's statement indicates, the role of individuals committed to the promise of next gen learning will be key to creating smart cities.

Students Deserve More
According to ACT, about a third of U.S. students graduate from high school ready to earn college credit without remediation; the study further reports that the numbers are even worse for black high school graduates—only five percent are fully ready for life after high school.[44] The country quickly needs to double rates of preparation for the idea economy to remain prosperous and reduce inequity. But these statistics indicate that the gap is bigger than traditional learning improvement strategies will be able to close. The learning students need and deserve is personalized, deep, flexible, engaging, relevant, challenging, collaborative and supportive.

Unfortunately, today's schools, particularly high schools, are not simply failing to prepare many students for their future; their basic design elements are obsolete. Consider legacy practices of grouping students by birthday, progressing at a uniform rate through a 180-day school year organized around the agrarian calendar, and tracking learning through courses and credits. The siloed structure requires many teachers to work in isolation; adopted approaches rely on textbooks and didactic instruction; and assessments reinforce regurgitation. The problem, according to Digital Learning Now, is that "grade level promotion has historically been dictated by birthdays, attendance and minimum achievement. Instructional pacing, aimed at the middle of the class, may be too fast or too slow for some students who become frustrated, disengaged and unmotivated."[45]

State standards and year-end tests introduced in the '90s highlighted big gaps and inequities in the system but in too many places resulted in routines of recall and regurgitation—a narrow preoccupation with low-level skills. While the basics are important, a survey of chief executives conducted by The Business Council and The Conference Board makes clear that executives placed priority on work skills and work ethic.[46] The next four priorities describe the demands of the new workplace—teamwork, decision-making, critical thinking and computer literacy. The "3 Rs" come next on the priority list.[47]

As Tony Wagner notes in his book, Creating Innovators, there is often a mismatch between what is taught and tested and what is required by the new economy. Wagner suggests the skills required for work, learning and citizenship are converging. "Schools aren't failing and don't need reform," says Wagner; instead, he says, "We need to re-invent, re-imagine our schools."[48]

Similarly, on his Dangerously Irrelevant blog, Scott McLeod advances a vision of student empowerment—"kids as autonomous, self-directed learners who are thinking deeply, collaborating to make societal contributions, and using digital technologies to do powerful, meaningful, and authentic work."[49] Suggesting a move away from cultures of fear and compliance, McLeod outlines the three big shifts our schools need to make: from low- to high-level thinking, from analog to digital, and from teacher- to student-directed.

Scott McLeod:
3 Big Shifts That Our Schools Need to Make

- **From low-level thinking to high-level thinking.** From an overwhelming emphasis on students doing lower-level thinking tasks (factual recall, procedural regurgitation) to students more often engaging in tasks of greater cognitive complexity (creativity, critical thinking, problem solving, collaboration, effective communication)
- **From analog to digital.** From local classrooms that are largely based on pens/pencils, notebook paper, ring binders and printed textbooks to local and global learning spaces that are deeply and richly technology-infused (devices + Internet)
- **From teacher-directed to student-directed.** From classrooms that are overwhelmingly teacher-controlled to learning environments that enable greater student agency (ownership and control of what, how, when, where, who with, and why they learn)[50]

What Is Next Gen Learning?

In these early innings of what is next, it is common for people to use terms including blended learning, competency-based learning, personalized learning, digital learning, Deeper Learning, next gen learning, optimized learning and more without clarity of where one stops and the other one ends. Simply stated, next gen learning is when students are helping chart the course, learning anywhere, learning anytime (and on a schedule), making connections, going deep, constructing solutions, writing—a lot, publishing, and presenting. Andy Calkins, Deputy Director of Next Generation Learning Challenges, suggests a framework for clarity.

Andy Calkins:
Toward Next Gen Learning

The graphic here builds on the taxonomy of blended learning developed by the Christensen Institute. It creates a landscape map of current efforts in the blended, competency-based, personalized learning space using four key dimensions of their taxonomy: degree of variation in, and student input into (even control of), the time, pace, path and place of learning. Time and place are being stretched these days through digital, online media (the X axis); path and pace are being stretched in models (up along the Y axis) that make students the organizers and managers of their own learning.

The goal is to see more Quadrant IV implementation, and that will be increasing nationwide soon, as that is the type of activity NGLC is seeking to grow. They will be seeking to lift student outcomes through the marriage of two ideas: next generation learning as the expression of what could be happening in schools, and the kind of dynamic ecosystem support that is being written about in this book.

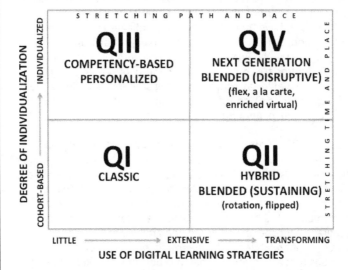

Quadrant I: learning in traditional school structures and classroom settings, increasingly with some level of digital support. This is probably where most of the country is these days: use of digital and online content and tools (including quite extensive use), but tucked inside of pretty recognizable age-based classroom models.

Quadrant II: blended learning in its most common forms (lab and station rotation), by which practitioners are using digital learning to transform some aspects of the traditional model. There's a lot of healthy innovating around *time* and *place* in this quadrant, lately around flipping what transpires in classrooms and what's being asked of students at home. Quadrant II is also where a growing swath of schools *believe* they are, but in truth, many haven't migrated that deeply out of Quadrant I. This quadrant is where Rocketship and Florida Virtual live, and is what resources like Khan Academy are being most widely used to support. The Christensen Institute has recently updated its taxonomy to suggest *hybrid learning* as a term for "sustaining" forms of blended learning innovation that would land in Quadrant II, as opposed to disruptive forms.

Quadrant III: personalized and competency-based learning, which may or may not be digitally supported, where learning becomes stretched by *path* and *pace*—moving toward more individual customization for (and by) each student in the design and management of his/her learning pathways. Not many schools (yet) have moved entirely beyond age-based student progression, but a number of school networks and districts are experimenting. Big Picture is here, along with New Tech Network and Expeditionary Learning, and a handful of school districts; all of them would say they're enlisting students in building their own competencies, to a degree at their own pace, through active, project-based, experiential learning.

Quadrant IV: disruptive forms of blended, next generation learning, all of which combine elements of the other quadrants, encompassing innovation in the use of all four elements—*time, place, path, pace*. Personalized learning, which some might include in this quadrant, incorporates variation and student enlistment in the time/pace/path/place of learning while being generally agnostic on its degree of digital support. We would propose that *next generation learning,* on the other hand, includes that assumption—that in order for personalized learning to be implemented effectively, affordably and equitably, it must include a strong digital component.[51]

A number of organizations are also working to describe what next gen learning will look like. As their website states, The William and Flora Hewlett Foundation "envisions a new generation of U.S. schools and community colleges designed to give all students—especially those from underserved communities—the knowledge and abilities necessary to succeed in this new environment." These schools would create opportunities for students to develop the Deeper Learning competencies described and defined by The Hewlett Foundation that are essential to prepare students to achieve at high levels: master core academic content, think critically and solve complex problems, work collaboratively, communicate effectively, learn how to learn, and develop an academic mindset.[52]

Shared characteristics. As outlined in the paper "Deeper Learning for Every Student Every Day," the Getting Smart team studied and profiled 20 schools that exhibit the Deeper Learning competencies—core to next gen learning—and found that they share 10 characteristics.

- **Good goals.** Danville Schools in Kentucky is a great example. Their goals focus on powerful learning experiences, growth, global preparedness, communication and community.
- **Equity focus.** All students are engaged in experiences that help them master content, develop academic mindsets, promote collaboration and critical thinking, and develop communication skills.
- **Powerful designs.** Everything—structure, staffing, schedules and supportive technology—works together for students and teachers.
- **Teacher Support.** A teacher support web includes common instructional frameworks, learning platforms, and strong development systems for adult learners.
- **"Show what you know."** Students are asked to demonstrate learning in a variety of ways, including public presentations, and matriculation is based on demonstrated mastery.

- **Strong culture.** A powerful and intentional climate lets students (and adults) receive regular feedback on shared values and habits of success.
- **Good habits.** Habits such as work ethic, perspective, participation, collaboration, asking questions and making connections are cultivated.
- **Sense of place.** Schools cultivate a sense of place through an extended learning day, inviting resources in, leveraging community assets, encouraging service learning and taking students on learning trips.
- **Powerful projects.** Often derived from student interest, good projects always incorporate standards-based assessment and periodically result in public demonstrations of students' work.
- **Great questions.** Schools encourage great questions by embracing curiosity, integrating subjects and assigning challenging work.[53]

In order to ensure students achieve the Deeper Learning competencies, schools and districts need to tie the competencies together. "From the minute students join The Springfield Renaissance School, be that as rising sixth graders or transferring juniors, they are asked to accept our 'college-bound' aspiration for all students, and to commit to 'working hard, being nice, and getting smart,'" according to Principal Stephen Mahoney. Part of the Expeditionary Learning network, the Springfield, Massachusetts, secondary school has been designed to provide a rigorous college-bound program that impels and supports students to use their minds well, care for themselves and others, and rise to the duties and challenges of citizenship. The school's explicit and consistent attention to character traits like self-discipline and perseverance serve to reinforce the academic mindset.[54]

Another example is the Mooresville Graded School District, which recently adopted requirements for four large-scale multimedia projects in third, sixth, eighth and 12th grade.

Beginning with the 2014-2015 school year, students will add products from these projects to their digital portfolios. "A major project that a student has to struggle through is one of the best forms of assessment and leads to future success," said Superintendent Mark Edwards.[55]

The 160 schools in the Expeditionary Learning network require presentation of year-end Passages projects.[56] Similarly, students in the 135-school New Tech Network learn through integrated projects. The lessons taught by these schools are that good schools start with good goals and a mindset that effort matters and everyone can innovate. Accordingly, good schools that foster next gen learning can be developed in every community.

In this chapter and book, next gen learning will refer to learning that is personalized, blended, interactive, relevant, data-informed, collaborative, agile, challenging and accessible.[57]

Attacking Poverty
It is critical that next gen learning be provided for all students, and not create a further divide between the "haves" and "have-nots."

Poverty can be a source of debate between educators and reformers, so any discussion of next gen learning should address its intersection with reform. Some advocates say education cannot be fixed education until poverty is fixed. Reformers point to new school development as the best intervention for a historically underserved neighborhood.[58] Whatever position one holds, new scientific literature indicates that students who grow up in poverty "bring adverse childhood experiences into schools in the form of traumatic stress," which "can cause children to be tuned out, preoccupied, impulsive, unable to concentrate, distrustful, and nervous," as noted in a recent literature review by Turnaround for Children, a NYC nonprofit focused on addressing the root problems faced by struggling schools.[59] Turnaround CEO Pamela Cantor says the "fight or flight response to stress impacts brain development, maturation of key learning and emotional centers and impacts the developing immune system of children." Predictable responses to trauma represent a risk to student development, to classroom learning, and to school wide culture.[60]

Turnaround occupies a thoughtful middle ground and believes that "until high-poverty schools have practices and supports that specifically address these risks, they will continue to underperform and millions of children will never reach their full academic and personal potential."[61] The Turnaround model includes high-capacity student supports, teacher training in specific behavioral and instructional skills, leadership for a high-engagement culture, and a conviction that next gen learning environments can extend opportunity and address the crippling effects of poverty.

Recuperative power. Some schools promote powerful learning for students, but according to the Alliance for Excellent Education, "For years, U.S. schools have tended to offer a two-tiered curriculum, in which some students, primarily white and relatively affluent, have had opportunities for Deeper Learning; while others, primarily low-income and students of color, have focused almost exclusively on basic skills and knowledge."[62] Urban educators nationwide are struggling with demands to help students living in poverty achieve higher standards. "We won't get more kids to Common Core expectations without personalization," said Carnegie Corporation Program Director Leah Hamilton. "Schools need to change very dramatically," says Hamilton, continuing, "Every high school needs to get better at recuperative work as well as pathways for acceleration."[63] The foundation is supportive of high college- and career-ready strategies but concerned about the dual demand of lifting standards and helping students catch up.

Recuperating and accelerating often starts with re-engaging disconnected youth. Nationwide there are 5.8 million young people that are neither in school nor working, and youth unemployment remains stubbornly high across the country; the unemployment rate among 16- to 24-year-olds is often more than twice the national unemployment rate.[64]

Responding to the daunting challenges of poverty and unemployment, Carnegie developed a set of principles, outlined in a report called Opportunity by Design, combining the best of new school development and youth development to create high-demand and high-support learning environments. The report outlines 10 design principles with the power to both recuperate and accelerate student learning. A high-performing secondary school:

1. Integrates positive youth development to optimize student engagement and effort
2. Prioritizes mastery of rigorous standards aligned to college and career readiness
3. Continuously improves its operations and model
4. Develops and deploys collective strengths
5. Manages school operations efficiently and effectively
6. Maintains an effective human capital strategy aligned with school model and priorities
7. Empowers and supports students through key transitions into and beyond high school
8. Remains porous and connected
9. Has a clear mission and coherent culture
10. Personalizes student learning to meet student needs[65]

To support work around this frame Carnegie tapped JoEllen Lynch to provide assistance to educators in New York, Denver, Philadelphia and Cleveland. Given the debate about poverty, Lynch, the Executive Director of nonprofit school support organization Springpoint, addresses the role of good urban schools using a school she founded in New York as an example.

JoEllen Lynch:
The Job Good Schools Fulfill

Across the board, research shows that the best urban high schools scaffold pathways for adolescents that take into account their need to develop and practice a range of competencies within and outside of school, developing adolescent ecosystems in which students feel safe, respected and engaged.

The job of a good school is creating the partnership between teens and adults that scaffolds this experience and recognizes the multiple ways that adolescents master these skills. While the ultimate recognition is the diploma—"the ticket" to the next step—students can only excel when they are sure of their skills and confident in the person they bring forward.

We recently celebrated the attainment of an 80 percent graduation rate in the United States. When we look at that data, we begin to understand that achievement increased as we boldly addressed the failure of our large comprehensive high schools and replaced them with intentionally designed schools where learning and development could be supported by intentional relationships between adults and young people.

In my experience designing and leading secondary and transfer schools throughout New York City, I've learned a lot about how to support young people as they work toward college and career. At South Brooklyn Community High School, students chose to attend after dropping out of high school. So, the journey began with a decision, a choice, and then was supported at admission by an adult who sought to understand the student's strengths, needs and vision. The instructional model and the youth development model were one and the same. "School" included life outside the brick and mortar through community involvement, family involvement, friendships and work. While we cannot "fix" the problems that teenagers encounter, we can help them build the skills to address them and support them in gaining the help they need. The school was a partnership: young people and adults, school system and community-based organization.

If we intentionally design schools that meet students where they are—accommodating young people's schedules, building on their strengths, and becoming an integral part of their lives—we can recuperate and accelerate learning, empowering young people to succeed in college and career. That's our job.[66]

Bill Bell, mayor of Raleigh, North Carolina, said it was time to stop waiting for "some wealth that will trickle down or that a rising tide will lift all boats" and time to attack the problem of poverty "neighborhood by neighborhood."[67] As Pam Cantor and JoEllen Lynch note, good schools can begin to recuperate the devastating effects of poverty; they can also spark a positive cycle in a neighborhood and raise property values.[68]

Blueprint of the Learning Revolution
With an understanding of what next gen learning is and its power to change lives and communities, it is important to look at emerging models to make next gen learning a reality for every student and city.

Here is what this revolution looks like: customized learning is replacing a one-way slog through a print curriculum. Engaging media is motivating students to work harder and longer. Mobile technology is extending and expanding learning opportunities, especially for low-income students. Customization, motivation, and equalization will boost achievement, narrow gaps, and prepare more students for the idea economy.[69]

This description of next generation learning from Getting Smart banks on customization boosting learning productivity (*i.e.*, students will learn more per hour in personalized pathways) and motivation building persistence (*i.e.*, students working harder and longer). New school models appear to bear out these predictions.

New models. Next Generation Learning Challenges (NGLC) is a series of secondary and postsecondary grant programs funded by the Bill & Melinda Gates Foundation and administered by EDUCAUSE. The national grant competitions seek to accelerate educational innovation through applied technology to improve college readiness and completion in the United States. The program provides a useful description of next gen learning from a student's perspective:

- Personalized to the ways I learn best
- Flexible so that I can try different ways to learn
- Interactive and engaging so that I participate in the learning
- Relevant to the life I'd like to lead
- Organized around my own progress against goals I understand
- Constantly informed by different ways of demonstrating and measuring my progress
- Collaborative with teachers and peers, unlimited by proximity
- Agile and supportive when I need extra help
- Challenging but achievable, with opportunities to become expert in an area of interest
- Available to me as much as it is to every other student[70]

After several rounds of national grant competitions aimed at catalyzing new designs for middle schools, high schools and colleges that reflect those next gen learning principles, NGLC is now working with local incubators to develop "breakthrough" schools in six cities and regions around the country: Chicago, the District of Columbia, New Orleans, Oakland, Colorado and New England. The idea is to leverage NGLC's national investments, and the more than 40 pioneering schools that have resulted, to help the regional incubators accelerate clusters of redesigned schools and foster smart city-style ecosystems that enable those schools to succeed and scale up. This ecosystem development work is also being supported by CEE-Trust, which runs a network of entrepreneurial, city-based school reform organizations. The Gates, Broad and Dell foundations are providing national grants to the initiative, which also calls on the local incubators to provide matching dollars. The goal is to build on the work of local educators and innovative organizations to generate student-centered, personalized, blended, competency-based educational approaches that are ultimately sustainable on public funding. NGLC hopes to expand the network to additional cities and regions in the future.

Directional evidence. The benefits of early next gen tools and schools are clear. Public Impact, which can be called an "action tank" as opposed to a think tank, estimates that new school models that use technology to leverage great teaching should gain 3.4 more years' worth of learning than a traditional school model in the K-12 years.[71] These new learning tools are beginning to be incorporated into elementary and secondary education, and hundreds of pieces of evidence indicate that they are enabling the development of productive new learning environments. Nearly all of the high-performing districts and school networks serving low-income students have adopted strategies that blend technology-enhanced and face-to-face learning. Digital learning is boosting achievement and examples abound in schools and networks such as Rocketship Education, KIPP, Summit Public Schools, Aspire Public Schools, Carpe Diem and more. Rocketship elementary schools, for example, are in the top five percent of schools serving low-income students in California.[72]

New tools are driving these exciting school models with particularly engaging and adaptive math and reading products. In math, Dreambox, which is used at Rocketship Education, has been found highly effective. A RAND study of Carnegie Learning's Cognitive Tutor Algebra I involving 17,000 students showed positive results from blended delivery. ST Math, a visual game-based program from nonprofit MIND Research Institute, has demonstrated results at scale in more than 2,050 elementary schools nationwide. A WestEd evaluation of schools in the Los Angeles Unified School District found "significantly higher math scores" associated with the use of ST Math, and Change the Equation recognized ST Math as a program that consistently yields positive outcomes. The Business Roundtable also recognized ST Math "for their outstanding work to improve U.S. student achievement."[73]

READ 180 from Scholastic incorporates small group instruction, modeled and independent reading, and adaptive instructional software. A "Compendium of READ 180 Research" summarizes more than a decade of validation of effectiveness for general student populations as well as for specific demographic groups.[74] The International Association for K-12 Online Learning provides reports and reviews on effective practices in online and blended learning. The resource section links to additional research on this topic.

Blended learning is improving the ability of teachers to meet the needs of students with special needs. PresenceLearning matches students with the right therapists for their situation. "With online therapy, we've proven that this is scalable, effective, and efficient," said CEO Clay Whitehead. Students exit therapy more quickly, districts save money, and therapists work when and where they want. "We see special education as leading the way of next generation learning toward a future of personalized learning for all students, not just those on IEPs," continued Whitehead.[75]

Blended and competency-based approaches are not only creating more personalized, engaging and relevant learning experiences for students, they are also generating results.

Learner in the driver's seat. "In the new world the learner will be in the driver's seat, with a keen eye trained on value."[76] That was the conclusion of Pearson's senior academic team who said An Avalanche is Coming to higher education. They also noted "an increasing acceptance of non-degree credentials that don't rely on traditional universities." Coursera is a case in point; at this writing, its website claims to serve up 718 free courses from 110 partners to 8.7 million learners.

For growing fields like Web development and coding, it is often faster and cheaper to learn outside a formal degree program. Experts point to resources including Code.org,

CodeAcademy and Bloc; General Assembly is raising the bar for startup management, tech and design.[77] The leading online learning marketplace Udemy, with short courses ranging from SEO to statistics and Spanish, boasts 3 million learners and 16,000 courses on its website. Digital learning is enabling postsecondary innovation in delivery, pedagogy, organization, matriculation and business models.[78] Accordingly, students have more options than ever before.

Learners as consumers. Higher education is unbundling, and students are responding as wise consumers. It is becoming rare that a higher education experience is four years at a university immediately following high school. On many campuses "non-traditional" learners are in the majority. It is not uncommon for a student to earn college credit in high school, attend a community college, take some courses online, and graduate from a baccalaureate institution. Almost half of all U.S. college students take some of their coursework online with credits coming from several providers. About 90 percent of public institutions offer some online offerings. The unbundled higher education world includes very low-cost general education alternatives including StraighterLine, Propero, UniversityNow and free preparation programs for the College Level Examination Program (CLEP), college credit tests from the College Board.

Learners increasingly bundle credits from multiple providers with portable, stackable credits, and credentials are becoming more common, particularly in career training. Alternative market signaling strategies including badging, certificates, portfolios and references may augment or even replace degrees in dynamic job categories like Web design and development.

Likewise, there are more P-12 options for students and families than ever, and online learning programs, traditional schools, charter management organizations (CMOs) and others are competing for all or part of students' FTEs. With so many options, students often need support in navigating their alternatives. As noted in a recent Digital Learning Now report, "Many of the emerging blended and online learning opportunities offer the complementary potential of stronger engagement, customized pathways and equalized opportunities; it will require more robust guidance and support services as well."[79] College and career pathways begin early, so students are well served to understand the expanding options in the P-12 and higher education marketplaces.

Changing business models and markets. Dynamic job clusters are served by rapidly growing informal online learning markets like General Assembly, Skillsoft and Udemy, learn-to-code sites like Bloc and CodeAcademy, and expanding open education resources (OER) including Saylor.org, CK12, Monterey Institute's NROC Project and Khan Academy. Online and blended learning are expanding free access to college credit opportunities in high schools. Employers often find that college graduates lack basic job skills leading to the rise of post-baccalaureate training shops like Fullbridge and Koru.

Bringing online learning to top-tier colleges and universities, 2U works with existing schools to create interactive and high-quality online programs. The company held its initial public offering in March 2014 and has a market capitalization above $600 million. With less fanfare, Pearson Embanet manages over 125 online higher education programs.[80] In June 2014, Starbucks baristas gained free access to ASU Online.

Traditional higher education has responded to new competition by incorporating online and blended learning into existing offerings with new platforms including Canvas by Instructure and Echo360. Adaptive learning systems are creating rapid pathways through developmental education. Some startups are finding opportunity by rebundling services in unique ways. Michael Staton, former teacher-turned-entrepreneur and venture investor, describes below how this shift is impacting both student options and business models.

Michael Staton: Unbundling & Rebundling Education—Emerging Business Models

Some of the strongest current business opportunities are in rebundled form. Below are six broad categories for these opportunities.

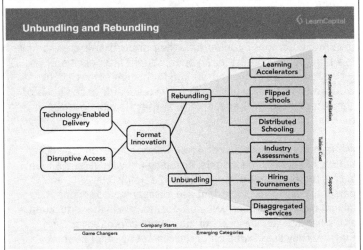

Career and learning accelerators. Immersive programs combined with technology-enabled learning can speed up knowledge and skill acquisition so that programs are short and inexpensive, relative to two- and four-year programs. Examples: Dev Bootcamp, Fullbridge

Flipped schools break the model of professor, classroom and library. They assign material to students prior to engaging with them experientially and expect that students will gain a level of understanding prior to showing up that allows more advanced participation. Example: Minerva

Distributed schooling captures several converging market themes and models of organizations that educate. It leans towards deinstitutionalization, decentralization and hacking school models, though still leans toward the creation and replication of physical schools and classrooms. These "schools"—to the extent they still look like schools—pursue scale alongside excellence and consistency. Examples: General Assembly, mSchool, Gap Year

Industry assessments are ways to evaluate competency or proficiency of knowledge to estimate aptitude and capability for particular jobs and industries. Because of the need for format and content specificity, it's likely that each industry would need its own company to deliver the best assessments. Once delivered, assessments can be a link to employment. Examples: Kalibrr, Knack, PyMetrics

Hiring tournaments provide a platform for interested candidates to compete for jobs by submitting their projects and work samples in a time-bound contest for an open, sought-after position. Hiring tournaments are appropriate for complex knowledge work and competitive positions. They create authentic signals of competency and work speed, making them much more effective than resumes. Examples: HireArt

Managed, disaggregated services. Higher education provides a bundle of services to students, including knowledge acquisition, access to opportunities, cognitive and employable skills, and personal transformation. Managed, disaggregated services take advantage of unbundled value propositions in higher education, as well as individual aspects of education, affordably or even for free. They are playing off of the market need for content learning, access to opportunities, skill acquisition and personal transformation. Examples: Thinkful and Degreed[81]

For students, institutions, and investors, a ballooning number of options means that students, more than ever, need to be wise consumers in addition to being focused learners.

Next Gen Learning at Scale

Ten years ago, a handful of reformers realized that a portfolio approach was the best response to urban challenges. The multi-provider approach involves partnerships to open innovative new schools, close failing schools, and work aggressively to improve the rest. Multiple-provider portfolios have gone mainstream and are powering improvements in three dozen urban centers with support of think tanks like the Center for Reinventing Public Education.

It helps to have outside partners "that act as either a nonprofit or foundation, have deep ties to the community and can raise money, invest in teacher programs, and provide inroads to building ecosystems in cities," said Ethan Gray, founder and CEO of CEE-Trust, an organization that helps develop strategies to ensure access for all to high-quality public schools. The 34 foundation and nonprofit members of CEE-Trust serve as "harbormasters" in their communities, working on three conditions for success: great talent, great schools and the policy and advocacy that build the right conditions for talent and schools to take root.

Ethan Gray on Talent Development

While all of the CEE-Trust harbormasters have focused on proven improvement strategies, a few have become local and national leaders on next gen learning, including CityBridge Foundation in the District of Columbia, Rogers Family Foundation in Oakland, Donnell-Kay Foundation in Denver, New Schools for Chicago, New Schools for New Orleans and Excellent Schools Detroit. It is inevitable that all harbormasters and city ecosystems will embrace an innovation agenda as well as an improvement agenda.

Despite the obstacles, what American Enterprise Institute scholar Rick Hess calls cage-busting leadership can overcome barriers and inspire improvement *and* innovation at scale.[82] Leadership, productive partnerships and stable governance have had more to do with the extent to which schools incorporate innovative tools and methods than proximity to the tech economy.

Innovation takes an ecosystem. Most innovation comes from startup companies, and most startups are launched in a technology ecosystem that includes successful companies, talented engineers, world-class universities, venture investors and high quality of life. New York City, the San Francisco Bay Area, and Chicago are the best examples of powerful innovation ecosystems producing network effects, which make them the best places in the world to start a company. If education were like Internet businesses, most innovations would be clustered in these three markets, but things are a little more complicated in education. Because learning is so relational, education innovations often involve new organizational designs and pedagogical strategies, and those can happen anywhere there are talented teacher-leaders.

Much of the widespread improvement in urban K-12 education over the last decade is a function of human capital initiatives and charter school networks—they improved talent and execution while creating environments—or ecosystems—conducive to such change. Teach for America, New Leaders and smart district leaders like Terry Grier in Houston have demonstrated that an aggressive talent development agenda produces results. When combined with data-informed, high-fidelity implementation, the results of a talent ecosystem can be quick and dramatic improvements in student achievement.

Since architecting many U.K. reforms, Sir Michael Barber has had the opportunity to study and influence education globally. Barber and his team recently outlined the path forward for the state of Massachusetts: whole-system reform, an innovation agenda, and a focus on implementation. The author of Deliverology says high-fidelity implementation is "the biggest challenge of all."[83] Barber suggests that a city or state has the opportunity to make dramatic improvement in educational outcomes.

 Sir Michael Barber:
The Path to Systemic Innovation

The era of standards-based reform has brought significant progress to America over the last 25 years. The results are clear, particularly in states that pursued reform with consistency, such as Massachusetts, Maryland and Texas. The Common Core and its associated assessments might be seen as the culmination of that era of U.S. educational development.

Alongside the progress brought by reform, the U.S. has seen globally-relevant innovation in other areas, too. Promising blended learning models, MOOCs, an array of startups showing potential, some excellent charter chains and Teach for America are examples.

So far, however, no place in the U.S. or the world has combined system reform with systemic innovation at scale. Even celebrated global systems such as those in Ontario, Singapore and Finland struggle with the innovation angle. And while California, Israel and England have innovation capacity, they have more to do on system reform.

Sometime soon, some system in the world will get this combination right and achieve lift-off in performance. Why not a large city or a state in the U.S.?

This is what we set out to recommend in the report for the Massachusetts Business Alliance for Education (MBAE) published in March 2014. The proposals are relevant to any U.S. system pursuing these objectives. The most important are:

1. **Expect all students to achieve** high standards and not just in core courses. Languages, history, the arts and learning leadership all matter, too.
2. **Devolve more power** and funding to schools and incentivize them to collaborate within and across district boundaries. Intervene effectively where there is failure.
3. **Redesign the teaching profession** along the lines advocated by Jal Mehta and others. To enable that redesign, have one statewide "thin" contract, which offers teachers new opportunities to grow and develop as professionals and to reap rewards for the contribution they make in return for removing the barriers to innovation that current contracts often include (*e.g.*, class size limits).
4. **Establish an annual competition** that would encourage educators, venture capital and EdTech innovators to collaborate to solve the major performance challenges facing the nation.
5. **Work on narrowing achievement gaps** not just through the school system but more widely as well. Introduce universal pre-K, for example.
6. **Focus on productivity as well as performance** of each school and district. How much performance is being delivered per dollar? Not only would this assure citizens that tax dollars were being used wisely, it would also encourage innovation, which has been a means of doubling output while halving cost in other fields. Gains of that scale may not be possible in education, but in an era of continuing pressure on the resources available we should surely ask whether it is possible.[84]

Smart Cities

The anywhere, anytime learning revolution started 20 years ago with the birth of the World Wide Web but did not reach most U.S. classrooms until after the widespread introduction of tablets and the explosion of mobile applications in 2010. Education venture investment accelerated, EdTech incubators and accelerators opened in major cities, and foundations funded innovative pilot projects.[85] Teachers, parents and students began adopting learning tools and resources at an unprecedented rate—the revolution became an undeniable bottom-up, outside-in change force.

Cataloging next gen learning in America's great cities makes it clear that mindset is the foundational condition for improvement and innovation for next gen learning. Shawn Rubin in Providence[86] or Andrew Coy in Baltimore[87] illustrate that one teacher on a mission can ignite a city. It is interesting to watch a principal in Columbus help change the energy level in a city. Now cage-busters like them are asking, "Can an urban district remain relevant if not connected to current needs of the tech economy?"

Chapter Summary

- Next gen learning combines blended and competency-based approaches to create personalized, challenging, engaging, relevant, collaborative and supportive learning environments.

- Next gen environments extend opportunity and address the crippling effects of poverty.

- Learning in general, and particularly postsecondary learning, is unbundling. Most students are learning online from multiple providers; some providers are innovating by rebundling services.

- Harbormasters coordinate regional talent, school development and advocacy efforts; some (and soon all) will embrace and lead an innovation agenda.

- It takes cage-busting leadership to overcome barriers and inspire improvement *and* innovation at scale.

1: Innovation Mindset

 Innovative Project-Based Learning:
Palo Alto High School

A few years ago, two Palo Alto High School newspaper staffers wanted to be able to write about food, styles, music and dance, and the traditional school newspaper just did not offer those opportunities. The students advanced the idea to start a full-color glossy supplement and call it *C Magazine*, imitating the *New York Times T Magazine*. They figured all costs could be borne by advertising but had little idea how to do that.

Going forward was a pretty gutsy decision on the part of the students and the newspaper adviser, Esther Wojcicki, who figured it would give them some important learning opportunities even if they failed. Allowing them to try was literally the only way to give them this writing opportunity they craved.

Their experience was much like a startup. They had to recruit other students in the class to work with them and sell their idea. They had to meet with their team and come up with a concept for the magazine, establish a plan, select leaders, and figure out how to fund it. They brainstormed about businesses that would be most likely to buy ads based on which ones teenagers frequented, and then they ran a training session on how to sell ads.

This was an entrepreneurial experience for all the students on the staff and one that empowered them in ways that other classes never did. The year taught them more about critical thinking, risk taking, organizing and meeting deadlines than any textbook or video could have. They learned collaboration skills, managerial skills and technical skills, just to mention a few. These skills were invaluable no matter what profession they chose.[88]

"Employers and parents want students who are creative, come up with new ideas, and are willing to take risks," according to Wojcicki, adviser for the Palo Alto students mentioned above and arguably America's best journalism teacher. A consultant and Edupreneur, Wojcicki believes the desired skills and dispositions are developed by doing, not by listening. "No one learns to swim by watching swimmers, or to write by watching someone else write. If we want students to learn entrepreneurial skills they need to practice," she said. "If we want to engage them and get them passionate about learning, give them an opportunity to do an entrepreneurial project of their choice that embeds the skills they need to learn. Imagine a classroom where students come up with their own project idea, have educational support from the school, and learn entrepreneurial skills by having to raise funding."[89]

Give students an opportunity to be creative, to fail, to recover, to learn communication, language and tech skills, as well as to be passionate about a project—that is what entrepreneurial opportunities offer.

It All Starts With an Innovation Mindset

There is a lot of talk about college and career readiness these days, but the focus remains on the reading, writing and math skills to gain college acceptance. Beyond the basics, the most important aspect of career readiness may be developing an innovation mindset—being prepared to create one's own job and the curiosity, self-direction and commitment to add value in every circumstance.

Wojcicki created a learning environment that cultivates an innovation mindset. Effort and determination are required and rewarded, entrepreneurship is supported, and collaboration is required. The best human development systems—from preschool to professional learning—have a culture, pedagogy and flexibility to support these dispositions. A growth mindset recognizes that talent is not fixed and that effort matters. A maker mindset embraces the value of creation and connects the initiative of entrepreneurship with the rewards of impact. Collaboration in diverse and dynamic settings requires a high level of social-emotional intelligence that may be called a team mindset. This formula for success:

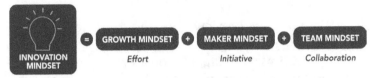

INNOVATION MINDSET = GROWTH MINDSET *(Effort)* + MAKER MINDSET *(Initiative)* + TEAM MINDSET *(Collaboration)*

This chapter explores this formula in student learning, in organizational development and in economic development. Some argue that a portion of the innovation mindset comes naturally to young people because the environment in which they have grown up has rewarded them for trying new things and supported them in failure. According to Sanjeev Agrawal, the founder and chief executive of Collegefeed and former head of product marketing at Google, "Today's young job seekers have grown up with a startup mentality. The value of embracing failure has been etched into their psyche."[90]

Growth mindset. What do young people need to know and be able to do be successful? Reading, writing and problem solving are obviously important to just about every family wage job. Content knowledge gives something to work with, but what else is important for success in life? It turns out there are a number of factors that schools seldom talk about, teach or provide feedback on that are at least as important as academic skills.

According to University of Pennsylvania professor Angela Lee Duckworth, two traits predict success in life: grit and self-control.[91] On the other coast, Stanford University professor Carol Dweck uncovered the importance of a "growth mindset," the belief that abilities can be developed through dedication and hard work; Dweck says that people with a growth mindset "believe that their most basic abilities can be developed through dedication and hard work."[92] This stands in contrast to talents that are fixed traits. Both Duckworth and Dweck's research findings were applied to education in 2013 in Paul Tough's book, _How Children Succeed: Grit, Curiosity, and the Hidden Power of Character_.

A 2012 literature review _"Teaching Adolescents to Become Learners"_ from the Consortium on Chicago School Research (CCSR) said that grades do a better job than tests at measuring life success habits including study skills, attendance, work habits, time management, metacognitive strategies and social and academic problem solving that allow students to successfully manage new environments and meet new demands. The CCSR report outlined evidence for other success factors including the beliefs young people have about their own intelligence, their self-control and persistence, and the quality of their relationships with peers and adults.[93]

This research emerged as top performing school networks saw their graduates complete college at lower-than-expected rates. Many concluded that the success formula was more than high test scores and included traits of perseverance built up through productive struggle—reinforcement to the advocates of social-emotional learning, character development and so-called 21st-century skills.

The Hewlett Foundation advocates for Deeper Learning—an antidote for a thin test prep curriculum—including development of academic mindsets. "Students develop positive attitudes and beliefs about themselves as learners that increase their academic perseverance and prompt them to engage in productive academic behaviors."[94] The definition is a bit broader than growth mindset adding, "Students are committed to seeing work through to completion, meeting their goals and doing quality work allowing them to search for solutions and overcome obstacles."[95]

There are a variety of pedagogical approaches to building persistence. Learning games and game-based strategies that incorporate productive failure and instructional feedback are a good start.[96] When well-constructed and applied, learning games and game-based strategies can boost motivation, extend persistence, build automaticity and deepen learning.

Maker mindset. While determined effort may be a foundational characteristic for academic success, there are other dispositions key to success in the idea economy. A study from Deloitte Growth Enterprise Services supports the idea that entrepreneurially minded individuals and companies are essential to economic growth.[97] A Deloitte executive observed that "entrepreneurial behavior matters to performance, and any company, regardless of its size, can adopt the kind of entrepreneurial approaches that can help them outperform across a variety of metrics."[98]

The Kern Entrepreneurship Education Network (KEEN) is a network of U.S. universities that, as noted on its website, "strive to instill an entrepreneurial mindset in undergraduate engineering and technology students." The network aims to graduate engineers who will contribute to business success. The framework includes entrepreneurial mindset, multi-dimensional problem solving, productive collaboration, and integrity.[99]

The KEEN framework is great, but it could use a dose of maker. "The baseline for a maker mindset is curiosity and creativity—both of which are often stifled in our current education system," said Ingrid Ellerbe, MIND Research Institute. "When you allow students to construct and test their own theories in a non-threatening environment it opens the floodgates for the 'what's next' challenge, thereby creating a sense of ownership and accomplishment that can't be 'taught.'"[100]

A survey of 1,500 CEOs from 60 countries and 33 industries identifies creativity as the "most crucial factor for future success."[101] Several organizations are doing good work in this area. As their website notes, the Imagination Foundation envisions a world "where creativity and entrepreneurship are core social values nurtured in schools, homes and communities everywhere; where all children are taught to be creative thinkers and doers, and encouraged to make their very best ideas happen." And MIND's visual game-based ST Math encourages hypothesis development and supports failure with instructional feedback.

In *Makers: The New Industrial Revolution*, *Wired* editor Chris Anderson notes a re-emergence of tinkering and building made user-friendly for the Internet Age. In the narrowest sense, the term "maker" refers to a new category of builders using open-source methods and new tools like 3D printers to move manufacturing from the factory to the desktop. More broadly, this new-age hacking is related to the growing interest in learning to code and working as a freelancer—the reality that many young people will need to "make" a job, not just get a job. Whether making a living, coding an app, or printing a gear, it is the maker mindset—self-directed, purpose-driven and iterative.

Matt Candler runs what is arguably the best education innovation incubator in the country, 4.0 Schools. They introduce entrepreneurial thinking to educators and help turn ideas into impact organizations. Candler "bakes" three big ideas into each 4.0 experience—be user-centric, be curious and iterate. In other words, embrace the fact that most kids are being prepared for jobs that do not currently exist, try some new strategies, and make many more smaller, faster bets.

David Dockterman would like to see more productive failure.[102] But as a lecturer at Harvard's Graduate School of Education, Dockterman sees students afraid to blemish a polished transcript. As Scholastic's chief architect of learning sciences, he sees K-12 students all too familiar with failure and schools that do not know how to support productive struggle. "We need to shift the student point of reference for struggle," he said, making four specific suggestions:

- Words matter. For example, rather than "Let's start with an easy question," which will not be true for every student, Dockterman suggests, "This may take a few tries."
- Model failure. Let students see you struggle; let them know you fail sometimes.
- Use stories of perseverance. Success is almost always the product of lots of practice, failure and struggle.

Teach children about their brains. Brainology, from Mindset Works, is a great example.[103, 104]

"Maker projects can give kids the experience of learning from failure and working collaboratively," Dockterman. "Games can similarly demonstrate the value of perseverance and challenge seeking," he said, adding, "Now we want to use those experiences intentionally to support other parts of the curriculum." Dockterman helped Scholastic build growth mindset into MATH 180, a math intervention for secondary schools.[105]

Developing and applying growth and maker mindsets requires variety and practice. "Coming up with a writing topic might be like generating an idea for a maker project," he said, adding, "Puzzling through a math problem might be like trying different strategies to complete a game level." It is important to help students make the connections because, says Docterman, "We can't rely on them happening on their own."[106]

Edupreneurs like Summit Public Schools CEO Diane Tavenner apply lean startup and iterative development strategies to building new tools and schools.[107] Summit's culture of innovation "encourages ideas and exploration, but does so through an intentional and thoughtful process to enable a laser-like focus on our mission." Innovation at Summit follows Lean Startup's Build-Measure-Learn approach.[108] According to Tavenner, they "rigorously and regularly explore data, identify problems and challenges, develop and implement solutions, and then check back with the data" to offer the best education possible. Summit not only applies these strategies to running schools, they provide regular feedback to students on what Summit calls "habits of success."

College for America (CfA) at Southern New Hampshire University (SNHU), which boasts what it calls a "most valuable, least expensive" Bachelor of Arts degree on its website, is a great example of next gen learning outcomes that embrace and exemplify an innovation mindset. CfA at SNHU offers a competency-based $10,000 bachelor's degree program with a well-structured set of outcome areas in an online, self-paced and self-directed model that encourages an innovation mindset.[109]

Team mindset. The Partnership for 21st Century Skills reinforces the focus on creativity and, like KEEN, adds collaboration. "Learning and innovation skills are what separate students who are prepared for increasingly complex life and work environments in today's world and those who are not. They include creativity and innovation; critical thinking and problem solving; communication and collaboration."[110]

The Hewlett Foundation adds, "Students cooperate to identify and create solutions to academic, social, vocational and personal challenges." They continue by saying that students should "communicate and understand multiple points of view and ... know how to cooperate to achieve a shared goal."[111]

Putting the Pieces Together
Compiling these dispositions, the best umbrella term (borrowing from business literature) is innovation mindset—a combination of

growth, maker and team mindsets. This assumes that complementary critical thinking, problem solving, and communication expectations are at least moderately well communicated through common standards. Below is a summary of emerging and advanced skills and dispositions for an innovation mindset.

	Emergent (Student)	Advanced (Teacher/Edupreneur)
Growth mindset	-Knows effort matters, takes initiative around opportunity -Meets goals by doing quality work and aiming for deep understanding -Knows how he or she learns best	-Defines problems, opportunities and solutions in terms of value creation -Has resilience to overcome failure -Utilizes strategies to foster Deeper Learning
Maker mindset	-Exhibits curiosity and resourcefulness -Locates/uses tools to complete tasks -Learns from setbacks	-Leads design thinking; uses "and" thinking to resolve tough dilemmas -Uses user-centric, iterative strategies -Pursues personal fulfillment by defining purpose and creating value
Team mindset	-Collaborates to identify and create solutions -Understands multiple points of view -Asks for help when needed	-Proactively "expands the pie" to make an impact -Substantiates claims with data and facts -Develops social capital by delivering value and exhibiting trustworthiness

What it sounds like. Author Bernie Trilling has been thinking and writing about career preparation and powerful learning experiences for a long time. He compiled a set of critical dispositions and turned them into "I" statements, which turn rather abstract concepts into statements that young people can be imagined speaking. Adapted for this growth + maker + team frame, following are the kinds of statements young people should be able to record in a digital portfolio.

Growth Mindset Dispositions
- Growth mindset: I can learn.
- Self-efficacy and confidence: I can do this.
- Goal setting and managing: I can reach my goals.
- Persistence and resilience: I can overcome setbacks.
- Metacognition: I know myself and what I need to do.

Maker Mindset Dispositions
- Curiosity: I'm interested in learning.
- Creativity: I ask, "What if? Why not?"
- Purpose and relevance: This is important to me.
- Contribution: I can create value.

Team Mindset Dispositions
- Social belonging: I belong here.
- Understanding: I appreciate that point of view.
- Social capital: I can get the help I need.[112]

There is widespread agreement that effort matters and that collaboration skills are absolutely vital. It also appears that an entrepreneurial bent is extremely valuable. States, districts and schools should embrace innovation mindset in their goals and definition of college and career readiness. Students should have access to learning experiences where they can develop these dispositions and the associated skills, and they deserve regular feedback on their development.

Developing Student Mindsets
"Students, or any of us for that matter, can have a growth mindset and demonstrate gritty behaviors in one context but not in another," said Dockterman.[113] Transfer can be a challenge. "Developing the underlying beliefs that foster general behaviors of resourcefulness, innovation, curiosity, persever-ance and so on are great, but getting those behaviors to manifest themselves across disciplines, in history as well as in maker projects or science labs, takes work." The academic setting matters even within a domain: "The culture of one math classroom can foster academic mindsets while another undermines them," said Dockterman.

Applying an innovation mindset requires domain specific knowledge and skills. "The strategies one uses to get started on a three-paragraph persuasive essay are not the same strategies one uses to decipher a baffling math word problem," said Dockterman. "Having a growth mindset primes us for learning, but learn we must." Innovation mindset should be integrated into the curriculum and classroom and school cultures. It cannot be developed on a field trip with the hope that it spreads.

Dockterman said, "Knowledge needs to be useful and tasks need to be challenging" to develop an innovation mindset.[114] Overcoming obstacles takes strategic know-how tied to the content domain. Ryan Olson, Team Leader for K-12 education at The Kern Family Foundation and a Center for Hellenic Studies (CHS) Fellow at Harvard University, provides practical strategies for developing an entrepreneurial mindset in students.

 Ryan Olson:
Forming an Entrepreneurial Mindset in K-12 Students

An entrepreneurial mindset is useful for anyone, for all of life. This mindset exercises a relentless curiosity about the surrounding world and draws from a diverse set of wells to find solutions to problems. An entrepreneurially minded person leans into change and complexity, finds insights and opportunities, and continuously seeks a broad understanding of the contemporary world.

Some students may be more entrepreneurially minded by nature. But aspects of the discipline can be learned. Here are a few suggestions for you and your students.

1. Zoom out to gain context and experiment with connections. What relevant events, trends, narratives or statistics can you find in history? Economics? Law? Material culture? Arts? Demographics? The entrepreneurially minded see and implement these connections.
2. Memorize your field's fundamentals. That's right: rote learning. Ephrem the Syrian said, "The eye as it read transported the mind; in return, the mind too gave the eye rest from its reading, for when the book had been read the eye had rest, but the mind was engaged." How can you imagine new ideas if you don't know the basics cold?

3. Become an "anthropologist." What problems and challenges exist around you? Observe in novels as much as news sites.
4. Practice describing your interests and observations so that unfamiliar people can engage and help you sharpen them.
5. Create projects in different contexts. Build something to apply your ideas at home, work, and in your neighborhood
6. Flex your mind by asking what you're missing today

Educators earnestly desire to serve their students. Fostering an entrepreneurial mindset will help young people thrive in a rapidly changing world.[115]

Projects. Big gateway projects, like those central to Expeditionary Learning (EL), can be a great way to promote successful struggle. However, balancing struggle and support is a critical judgment. EL's Chief Academic Officer Ron Berger said that many teachers consider the final product to be a sufficient form of assessment but cautioned, "If the teacher isn't assessing all along the way then the final product will not typically show the high quality of success." He explains, "You don't want to undermine the quality of the final product by taking away the scaffolding, but you want a sense of individual student levels of understanding throughout that flow."[116]

Jim Stephenson is the history teacher at Stapleton High School, part of the DSST Public Schools (DSST) in Denver, top-performing science- and math-focused schools serving low-income students. The data-driven network tries to provide brain-based learning by creating "an environment where students have to learn something where we didn't provide direct instruction," said Stephens.[117] He explained that the school's core values of "doing your best, being responsible, and practicing integrity are all related to learning the skills required to be a learner." DSST was established on the philosophy that learning how to learn is more valuable than any content alone. "We want our students to be thinkers and doers, not Jeopardy champions."

Stephenson teaches an integrated block covering the history of the universe, the planet and human history using open content from the Big History Project. "Students have to have an understanding of how the earth works in order to decide how humans have interacted with it. They need to look at the history of the problem, and solutions that have been tried or suggested already, before they can try to solve it. This is problem-based learning," said Stephenson.

The focus on inquiry evident in classrooms at DSST is the mindset necessary to transform schools, systems and cities. Digital tools can support powerful learning experiences by providing personalized skill building, by enabling deep integrated explorations like Big History, by powering dynamic collaboration, and by supporting the development of professional-quality work product.

Reynoldsburg High School converted their library into a "fab lab" to promote hands-on learning. Their triple block capstone experience incorporates applied and personalized learning by combining a big team-based, real-world investigation with individualized supports and culminating with an exhibition. Reynoldsburg High has four academies, each with a career theme. Through projects supported by partnerships, Reynoldsburg High is a great example of promoting Deeper Learning, developing real career readiness, and cultivating an innovation mindset.

Robotics competitions are a great way to combine science, entrepreneurship and, typically, teams. Coding opportunities, Maker Faire and maker apps, DIY projects and the Cardboard Challenge can all boost engagement. Network for Teaching Entrepreneurship (NFTE) and Junior Achievement are also great resources for developing an innovation mindset.

NFTE ran two-week BizCamps in 11 cities during the summer of 2014. The intensive entrepreneurship program is designed to unlock the entrepreneurial mindset in youth, as all participants build a full plan for an original business idea of their own. Students cover all aspects of what it takes to start a business, including learning about opportunity recognition, market research, sales and business financials.[118]

Developing Educator Mindsets

Producing different and more relevant student outcomes requires a new educator mindset. According to Candler, "For the first fifteen years of my career, I had a stubborn 'kids' lives are at stake' mindset that championed certainty and perfection."[119] Candler was arguably the best in education at incubating new "no excuses" charter schools, but he "realized that what kids' lives really depend on is me having a growth mindset that champions curiosity over certainty and iteration over perfection."[120]

Candler left New Schools For New Orleans and launched 4.0 Schools, "a skunk works" for education. Candler explains, "Since Lockheed coined the term in the 1940s, these internal R&D labs are built within organizations and given broad autonomy to question the status quo and pursue bold ideas too wild for the existing org to pursue."[121] Candler's group hosts a range of community events geared toward honing hunches about the future of school. They offer prototyping bootcamps, feedback sessions and design workshops to build key innovation skills and learn helpful new approaches and mindsets. What 4.0 Schools does really well is incubate new organizations—testing ideas on a small scale and fine-tuning what works. Candler "bakes" three big ideas into each 4.0 experience—be user-centric, be curious and iterate.

Matt Candler:
Three Shifts in Educator Mindset

Effectively serving students and fixing an obsolete system requires at least three shifts in mindset for educators:

1. **Be user-centric.** Focus on the problems that face those you serve—your users. The problem our users face is that 65 percent of the jobs they will choose from a decade or two from now don't even exist yet. The more we embrace that real problem as our own, the less likely we'll be to assume what worked for us when we were in school will be best for them.

2. **Be curious.** Kids don't need to hear me say things like, "I know what works, just let me show you." They know the world's changing. What they need to hear me saying—and modeling—are things like, "Wow, this is hard. I don't know what the future will hold; let's get to work trying some new ideas." Curiosity is critical to preparing kids to be confident, gritty, joyful lifelong learners in a world changing too fast for us to tell them what the future will hold. Choosing curiosity over denial in this situation is key to creating schools that better prepare kids for the exciting, big world they're growing up in.

3. **Iterate.** In the pursuit of a better way, we must make many, many more smaller, faster bets. This requires a bias to action, not a bias to certainty. Shipping an early version of a new idea to your user is scary. But when you get this right, your user appreciates that you've involved them in the process of finding new ways to meet their needs. And if you respond quickly to their feedback, you'll create deeper loyalty and investment than you ever could trying to read their minds.[122]

Difficult work. Creating innovative new schools is such difficult and often contentious work, it takes an innovation mindset. This is particularly true for schools inventing new competency-based progressions where students advance based on demonstrated mastery. Rather than one school advocating for the opportunity to innovate and attempting to build all the components alone, it helps to collaborate with other schools, perhaps in a regional approach like the New England Secondary School Consortium. Chris Sturgis, co-founder of CompetencyWorks, describes the educator mindset needed to create next gen learning environment.

Chris Sturgis:
Growth Mindset Key for Kids and Educators

Competency education starts with a growth mindset, a belief that we can all learn, we can all get smarter. In competency education, the vibrant culture of learning ensures that within schools educators are collaborating and sharing their expertise in order to better support students in their learning. The culture of learning lays the groundwork for schools and districts to form networks that expedite the transfer of effective practices, create avenues for leadership development, and facilitate innovative problem-solving to tackle larger systems issues. When converting to competency education, schools will need to follow a two-pronged strategy of nurturing a strong internal culture of learning while also forging relationships with other competency-based schools.[123]

Companies like Google doing difficult work on many fronts hire innovative people. They create and actively maintain a culture that supports innovation, including leadership modeling, expectations for innovation, and a culture of creativity, fun and feedback. Innovative companies maintain a culture of "launch and iterate." They design organizational structures that support innovation; they give employees a voice, and they listen. They reward employees for innovation.

Developing Community Mindsets
The city and schools of Anaheim, California, are an emerging example of a values-based partnership. Anaheim mayor Tom Tait ran on a platform of kindness. It undergirds a million acts of kindness in Anaheim elementary schools and service learning in secondary schools.

In October 2013, hundreds of high school students attended a City Council meeting and encouraged support for Anaheim to become a Partnership for 21st Century city. The Council said yes to supporting collaboration, critical thinking, creativity and communication. Working with new high school district Superintendent Michael Matsuda, the mayor's staff launched a business partnership for mentoring to boost career awareness and employability.

Can the mindset of a community be changed? Tait and Matsuda think so. "It starts with a smile and handshake and then goes deeper," said the superintendent. Commenting about the culture of kindness, Mayor Tait said, "It's the mortar that holds it all together."

 Mayor Tait and Superintendent Matsuda on Innovation Mindset

Tait and Matsuda are not the only ones working on culture change at scale. Twenty-five year-old Brazilian entrepreneur and MIT graduate Bel Pesce is passionate about teaching people business-building skills. She founded FazINOVA to spread the entrepreneurial mindset.[124] Her message suggests, "You have much more control on things in your life than you imagined," as well as "Find what you are good at and be better at it."[125]

Pesce offers classes at 13 locations in Brazil. Classes will soon be offered online. "My big vision is to find, develop and connect talented people to create a more entrepreneurial country and a more entrepreneurial world."[126]

As modeled by these leaders, an innovation mindset—focusing on growth, maker, and team—can be fostered at multiple levels. Developing innovation mindsets has the potential to change a classroom, community, city, or country.

Whether fostering an innovation mindset in a country, as with Brazil, in a city, as with Anaheim, or a classroom as with Palo Alto High School, the power to change becomes real. It is this foundational key that unlocks the power of subsequent keys to education and employment.

Chapter Summary

- An innovation mindset includes three dispositions: growth mindset, maker mindset and team mindset. Effort, entrepreneurship and collaboration matter.

- These dispositions can be developed in students, educators and communities.

- An innovation mindset can be transformational. It begins with leaders choosing words carefully, modeling openness and humility, encouraging risk taking, and rewarding innovation.

2: Sustained Leadership

 Beating the Odds with Buzz:
Mary Esselman

The most innovative work being done in education today uses new tools to develop new schools—stretching the capabilities of a learning platform to support students and teachers in a personalized learning environment. It's not surprising that this two-pronged innovation is happening in Silicon Valley, but you may not expect to find it amid disaster recovery work in Detroit. In 2011, as chief academic officer of the struggling Kansas City Schools, Mary Esselman formed a partnership with both the School Improvement Network and platform builder Agilix and launched an ambitious personalized learning pilot. After a move to Michigan, she helped start the state's Education Achievement Authority (EAA), an effort to improve the lowest-performing schools in the state, and bring the personalized learning platform there.

Esselman's work to implement the new school design and learning platform called Buzz took place in difficult conditions and was not without controversy —12 Michigan schools that were closed, redesigned and re-staffed. While the EAA continues to struggle with daunting conditions, community questions and early versions of the school model and software, the work is of national significance and required courageous leadership.

The Buzz platform organizes a variety of content into units of instruction. Students have the ability to choose how they learn, practice and apply. Students must present three forms of evidence for each learning target—they have options in how they show what they know. Student productivity is measured by the number of targets hit over an expected period of time and appears on a speedometer on their desktop. Teachers can monitor the progress of all of their students at a glance. The combination of student choice, engaging content and lots of feedback on performance and progress yields a motivating learning environment.[127]

Buzz is not an app coded over the weekend, it is a powerful learning platform developed by a team that has been at this for a decade. The school model reflects a collection of emerging practices not previously assembled at this scale and achieved through sustained leadership. If the EAA stays on track, it will join the Louisiana Recovery School District, which led reconceptualization of education in New Orleans, as one of the most important city turnaround projects. Both took bold and sustained leadership that challenged the status quo, developed talent, and built strategic partnerships.

What It Takes to Lead

Lyle Kirtman, leadership development expert and author of Leadership and Teams: The Missing Piece of the Educational Reform Puzzle, debunks the myth that instructional leadership is *the* answer. Kirtman writes, "We have once again focused too narrowly on symptomatic solutions. Yes, instruction is key to improving student achievement. However, our educational leaders need to broaden, not narrow, their leadership competencies to be successful in today's world. Other sectors are emphasizing innovation, external partnerships and customer service. Is education that different that the focus needs to be so internal?"[128]

Just as the terms instruction and leadership were used separately in the past and have since converged, the terms innovation and leadership need to converge. Systems, schools and students can be transformed with a broadened viewpoint that includes hiring innovative leaders who are focused on sustainable results. According to Kirtman, "These high-performing leaders embrace innovation and have the curiosity to learn from their teachers, colleagues, leaders in education and even other sectors about building truly creative learning environments for staff and students."[129]

Lyle Kirtman:
Competencies for High Performing Education Leaders

I have found in my research of 1,000 national leaders in education that we have already begun to transform our cultures slowly. In fact, our most successful leaders have a broad base of skills and competencies. Yes, they realize the importance of instruction and are skilled at developing teacher-leaders who inform decision making and create innovative opportunities for students. These high-performing leaders also embrace innovation and have the curiosity to learn from their teachers, colleagues, leaders in education and even other sectors about building truly creative learning environments for staff and students. The following competencies help leaders build creative, sustainable learning environments with high expectations and great results for students.

1. **Challenging the status quo.** Delegates compliance tasks, challenges common practices and traditions, takes risk and looks for innovations to get results.

2. **Building trust through clear communications and expectations.** Is direct and honest, confirms understanding, follows through and is comfortable dealing with conflict.

3. **Creating a commonly owned plan for success.** Takes input, ensures buy-in, sets clear goals, monitors implementation and makes adjustments.

4. **Focusing on team over self.** Hires the best people for the team, commits to ongoing development, seeks feedback and empowers staff.

5. **Maintaining a sense of urgency for change and sustainable results in improving student achievement.** Is able to move initiatives ahead quickly, can be decisive, builds strategies to ensure sustainability and is able to manage change effectively.

6. **Committing to continuous improvement for self and organization.** Maintains a sense of curiosity for new approaches, has a willingness to change practices, listens to all team members, takes responsibility and has strong self-management skills.

7. **Building external networks and partnerships.** Sees broad role as a leader, values external networks, has a strong ability to build partnerships, uses technology to manage a network of resources.[130]

 Lyle Kirtman on Sustained Leadership

"Testing is important for data but doesn't provide direction," said Kirtman, adding, "Leaders need to think, work, and partner with people."[131] His team has looked at enough leadership profiles that they can predict problems. Most frequently, his coaching focuses on getting leaders out of compliance mode, often half of how school administrators spend their time. Lyle is used to coaching "A" students; he often has to convince them that "it's OK to get a 'C' in compliance." He helps them move things off their plate and start building relationships and focus on results. Kirtman helps leaders "get away from being overwhelmed and focus on reallocating resources and building partnerships."

Innovation is Harder Than Improvement

Improvement focuses on doing things better, while innovation focuses on doing things differently. Both are important, yet innovation, by definition, is more challenging. By way of example, standards-based reform is a series of efforts focused on improvement, while online learning and new learning models are examples of innovation.

Improvement efforts usually leave the basic time-bound, cohort-based structure in place and attempt to improve course offerings, course-taking patterns, guidance services, academic supports and the quality of instruction. While not easy, these improvements can result in big system-wide advancements in achievement and completion rates as seen in Cincinnati, New York City and Kansas City, Kansas. These reforms require data-driven process management—a relentless focus on quality instruction in every classroom. It is common knowledge that an aggressive improvement agenda requires capacity and political capital. Education leaders make deposits in the political capital account by, as Kirtman suggested, creating a shared vision and plan, exhibiting trustworthiness, and building support with clear communications among stakeholders.[132]

Because innovation is even more challenging than improvement, it requires more political capital, even when working from the edges (or as Michael Horn describes it, areas of nonconsumption[133]). Innovations have emerged from alternative schools, credit recovery and turnaround schools, whose students are generally poorly served by the traditional system. But as controversy swirling around Michigan's EAA suggests, when innovation disrupts employment, it becomes highly controversial.

Innovating by developing new schools is extremely challenging for leaders, especially when it is likely to cannibalize enrollment, but it is also much more likely to provide improved results when based on thoughtful design principles such as Carnegie's Opportunity by Design or Next Generation Learning Challenges.

Following are a few examples of the differences between improvement and innovation in the K-12 context:

	Improvement	Innovation
Goals	Boost graduation rates	P-TECH schools: diploma, AA degree and a computer science job
Time	Double block math	Flipped classroom strategies to extend learning
Personalization	Differentiated instruction	Blended format with adaptive learning
Progress	Remediation to avoid retention	Competency-based progressions where students show what they know
Path	Internship	Career Technical Education (CTE)-linked flex academy (*e.g.*, GPS Education Partners)
Providers	Local school	Multiple providers full- and part-time
Teaching	Station rotation model	Extended reach strategies including teaching online
Books	Doug Lemov's Teach Like a Champion	Clayton Christensen and Michael Horn's Disrupting Class

Education leaders need to consciously gauge their community's appetite for change and their internal capacity to deliver. They need to consider the amount of political capital they have earned and what they will need to do make deposits sufficient to support an aggressive change agenda. They need to balance the amount of improvement and innovation they can phase in over several years.

Improvement can be likened to playing a baseball game to hit a single or a double. Innovation can be likened to swinging to hit the ball out of the park. Education leaders need to facilitate community conversations that create the right balance of the two.[134]

Leveraging Broad-Based Leadership

Given the complexity and importance of both improvement and innovation efforts, it is vital that a broadened definition of leadership is assumed. While an improvement lens may look primarily to superintendents or mayors for leadership, innovation requires a broad base of leaders, with teachers, principals, parents, businesses, and yes, even students, assuming leadership roles. These groups and individuals take on different roles including that of advocate, instigator, builder and investor.

Many districts have delegated—really capitulated—leadership to the school level, hoping they will figure out how to leverage technology to reach higher standards. Mooresville Graded School District, on the other hand, is taking a systems approach with common goals and a collaborative culture, as well as shared practices, tools and information systems. This sort of enterprise approach usually feels top-down, but Superintendent Mark Edwards developed a system of distributed leadership where teachers have a say and feel supported. And it is evident at their annual summer institute, where teachers and principals clearly have important roles in defining challenges and solutions.[135]

Mooresville recently adopted requirements for four large-scale multimedia projects in third, sixth, eighth and 12th grade. Beginning in 2014-2015, students will add products from these projects to their digital portfolios. The rationale for projects, according to Edwards, is to broaden the experience base of all students. He observed the influence of socioeconomics on results as North Carolina adopted Common Core State Standards (CCSS): performance among affluent students' scores rose, while results for in students in poverty declined. Edwards said, "We're excited about the stretch goals and the impact they have on student knowledge and understanding."[136]

Values first. Regardless of circumstances or location, effective leaders cultivate, communicate and make decisions based on shared values. A couple of examples are found in Denver and New Orleans.

"We're a values-first organization," said Bill Kurtz, CEO of DSST Public Schools. "Each human being strives to be fully known and affirmed for who they are, and to contribute something significant to the human story."[137] That may sound more like a humanities network than a group of STEM schools, but the DSST team embraces the big questions.

Kurtz has created a collaborative environment known as a "distributed leadership" model that attempts to leverage each person's individual talents. In hiring their team of teachers, Kurtz said DSST looks for leaders, and "there has to be a commitment to demonstrated leadership without a title."

"Character starts with the adults," said Kurtz. That means core value commitment, modeling, 360-degree evaluations, and celebrations. "We're working hard to scale culture as we grow 35 percent per year." The seven DSST schools serve 2,800 mostly low-income minority students who receive a grade on each of the school's core values each trimester. The shared values include student decision-making to determine whether students return from a suspension. Kurtz sums it up by saying, "It's a high-care, high-accountability culture."

Smart Cities

Before becoming CEO of <u>New Schools For New Orleans</u> (NSNO), Neerav Kingsland was tutoring kids in a central city elementary school in 1999, when about 80 percent of the schools were failing. The figure is down to 10 percent now, and it is quite possible that in a few years there will be no failing schools in NOLA. The same could not be said for any other urban center in the country. Graduation rates have climbed from 45 to 78 percent—from disaster to U.S. average. The system of charter networks is a great turnaround example.

While the city's <u>Recovery School District</u> (RSD) required pre-storm insight and action by the state board, Kingsland argues that it is humility not brashness—and openness not certainty—that is required of leaders.[138]

 Neerav Kingsland:
<u>Humble Cities</u>

It is tempting to believe that smart cities need "smart systems"—systems where technocrats attempt to implement the best practices of a given era; systems where government officials review the research, design strategies, and then push the bureaucracy to implement.

But the limit of this model is clear. At best, it freezes innovation until the next technocratic makeover. At worst, it inhibits innovation from ever occurring. It is humility, and not smartness, that must be the primary design principle of a smart city's educational system.

How are humble systems different? Humble systems are not designed to implement the current best practice—rather, they are designed to nurture an ecosystem that allows innovation to flourish. Humble education systems should be built upon three principles:

1. Educators must be able to form their own organizations to operate schools. Educators should not simply be given school site autonomy or increased decision-making power. They should be given the power to start and scale their own organizations. Entrepreneurs are the source of innovation. And if we do not trust educators to be entrepreneurs, then, at the end of the day, we simply do not trust our educators to innovate.

2. Families must be given choice among these educator-run schools. The best entrepreneurs develop solutions to solve the needs of others. But if families have no power—if they have no choice—it is very difficult to test and scale solutions that can meet their needs. By banning choice, we are implicitly saying that every student can thrive in the same kind of school, which is another way of saying that it is only scale, and not innovation, that is important. Forced assignment of schools is antithetical to innovation and differentiation.

3. Government must regulate the system for both performance and equity. Changing the structure of public schooling should not make it any less public. Both the public good and taxpayer dollars remain at stake. Government must ensure that only the best educator-run organizations are allowed to expand—and it must revoke the school operation privileges of those organizations who do not serve students well. Additionally, it must ensure that all schools meet the needs of our most at-risk students.[139]

RSD creator Leslie Jacobs notes, "There is 50 times more involvement with school governance than there was before Katrina," largely a function of "350 local charter board members, representing every neighborhood and ethnicity and coming from very diverse backgrounds and experiences."[140] Jacobs and others also note how important the strong state accountability system was to creating the RSD and quality options. Caroline Romer Shirley and the Louisiana Association of Public Charter Schools were critically important in community engagement and charter school development.

The first decade post-Katrina was enabled by governance reform and powered by an amazing confluence of talent; the second post-storm decade will be characterized by autonomous school networks with highly engaged community boards, a harbormaster like NSNO, and a thick web of support for Edupreneurs. New Orleans will continue to be one of the best examples of what is possible in urban education because of its broad-based leadership. It also suggests that smart cities require leadership from a coordinated cast of characters: instigators, advocates, builders, educators, investors and harbormasters.

Making Way for Innovation

A recent report, "Great Principals at Scale," found that the lack of autonomy for principals is a major deterrent to finding and developing school leaders.[141] For example, the lack of autonomy shows up in hiring teachers, when principals typically have to select a team based on collective bargaining agreements that value seniority over results. Effective districts give principals the authority to build their own teams. If districts want a principal to get the job done, they have to give them the freedom to hire, reassign or dismiss staff.[142]

This theme of clearing a path for innovation rings true not only for principals, but for teacher-leaders as well. Rick Hess, Harvard professor and author of Cage-Busting Leadership, describes setting people free from restraints through his concept of cage busting.

 Rick Hess:
Cage-Busting Leadership

Creating a great education system isn't just a matter of practice, because rules, regulations, contracts and cultures can stymie even the most committed educator. But it can't just be a matter of policy, because what really matters is what educators do in schools—and policies can make people do things, but they can't make them do them well. Successful education reform ultimately requires both policy change *and* the kind of school, system and teacher leadership able and willing to deliver on new possibilities.

Leadership is not just a matter of "instructional leadership." It's not just about curriculum, instruction and mentoring. It's also about understanding how to unwind old norms; rethink the use of time, tools, money and talent; and dismantle the barriers that stymie teachers and leaders. Now, it's true, as would-be reformers often argue, that old policies make it tougher than it should be for school and system leaders to drive improvement. However, it's also true that leaders have far more freedom to transform, reimagine and invigorate teaching, learning and schooling than is widely believed.

The problem is that in selecting, training, socializing and mentoring leaders, we have unwittingly encouraged "caged" leadership. You need only to talk to school and system leaders or school board members, observe education leadership courses, or read texts by education leadership icons to understand that leaders are expected to succeed via culture, capacity building, coaching and consensus—no matter the obstacles in their path. Indeed, talking about how to address or trample those obstacles is typically dismissed as a distraction by leading thinkers on education leadership.

The problem is that administrators are routinely trapped in "cages" of their own design by urban legends or not knowing what they're already free to do. Much as we wish it were otherwise, great schooling can't just be about policies or systems, or even about impassioned leadership—it needs to be about community leaders, district leaders, school leaders and teachers working to solve problems in smarter, more imaginative ways. And, on that count, cage busting becomes critical.[143]

 Rick Hess on Sustained Leadership

Portfolio Strategy

By 2005, it was clear that regional charter management organizations were achieving quality at scale and were an important development. It was also becoming clear that a portfolio strategy was, in most cases, the urban path forward. A portfolio strategy seeks good options for every family through school autonomy, pull-based funding, talent development, new school development, engagement and accountability. The high-demand, high-support combination of school improvement and new school development includes a multi-provider partnership of district and charter schools, and it empowers families to make choices.[144]

Most K-12 portfolios start with interlopers creating educational options. Tensions often rise with fights over enrollment, facilities and funding. At that point, either options are blocked, or partnerships are created. A portfolio strategy requires district leaders committed to student success with a "whatever it takes" attitude; it requires outsiders to come to the table and collaborate. Leadership is both a prerequisite for, and a byproduct of, a portfolio strategy. Leaders are required to ensure options are innovative and equitable, and with the opportunities for new schools, leaders are born through the process.

Paul Hill, founder of the Center for Reinventing Public Education (CRPE) at the University of Washington, was an early and important advocate for this approach. CRPE has defined seven portfolio strategy components.

1. Good options and choices for all families. Families have the freedom to attend their neighborhood school or choose one that is the best fit for their child. Portfolio districts make sure there are good schools in every neighborhood. They also give families useful information and support to make enrolling clear and simple.

2. School autonomy. Principals and teachers—the people who work with kids every day—can decide what and how to teach to bring out the best work in their students.

3. Pupil-based funding for all schools. This school funding model links money to each student in a school, rather than to school positions. It allows principals to make spending choices that make the most sense for their school and to make sure as much money as possible is spent directly in classrooms, rather than at the district.

4. Talent-seeking strategy. The most important element of education is the people who teach and lead the schools every day. Every city needs smart, compassionate, motivated, creative people working in the schools and district offices. Portfolio districts focus on developing the strong people they have and seeking new talent from the best districts, charter schools and training programs.

5. Sources of support for schools. Schools need to be able to make use of the best ideas and materials available. Those things may come from the district, but they also might come from local organizations or from online providers. Portfolio districts help schools find these best

ideas, training or materials and allow them to choose and purchase what they want within their budget.

6. <u>Performance-based accountability for schools</u>. Schools need to be caring, cheerful, exciting places. They also must be places where children learn the challenging things they need to succeed in the world. For all the possibilities that portfolio districts give to schools, schools must be able to show they are teaching all students, and that students are engaged and prepared for the next grade or transition.

7. <u>Extensive public engagement</u>. Districts need to know what families want, and they need to show them what they'll get. This strategy brings a lot of changes to schools. It works best if it channels the needs and dreams of communities for their children, and translates those into new opportunities for families, teachers and school leaders.[145]

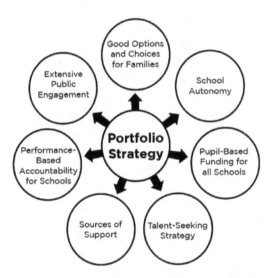

Andy Smarick, <u>Bellwether Education Partners</u>, outlines the concept of a "true portfolio" approach in his book <u>The Urban School System of the Future</u>. In a recent Getting Smart blog post, Smarick writes, "We start by seeing the district as nothing more than one of many school operators in the city, placing it on the same playing field as the city's charter school operators."[146] From there, Smarick describes the importance of applying the systemic innovations of chartering across the entire K-12 portfolio and empowering families with choice. Smarick asserts that elevating school quality above school provider, de-emphasizing the district role, and maintaining high fidelity to smart portfolio management allows for the greatest chance of developing "dynamic, high-performing, self-improving systems of schools that will put underserved kids on a trajectory taking them to the moon and beyond."

Ranging from competitive to cool to collaborative, the relationship between school districts and public charter schools is of growing importance now that more than 25 cities have more than 20 percent charter enrollment.[147] About 90 percent of New Orleans students attend charters; half of all students in Detroit and the District of Columbia attend charters. Almost 100,000 students attend charters in Los Angeles. In most urban areas, districts and charters compete for students, argue about facilities, and worry about budgets. But with more than 6,400 charters and growing pressure for achievement, there are more signs of collaboration. The most basic area of collaboration is a universal enrollment system for all public schools in a city. If the state accountability system does not have common metrics, it helps to establish those in order to help families evaluate all schools on consistent criteria.

The Spring Branch Independent School District near Houston is an example of district and charter school collaboration. They hired Elliott Witney, one of the six people who launched KIPP public charter schools, to be executive director of strategic initiatives and innovation. The collaboration is highlighted in Richard Whitmore's new book, On the Rocketship: How Top Charters are Pushing the Envelope. He notes that Witney's job is to bring in effective charters and help regular schools reach the same level of effectiveness. Best practices from top performing charters were incorporated into the Spring

Branch and Houston turnaround strategy. These collaborative examples could lead to more constructive district and charter school relationships.

In the last decade, many urban education leaders decided that a multiple-provider portfolio was the best way to create quality educational options. The new opportunity of the coming decade is innovation partnerships that personalize learning and expand access to digital learning. (See the chapter on collective impact for more examples of district-charter partnerships.)

Overcoming Obstacles
"No single school sector can adequately address the education crisis in our country's large cities," said Abby Andrietsch. "We need meaningful collaboration and resource-sharing among all types of schools, leaders, and teachers who have in common an intense desire to improve and a fiery belief that all children are capable of achieving at a high-level."[148] Several cities and school networks, including Schools That Can Milwaukee (STCM) where Andrietsch serves as a leader, are rising examples of overcoming obstacles by leveraging strengths—including vision, teacher leadership and design thinking—to overcome the obstacles to innovation.

Leveraging vision. "Leaders remind people what is important," said Bill Hughes, also of SCTM. Hughes and Andrietsch believe strong leaders are the linchpin of high-performing schools; they set a vision for their school, attract and develop talented teachers for every classroom, and lead the implementation of best practices. "Leadership is a learned skill," said Hughes. In Wisconsin, it must be learned in a master's degree program, so Hughes and STCM created a partnership with Alverno College.

Education leaders face obstacles on every front, but they push, persuade and persist; they include, improvise and innovate. They live in the future where things work better for learning, and they invite others to join them.

Leveraging teacher leadership. CityBridge Foundation was formed by Katherine and David Bradley in 1994 as a best practices shop for District of Columbia schools. In 2013, CityBridge and NewSchools Venture Fund launched the Education Innovation Fellowship, a professional development opportunity for 20 teacher-leaders. They meet monthly for a year, surveying all the sector knowledge about next gen tools and models and visit innovative schools. They bring their principals with them to three sessions to get them excited about the opportunity.

In September 2013, CityBridge announced Breakthrough Schools: D.C., a whole-school design grant program in partnership with Next Generation Learning Challenges.[149] Many of the Fellows have already created or joined teams to propose new or transformed schools. The combination of training teacher-leaders and then offering whole-school design grants is a unique and potent combination.[150]

Leveraging design thinking. With a headquarters in the heart of Silicon Valley, Summit Public Schools has absorbed some of the startup DNA. CEO Diane Tavenner leads a talented team that applies lean startup and iterative development strategies. Because they are leading their own platform development, the Summit team is able to iterate on their school model and tool set simultaneously.[151]

"We tend to think first about the needs of the system and create solutions from there," said Sandy Speicher, Managing Director of Education Practice at the design and innovation firm IDEO. "But what if we looked first to the needs of people, and then designed ways the system could meet its goals by serving these needs?"[152] Beginning with the user experience is the heart of design thinking and the beginning of most innovative solutions. Speicher describes how design thinking can produce win-win solutions.

Sandy Speicher: Design Thinking—
Human-Centered Approach to Innovation

Recently IDEO, the design and innovation firm where I work, collaborated with San Francisco Unified School District to develop a new vision for their food system. Instead of starting from a typical approach to food system reform— auditing equipment, aligning policies—we started by thinking about the students.

Through interviews, observations and workshops, we engaged hundreds of people, including students, parents, union leaders, nutritionists, teachers and community groups. We learned so much about today's kids—how many different taste palettes they represented, how desperate they were for time to connect with friends, how engaged they were with food outside of school (from cooking to blogging), and how much they were craving information to help them be responsible about food. Thus, our solutions included expanding food choices, eliminating long lines, and adding more places to get food. We also designed a technology platform that allows students to order food, give feedback and manage their nutrition and budgets, which of course helps the system be more efficient and effective.

Ultimately, our recommendations balanced an understanding of today's students with the realities of budgets, staffing and local and federal regulations.

As part of this collaboration, we prototyped our ideas with students. In one particularly revealing moment, a student told us what she thought about the new lunchtime experiences: "I love this so much. This would be amazing. I just can't believe you would do this for us."

Her words sound simple, but stop and think. Every day people show up at work in our schools because they care deeply about our kids. Yet we often end up designing experiences that don't actually meet these kids where *they* are. We unintentionally turn them off, so much so that they don't believe we would design something that they would actually like.

> People, and our understanding of them, are the heart of innovation.
>
> Designing with an understanding of people's needs and desires—what design thinking is all about—doesn't mean we compromise the system's desired outcomes. Rather, the design process takes the aspirations of a system and seeks ways we can achieve these outcomes through experiences that people actually want. If we really want to innovate in education, we must let go of our assumptions about how schools work and open up to what really understanding our students can teach us about what we should be creating.[153]
>
> Sandy Speicher on Innovation Mindset

Leveraging strong mayors. Over the last 20 years, schools in three of America's great cities—Boston, Chicago and New York City—benefited from a sustained partnership between a mayor and a K-12 system head.

Five-term Boston Mayor Tom Menino hired Superintendent Tom Payzant in 1995. Their 11-year partnership, bolstered by support organizations, made Boston Public Schools the best urban system in the country a decade ago. Tim Knowles learned the craft as Payzant's deputy in Boston before developing a fantastic example of a university-based school improvement engine, under the umbrella of the University of Chicago Urban Education Institute and working with Arne Duncan who took over from Paul Vallas as CEO of Chicago Public Schools in 2001. Hired by Mayor Daley, Duncan had crafted a coherent effort to support struggling schools and to close and replace failing schools. In 2004, Duncan, the mayor and the business community launched new school campaign Renaissance 2010, which resulted in 13 charter networks and 70 new schools, and laid the groundwork for the next gen model's work that New Schools for Chicago is currently supporting.

Duncan's agenda was similar to Joel Klein's <u>Children First</u> plan in New York City. Hired by Mayor Bloomberg in 2002, Chancellor Klein had the support to close failing schools and open new schools. Klein assembled a world-class team of educators including <u>Michele Cahill from Carnegie</u>. Klein's decade of leadership made New York City the most important and innovative in the country. Leaders from Klein's cabinet have gone on to lead districts and states around the country.

In addition to spearheading K-12 system partnerships, mayors—again with Boston as an example—can have a strong influence in workforce development at large. Initially created by former Boston Mayor Raymond Flynn, the <u>Mayor's Office for Jobs & Community Services</u> (JCS) has the goal of "promoting economic self-sufficiency to ensure the full participation of all Boston residents in the city's economic vitality and future."[154] Mayor Menino has built upon that structure, enabling the agency to develop and expand with the addition of summer jobs, programs targeted at court/gang youth, and other employment initiatives.

Blended, Lean and Iterative
Lyle Kirtman's leadership competencies (featured earlier in this chapter) include timeless qualities of challenging, communicating, team building, partnering and trustworthiness. Rapidly changing technology and improving learning opportunities—for youth and adults— makes three leadership strategies a priority: blended learning, lean operations, and iterative development.[155]

New tools—particularly inexpensive Internet devices and adaptive game-based learning systems—have created new design opportunities for learning environments. Combining the best features of digital and face-to-face learning, the <u>Christensen Institute</u> says blended learning incorporates "some element of student control over time, place, path, and/or pace."

Blended classrooms can provide a boost to a group of students, but blended schools create a new world of opportunity for how a team of teachers interacts with hundreds of students and how students experience learning. Blended schools redesign roles and use technology to extend the reach of excellent teachers and the teams they lead.[156] Adaptive learning is a particularly important blended tool because it combines continuous assessment with targeted tutoring. And as discussed in the next chapter, blending personalized online learning with team-based development is also the best way to boost professional learning.

Leading lean. "Simply, lean means creating more value for customers with fewer resources," according to Lean Enterprise Institute.[157] A lean organization understands value and focuses its key processes to continuously increase and improve it. Lean thinking changes the focus of "management" from optimizing separate technologies, assets and vertical departments to optimizing the flow of "products and services" through entire value streams that flow horizontally across technologies, assets and departments to users. Lean is not a simply a new program or short-term cost reduction approach, but a paradigm for entity operation.

Lean schools allocate a high percentage of their budgets to classrooms and they invest in productivity-producing tools and initiatives. They use design thinking to reconsider everything in their quest to optimize learning.[158] Reynoldsburg City Schools in Columbus, Ohio, is a good example of a district that has rethought strategy, structures and systems to transform its schools and create new student learning pathways. The lean startup methodology has transformed how new products are built and launched within and beyond the education industry.

While common among education technology startups, iterative development strategies are also being used by some school networks. Summit Public Schools in the Bay Area and Michigan's EAA are simultaneously iterating on school models and learning platforms. Summit opens at least one new school each year and each school reflects a new version of the school model and platform. The combination of organizational design with technology design is yielding promising results in both cases.

Following is a summary of all three elements—reflecting new tools, new approaches and an innovation mindset—along with a comparison to a traditional approach.

	Traditional	Blended, Lean and Iterative
Strategy	Implementation-oriented	Hypothesis-driven experimentation
Experience	Step-by-step plan	Test, hypothesize, iterate
Design	Prescribed	Flexible, 90-day cycles of innovation
Communication	Top-down	Frequent shared reflection
Organization	Departments, individuals	Problem-solving teams
Development	PD to support plan	Continuously developing mindset/skills
Evaluation	Year-end results	Real-time, data-informed decisions
Failure	Avoided	Expected: fix it, iterate
Speed	Measured: compliance data	Rapid: hacks on "good enough" data

Leadership is critical to each of the seven keys to education and employment. Effective leaders practice and encourage an innovation mindset, find and develop talent, build authentic partnerships, seek and provide aligned investments, set the vision for new tools and schools, and advocate for policies that promote equitable access to quality education.

Chapter Summary

- Leaders challenge the status quo, build trust, create commonly owned plans, build partnerships and create momentum.

- Improvement focuses on doing things better, while innovation focuses on doing things differently. Leaders create the right balance between the two.

- Smart cities require leadership from a cast of characters: instigators, advocates, builders, educators, investors and harbormasters.

- Portfolio strategy seeks good options for every family through school autonomy, pupil-based funding, talent development, new school development, engagement and accountability.

- Leaders leverage advocacy, teacher leadership and design thinking to overcome obstacles.

- Leaders incorporate a lean, flexible and iterative approach.

3: Talent Development

Renee Hill:
Talent is Underrated

In any learning organization supporting innovation, our workforce, our talent, may be the single most important resource. An intelligent, capable, results-driven pool of individuals who are willing to act interdependently and accountably is essential for any school or school district to competently meet the needs of today's students, parents, professionals and communities. Talent is THAT important. Our district, Riverside Unified, has set sail on the course of personalized learning (PL). We are allowing our PL talent to design their own approach, respecting their own, their customers', and their community's assets, needs, interests and state of development. In addition to the attributes listed above, here are more essentials we have identified thus far.

A comfort level with loose and tight. Abundance of information and resources makes our most capable teachers and leaders as informed as anyone in an "official" instruction role. To adjust, we are doing our best to remain tight on some critical aspects of our instructional program and loose on all others. We are tight about the fact that grade-level, standards-based learning is the floor. We are tight about having common assessments across grades or subjects. We are tight about students having flexibility in delivery of learning resources and selection of device. We are loose about how quality content is presented to the student, and we are becoming more loose about how students show their learning. We know we'll have to let go of pacing altogether. Pacing is the student's, not ours.

An iterate attitude. Traditional teachers plan everything out and advance the plan. The speed of learning, the availability of resources, and the wealth of tools no longer support long-term execution. Now, we iterate. Start, check, modify, restart or continue, repeat. There is no time to fully develop solutions. We operate in outline form, draft outline form, even. Outline a plan and get busy! This creates the need to be able to listen well, to pivot quickly, and hold fast to desired outcomes while quickly releasing chosen methods of arriving at outcomes.

A refreshing "well" and a stance of selflessness. Transforming public schooling is hard work—physically, mentally and spiritually. PL talent must be able to go to the well. They must have ways to refresh, draw energy and fuel creativity, all while remaining in a stance of collaboration and professionalism toward students, parents and colleagues. A measure of selflessness allows these pioneers to put reactions into perspective and move on with their very good work.

Our teams that have made the greatest strides in personalized learning are able to live with both "non-negotiables" and "undefineds." They are able to begin work with mostly complete outlines and partial plans. They maintain focus on outcomes and are willing and able to adjust processes iteratively. Finally, their ability to be selfless protects them from being stopped by criticism and indifference. They are able to go to their well and gather the energy to fuel the work of pioneering.[159]

"Knowledge is more valuable than ever, and that has increased the value of learning from people in other cities," said Harvard professor Ed Glaeser, author of _Triumph of the City_.[160] Leveraging that ideal, CEOs for Cities identified the four areas most vital to city success in their 2006 report "City Vitals I": connections, talent, innovation and distinctiveness.[161] These factors are gaining importance in education—and are blooming in school districts like Riverside.

The development of managed school networks in the U.S. may have been the most important innovation in K-12 education over the last two decades, but the importance of hiring and developing talented educators and school leaders was the most important insight. Talent development may seem obviously important, but schools of education are typically non-selective, and prospective school leaders are self-identified. Add terribly ineffective professional development, little regard for developmental work experiences, and strong incentives to leave high-challenge schools, and there is a disastrously bad talent pipeline.

Talent Matters

Great leaders find and develop great talent at all levels of the organization. They realize the connection between talent and outcomes. Examples of innovative talent development practices can be found both within districts and around the world. Given a mobile workforce, talent is a regional issue—one where strong, focused partnerships can quickly make an enormous difference in the level of initial preparation of teachers and leaders.

Talent is key to closing the opportunity gap. According to Aaron Walker, founder of EXPERTLY, by "broadening the pool of people and ideas—particularly the leaders of color or those from low-income backgrounds—we will create an innovation ecosystem that multiplies our ability to close the opportunity gap."[162]

Prize-winning Houston. The Broad Prize for Urban Education recognizes the top performing big city district. In 2013, the Broad Prize was awarded to Houston Independent School District (HISD) noting that "[s]ince 2009, HISD has focused on investing in its principals, teachers and other employees and put in place a system-wide level of accountability. The increased emphasis on human capital investment led the district to become far more selective in hiring and more rigorous in evaluating personnel performance."[163]

According to Superintendent Terry Grier, they seek to improve internal talent through recruitment, opportunity and reward. They recruit often and early through partnerships with universities and Teach for America (TFA). Initially, it was difficult to attract great teachers to previously failing and sometimes dangerous schools. Grier and his team turned that around with the largest TFA partnership in the country by offering big signing bonuses and by marketing the opportunity. They made visible changes at each school and invited candidate teachers to visit and talk to students who could attest to the turnaround underway.[164]

Houston created leadership opportunities so that teachers who want to stay in the classroom do not have to move into administration, but instead can lead capacity-building processes in areas of instructional technology, assessment and other initiatives. Such opportunities, along with a reputation for innovation and rewarding good performance, have led to a 90 percent teacher retention rate.[165]

Houston principals receive extensive training in teacher evaluation. With three members of the central office team, principals participate in a staff review of every evaluation for each teacher, including academic results. Principals are required to place their teachers in one of four categories ranging from high to low. These evaluations provide accountability and aim to retain top teachers and exit low performers.

"The district provides multiple types of differentiated professional development to all teachers and instructional staff to help meet district and school goals," according to the Broad Foundation.[166] HISD also provides instructional coaches to first- and second-year teachers.

The district's goal to use technology to transform the nature of learning and instruction is now on the verge of widespread adoption. HISD's approach has combined thoughtful goal setting, thorough planning and robust support. Their process demonstrates the importance of starting with learning goals and keeping them at the center of key implementation decisions, including staff development and technology deployment.[167]

Big Apple talent. Another good example of talent development is found in the New York City Department of Education (NYC

DOE). Districts are using data to transform its human capital system through "Smart Retention Reports." According to researchers Sengsouvanh Leshnick and Tina Law, "NYC DOE is using data boldly to reinvent human capital systems by providing school leaders with access to data about their talent. In doing so, they gain greater context about the needs of teachers and the supports they need to improve their practice."[168]

Three key lessons can be gleaned from NYC DOE's effort. First, districts can use data to gain greater context about the needs of teachers and the supports they need to improve their practice. Second, districts can develop responsive interventions based on data available with a particular focus on retaining what might be considered "irreplaceable teachers." And, third, districts can use data to focus on rewarding excellence.

The Big Apple is home to two outstanding leadership development programs: New York City Leadership Academy, which develops great school leaders through applied and team-based programs, and Relay Graduate School of Education, which is an innovative, independent preparation program that intends to be an early adopter of micro-credentialing in teacher training by piloting badges in its clinically focused, competency-based program.[169]

 Caroline Vander Ark:
Every Community Should Be Developing Leaders

Advancing Leadership (AL) is a community leadership development program for adults and high school seniors in Federal Way, Washington. Launched 14 years ago by community and corporate leaders (including then-Superintendent Tom Vander Ark) and modeled after programs in other cities, AL brings together emerging leaders for in-depth examination of key community components, intensive leadership training and a chance to work with local change agents on a team project. Participants develop their own leadership skills while they explore their city. Every month they dive into another facet of the community: housing, health, education, environment or commerce. Most days include eye-opening field trips and visits with community leaders.

While many communities offer a leadership development program, Advancing Leadership was one of the first to add a youth program. It is open to motivated high school sophomores and juniors who show evidence of leadership potential and interest in serving the community. Students participate in a two-day opening retreat and monthly sessions during the school year that are similar to the adult program. For many, it is a life-changing experience that helps leaders learn more about themselves and their community.

As a board member and alumna of the program, I have witnessed firsthand the change this program has had on our city. As a leader in my organization, I appreciate the professional development for my employees who enter the program. As a resident of the city, I am thankful for the dedication of the hundreds of alumni to making our city safe, sustainable and economically viable.

Through community partnerships with city hall, the fire and police departments, the school district and companies like Starbucks and Weyerhaeuser, AL is a great representation of the city's residents, students, services and businesses. Leadership development opportunities should be available to both adults and youth in every city.[170]

The best entities focus on talent. Successful Silicon Valley technology companies are innovative in large part because they hire innovative people. In order to find the right people, they share common hiring practices, which are represented below:

Innovative organizations hire:	Innovative organizations avoid:
People who add to products, services and culture.	People they cannot learn from or be challenged by.
People who will get things done.	People who just think about problems.
People who are enthusiastic, self-motivated and passionate.	People who just want a job.
People who inspire and work well with others.	People who prefer to work alone.
People who are well-rounded with unique interests.	People with narrow skills or interests.
People who are ethical and communicate openly.	People who are political or manipulative.
Only when they have found a great candidate.	Hiring just to fill a position.

Such talent-centered practices can influence not only a company or a city, but a country at-large. Singapore's innovative human capital strategy has propelled the country's overall transformation. Singapore's strategy has been implemented across three core phases, moving from survival to efficiency toward the end of the 20th century, and now into knowledge as the emphasis at the turn of the century.[171] It is this knowledge phase that has changed the shape of their education system and from which there are lessons to be applied across all levels and types of education.

Recognizing that a shift in education practices would be necessary to meet the demands of the global knowledge economy, Singapore moved from a focus on cultivating technical skills to a focus on building innovation, creativity and research. This translated right down to the title of the country's strategic plan, "Thinking Schools, Learning Nation." This title captures the essence of Prime Minister Goh Chok Tong's belief that a nation's wealth in the 21st century will depend on the capacity of its people to learn.[172]

Cities and states have no choice but to act aggressively to build effective talent development systems to create a vibrant economy. Realizing a dynamic knowledge-based economy requires a redesign with 21st century skills and demands in mind. A Global Silicon Valley (GSV) commentary concludes, "Human capital is the foundation for success. And as Singapore can attest, it will take common sense, courage and vigilance to make the blueprint a reality."[173]

"Talent development must be a policy priority for city leaders, and should be explicitly owned by an entity or coalition to ensure success," according to a recent report by EdFuel, a K-12 talent development shop. The report goes on to say that there is work to do across the learning sector: "Leadership in the new ecosystem requires an increasingly complex set of competencies in every role, yet most organizations lack a sophisticated understanding of how to prepare team members for this environment."[174] Jobs are different; it is time to update job requirements, focus on talent, and recruit accordingly.

Blended and Personalized Development

While attending Stanford University, Jason Lange identified a big opportunity to use digital tools to improve professional development. As part of the first Imagine K12 cohort in 2011, Lange and Eric Dunn, former director of engineering at EdisonLearning, built and piloted a professional learning platform at several charter networks. Launched in 2012, Bloomboard is working to provide personalized mechanisms for observation, evaluation and support across 19 states.

"Just as we see with students, educators benefit from blended and project-based learning, as well as external work-based learning and simulations. Our ability to ensure that professional learning is highly relevant and personalized, incentivized, and largely self-directed for all teachers will be paramount to the success of our education institutions," Lange said.[175] He outlines results from a global study of best practices in professional learning below.

 Jason Lange:
New Trends in Professional Learning

A 2013 Australian study conducted by the government-funded Australian Institute for Teaching and School Leadership and the nonprofit Innovation Unit examined 50 high-performing corporations, educational institutions and nonprofit organizations from around the globe to identify common features of professional learning experiences. These commonalities include collaboration between participants, blended (remote and face-to-face) learning, as well as an emphasis on personalization and informality.

The study found few examples of compulsory classroom-style training. Instead, professional learning "is incentivized through recognition and sometimes tangible rewards, usually within a culture of high expectations." The study identified these five global trends in professional learning:

- **Integrated.** Learning and performance feedback are closely connected and embedded in the culture.
- **Immersive.** Intensive, holistic experiences challenge beliefs and radically alter practices.
- **Design-led.** Problem-solving process requires deep user engagement.
- **Market-led.** New providers stimulate demand and grow the market.
- **Open.** Ideas and resources are freely exchanged in unregulated online environments.

These finding suggest that education professionals should have an individual learning plan and access to a combination of collaborative and online learning experiences, all of which need to be reinforced by regular embedded feedback and assessment mechanisms.[176]

 Jason Lange on Talent Development

The benefits of blended, work-based and Project-Based Learning for students hold true for educators as well. In most cases, professional learning should be offered, incentivized and highly relevant. Complex roles such as teaching and leading require a progressive sequence of work experiences and personalized learning. Educators should advance based on demonstrated expertise and their contribution to a learning community. As discussed in the next section, initial preparation should work the same way.

Preparing Educators

The role of an intellectual hub is key to an innovation ecosystem: what Harvard and MIT are to Boston, what Stanford is to Silicon Valley, what Carnegie Mellon is to Pittsburgh, what Arizona State University is to Phoenix. University-based research has played a pivotal role in talent development and resulting innovations in technology, medicine and energy. Conversely, universities have played a lagging rather than leading role in education at a time when talent is more important than ever. There was a big but generally unrecognized educator preparation problem 10 years ago when Art Levine began researching his groundbreaking report, Educating School Teachers. The problem has grown exponentially worse with advances in technology, the development of new school models, diversifying student populations and the shift to new college- and career-ready standards and the next generation of assessments.[177] And there is also the problem of accreditation and certification of educators. Originally designed to promote quality, accreditation and certification now serve as a barrier to entry for quality applicants. A Heritage Foundation report concludes that, while some form of accreditation is necessary to protect students from low-quality providers, the current system is a "barrier to entry in a market, enabling existing providers to use licensing to thwart competition."[178]

According to the National Council on Teacher Quality (NCTQ) Teacher Prep Review, only a handful of the more than 1,100 teacher preparation programs reviewed perform at a high level, and a significant number are effectively failing.[179] Leading state education officers, Chiefs for Change, commented, "This report offers a sobering look at the state of teacher training and underscores the critical need for improvement. As state leaders, we must support a healthy teacher pipeline, starting with teacher training. Our states are raising the bar for students by adopting the Common Core State Standards. Teacher preparation programs must keep pace with these changes in order to equip all educators with the skills and knowledge they need to help children succeed."[180]

Carri Schneider:
Preparing Teachers for Deeper Learning

Imagine a map of what a learner needs to know, different ways to learn it, and a collection of their demonstrations of competence. You're probably picturing a blended learning environment for students. Instead, imagine that every teacher has access to his or her own professional map—reflecting common expectations differentiated by specialty, subject, level and school type—that offers a clear description of what teachers should know and be able to do. Imagine that the teacher is offered multiple ways to learn, differentiated pathways with opportunities to specialize, individual and cohort models, interactive communities, and aligned learning opportunities. Imagine a series of ways for teachers to demonstrate competence through peer and expert review, automated assessments, and observations, interviews and demonstrations. This is what the next generation of talent development looks like for teachers.[181]

Susan Patrick, President and CEO of the International Association for K-12 Online Learning (iNACOL), underscores the need for better preparation, highlighting the need to equip teachers with skills and methods to target individualized instruction and maximize research-based strategies around empowering students using the digital resources available to them. "Teachers need to be prepared with the tools to personalize instruction and expand open, digital content resources to help them succeed and meet each student's individual needs. This requires a call to action for schools of education to transform their educator and leadership preparatory programs—rethinking talent development for a modern workplace in education. Educator preparedness needs to examine how to implement digital learning models requiring students to engage deeper learning through personalized, mastery-based pathways." On professional development, Patrick added, teachers "need flexible options with personalized pathways that fit their own needs—and to demonstrate competencies for advancement, too."[182]

Progress in prep. One sign of progress in teacher preparation is the adoption by seven states of edTPA—a partnership between the Stanford Center for Assessment, Learning and Equity (SCALE) and the American Association of Colleges for Teacher Education (AACTE) that creates a multiple-measure assessment system aligned to state and national standards including Common Core State Standards (CCSS) and the Interstate Teachers Assessment and Support Consortium (InTASC). Another promising partnership is the Albertson Foundation-sponsored blended and competency-based approaches to preparation at the University of Idaho and Northwest Nazarene University.[183] Yet another example is competency-based Western Governors University that prepares the largest number of STEM teachers in the country.[184]

A spring 2014 report, Preparing Teachers for Deeper Learning, advocated for multiple blended competency-based pathways to the classroom, as Karen Cator describes.

 Karen Cator: A Competency-Based Approach to Preparing Teachers

As calls for improving achievement and increasing personalization of student learning echo across the national discourse, new adult learning models are creating the potential for personalized preparation and development pathways for teachers. As student roles change in a personalized learning environment, teacher preparation and professional learning should evolve accordingly in order to offer teacher control over time, place, path and/or pace; balanced goals; meaningful integration and competency-based progression.

Just as K-12 blended learning models offer students opportunities to learn in both in-person and online environments, blended teacher preparation and development could combine online learning with onsite experiences. New pathways could be part of a formal degree program or an alternative program, specific to a group of schools or particular models.

In the same way that student assessment is evolving to prioritize demonstrations of mastery over basic proficiency, competency-based teacher development would enable pre-service and practicing teachers to demonstrate knowledge and skills at regular intervals.

Micro-credentialing, or badging, is a competency recognition system aligned with a series of gates or milestones recognized by a community. Recent research and development efforts have focused on the use of digital badges or tokens to signify accomplishment and to measure and reward competency-based outcomes. A series of micro-credentials could be used to mark initial preparation as well as recognize and reward ongoing development and leadership in myriad aspects of the education profession.

A competency-based approach to high-quality teacher preparation and ongoing professional learning opportunities would offer:

- Some element of teacher control over time, place, path and/or pace;
- Balance between teacher-defined goals, goals as defined by administration through teacher evaluation efforts, and school and district educational goals;
- Job-embedded and meaningful integration into classroom practice; and
- Competency-based progression.[185]

Most states require principals to earn a master's degree; many districts require superintendents to earn a doctorate. Both are time-consuming and expensive for educators and only partially relevant to the task of leading a school or system. Like the teacher pathways described above, competency-based leadership development would be faster, cheaper and more relevant.

Informal Learning

Talent is everywhere and can be tapped through informal learning. The viral adoption of learning applications and resources by teachers and families is one of the most important trends of this decade. The EdTech revolution is equipping young teachers, rejuvenating veteran teachers, and inspiring education entrepreneurs. But while new apps may spread globally, many teachers and entrepreneurs lack local connections. Christopher Nyren is the Johnny Appleseed of EdTech, creating Meetups and Startup Weekends to connect and support Edupreneurs. "I continue to bang the drum to get more widespread recognition of over-looked centers of education innovation."[186]

 Christopher Nyren:
EdTech Ecosystem in a Bottle

Through the vehicle of Educelerate, we have sought to bring our EdTech "Ecosystem in a Bottle" model to local partners in other over-looked markets like the Upper Midwest, Los Angeles and Phoenix. Indeed, Southern California has seen nearly as many scaled successes among education technology companies as the northern half of the state, but it has lacked even a single Meetup group, let alone any EdTech accelerators. After launching Educelerate LA, we stepped in to help organize LA StartupWeekend EDU and a post-Startup Weekend Education (SWEDU) event featuring some of the most promising startups that tapped into the buzz around "Silicon Beach." That event drew 165 attendees and was one of the most heavily attended EdTech Meetups across the country!

It is my hope that this humble effort has helped bring more attention to the Midwest, Phoenix and Southern California. (Call it the "Route 66 of EdTech.") In so doing, we have created a scalable and replicable model that combines high-quality, in-person event programming.[187]

These informal online and onsite learning opportunities are part of the new talent development landscape. Bringing talent development opportunities to scale takes sustained leadership across multiple partnerships.

Chapter Summary

- Jobs are different; it is time to update job requirements.
- Preparation for complex roles like teaching and leading requires a progressive sequence of work experiences combined with personalized learning.
- Employment and advancement should be based on demonstrated mastery.
- Schools should signal requirements to formal and alternative preparation, and they should not hire anyone that does not fit the bill.
- Just as students benefit from innovative education opportunities like blended learning and Project-Based Learning, educators should, too.

For further information on this topic:

   Tim Hilborn on Talent Development

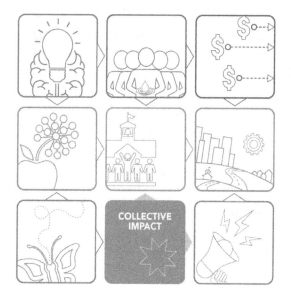

4: Collective Impact

 Partnership Success Story:
College, Career, and Technology Academy

"Many young people don't see the connection between high school and the rest of their life. And so there's a lot of time in high school that they spend maybe killing time," said Superintendent Daniel King, "Well, high school not only needs to be more challenging; it needs to be more real."[188]

King leads a McAllen area school district representing the Pharr, San Juan and Alamo communities in the Rio Grande Valley (RGV), one of the poorest regions of the country. In 2007, the district teamed up with South Texas College to create the College, Career & Technology Academy (CCTA), a college-connected dropout recovery school that builds on statewide success with schools and policies that connect high school and college.

Early college high schools blend high school and college in a rigorous yet supportive program, compressing the time it takes to complete a high school diploma and the first two years of college. Not just for advanced students, the early college proposition has proven effective as a dropout recovery strategy. "We not only get them back on track to complete their high school requirements, but also connect them to college," said CCTA principal Yolanda Gomez.[189]

CCTA is a partnership success story. It builds on the work of Educate Texas, a statewide nonprofit and one of the most successful public-private partnerships in the country over the last decade, yielding 135 new high schools serving 63,000 students—more than 70 percent minority and low-income.[190] Educate Texas built on the success of the national Early College High School initiative facilitated by Jobs for the Future (JFF).

Reviewing CCTA, JFF said, "Under the leadership of Dr. Daniel King, Pharr-San Juan-Alamo illustrates how Texas districts can use innovative state policy to improve graduation rates by reengaging and graduating out-of-school youth."[191]

Smart Cities

Spurred by a 2011 Stanford Social Innovation Review (SSIR) article and success in Cincinnati, Educate Texas formed regional collective action initiatives to focus community leaders around measuring a common set of indicators, to identify effective strategies and to direct resources toward helping spread these practices. A Rio Grande Valley collective impact team, RGV Focus, identified CCTA as a successful way to get high school dropouts on an accelerated pathway not only to earn their high school diploma, but to move them toward a college degree. "Other districts are beginning to replicate these efforts utilizing their own funds and resources," said George Tang, Educate Texas COO. "Collective impact can provide the type of adoption and spread that has been so elusive to the EdReform world."[192]

Social impact consultants John Kania and Mark Kramer wrote in SSIR, "Successful collective impact initiatives typically have five conditions that together produce true alignment and lead to powerful results: a common agenda, shared measurement systems, mutually reinforcing activities, continuous communication, and backbone support organizations."[193] Collective impact begins with a commitment to engagement and builds on well-constructed partnerships. This chapter investigates both and concludes with best practices in collective impact.

Family Engagement
Family engagement starts with a relationship, and supporting high expectations is key. Preston Smith, co-founder of Rocketship Education, knows that every student and every family matters. He has worked to develop character and enterprise by living this belief out every day.

Preston Smith:
What Would Real Parent Engagement Look Like?

It was a late night in April, after a long, warm San Jose day leading a local district school as the principal; I was now at a student recruitment event at a local church where I would meet with prospective families and students for the charter school that we were opening in a mere four months.

On this evening, only one family arrived. It would be a slow recruitment night, but every student and family matters. Maria had come this evening with her son, who was sick. He lay on the floor, moaning while his mother sat across the table from me— wary and dubious. She immediately began to pepper me with questions about the quality of the school and why I was doing this. I could immediately sense the challenges within this family, as well as her deep mistrust of the public education system.

Through home visits conducted by school staff with every family and monthly community meetings, Maria built trust with me and with our larger school community. She knew that her son was not merely *another* student and that we also cared about her story— as a person, as a mom.

Maria joined in the parent collaboration where parents help with staffing, planning and prioritizing. We invest in the innate leadership in each parent and train them to become powerful advocates for student achievement and excellence. We encourage them to meet with local public officials and to learn more about the public systems impacting their lives.

Rocketship's mission is to eliminate the achievement gap. We know this goal can only be achieved if we have a much broader base of parents in our country who see themselves as civic leaders with the tools to improve their local community, holding local school systems accountable to making sure all students succeed.

Maria's son is now in high school, and she shared with me that during a recent road trip, they discussed where he wanted to go to college. She is incredibly proud of him, but I could also see the pride she has developed in herself, the sense of voice, value, confidence and connection that had been nurtured through her deep engagement in the Rocketship community.

By taking the time to build a real relationship with parents like Maria and encouraging them to see their own leadership capacity, schools can become catalysts of broader community transformations.[194]

In April 2014, the W.K. Kellogg Foundation made grants totaling $14 million to 30 organizations implementing transformative family engagement models that emphasize starting when children are young. Unprecedented interest in the grant program was an indication of both the need and opportunity to invest in efforts that would result in increased family engagement in a child's academic life. One example of a funded program that will provide leverage for engagement was an award given to the Institute for Sustainable Economic, Educational and Environmental Design (I-SEEED). The grant proposal indicates that "the goal is to build an ecosystem of 'solutionists' to solve communities' most pressing social problems," and asserts "that through innovative economic, educational and environmental design and cutting-edge technology, they can create sustainable cities and schools so that people do not have to leave their communities to live, learn, work and thrive."[195] The focus will be on deepening partnerships between the nation's most vulnerable families and children and the schools that serve them.

Motivation and expectations gap. Despite the fact that much of the world's knowledge is widely and freely available, there are millions of unfilled skills jobs and a growth wealth gap. Contributing to the gaps are poverty and a lack of functional literacy, which are real barriers to learning. Access to devices and to broadband are issues, but the access divide is rapidly shrinking. The most important divide may be the motivational gap between those who, as Tom Friedman said, "[H]ave the self-motivation, grit and persistence to take advantage of all the free or cheap online [resources] to create, collaborate, and learn" and those who do not.[196]

The fact that the best professors in the world are making their courses freely available is an important milestone in learning opportunity, but MOOCs are largely serving the college-educated seeking additional education. They are super-efficient at surfacing and developing talent. The winner of the Hewlett Foundation-funded essay scoring competition in 2013 was a college senior from Ecuador who had benefited from Andrew Ng's machine learning course that kicked off the MOOC revolution, another sign that the transnational economy will go to the motivated.[197]

The motivation to learn is largely a cultural issue and is unevenly distributed, particularly in America. On one end of the spectrum, Tiger Moms are stressing out their kids with the race for selective colleges. On the other end, generational poverty has cut off entire communities from the innovation mindset that connects effort and life outcomes.

On a family level, a common trap is to think that what generally works is complex or that it would require a certain level of experience or education of the parent. In fact, new research suggests the list of what works is short: parents should expect their child to go to college, discuss activities children engage in at school and request a particular teacher for the child.[198]

Community Engagement

"Education is like the night sky; EdReform offers a few points of light and the rest is dark matter," said Nick Donohue. "The real opportunity is deeper public engagement—tapping the dark matter." [199] Donohue has been a high school head master, a college trustee and a state chief of education. As CEO of The Nellie Mae Education Foundation, Donohue thinks a lot about real public engagement. "We've been digging our own hole in the way we talk to the public."[200]

Nick Donohue:
Engaging Communities With Common Values

Recent research suggests that many public school leaders work on counter-productive assumptions about the readiness, interest and even the basic capacity of regular people to understand the changes our systems need to keep up with the times—never mind to keep up with other higher-performing countries.

The main assumption many have is that in order to enlist support, we need to ring the alarm. Familiar ways of rallying support include: "We are in a crisis." "Parents, kids, community members you need to step up faster and further to help us!" "We need our budget restored or else their children will suffer."

It turns out that when people think they are in this kind of crisis they are driven to familiar but counter-productive frames of mind. A crisis frame pushes people to look back to basics and tap values about individualism, merit and competition. If you are in a crisis, get out fast and make sure those closest to you make it, too. This stifles innovation.

However, the research also suggests that Americans are naturally drawn to other core values that can be tapped to advance innovation and renovation of schooling at its foundation. These other values include fairness, pragmatism and a deep interest in being prepared for a good future.

If you give regular folks a chance to think ahead and consider what their communities need in order to be prepared—to be vital places to live and work—they will of course talk about individual success but within the context of community well-being.

The public is more understanding, more generous and more adventuresome than we have given them credit for. So, maybe those who promote deep innovations in the name of universal, equitable public education might rethink assumptions about the public, take some risks and make a bet on many of the core values that have made us a great nation. The bet is a sound one because it is, at its core, a bet on America and its people—one that has the power to move educational change to warp speed.[201]

Nick Donohue on Collective Impact

Donohue supports the work of FrameWorks Institute and thinks founder Susan Bales has created "a sheet of music on how to talk about changes."[202, 203]

FrameWorks Institute: 10 Tips for Talking Change

Following are ten framing observations
from a FrameWorks "MessageMemo":

- Education systems are invisible, which makes reforms unimaginable.

- Unframed conversations about education blame parents, teachers and/or students.

- The reforms that are easiest to think are the most conventional.

- Crisis thinking, while common, leads to caution and conservatism, not innovation and transformation.

- A lack of agency with respect to changing the education system leads to a defensive posture that favors a consumerist "me and my kid" approach.

- Individualized and consumerist approaches to education make it difficult, but not impossible, for people to see education as an engine that drives national prosperity and as an investment we all make in the country's future.

- When the goal of education is explicitly described as the future preparation needed to maintain and support our country's quality of life, people understand that a new set of skills and experiences are necessary.

- When people can see the system of education and the need to coordinate its different parts for the good of the whole, they become more expansive in their thinking about how and where reform might take place.

- When people can see reform as a practical act or as a set of methodical steps toward an ultimate goal, they gain agency and become more enthusiastic about education reforms.

- Individual education reforms need to be contextualized by values and simplifying models if they are to avoid people's tendency to default to strong, entrenched patterns of thinking that undermine meaningful reforms.[204]

Smart Cities

The transition to personal digital learning makes parent and community engagement more important than ever. New tools are making it easier to connect, listen and inform, but it is still relationships that matter. Bill Kurtz, CEO of Denver Schools of Science and Technology, reflects on the importance of, and deficit around, real conversation. "The capacity for cities and communities to have real conversations about real issues is a huge deficit in cities today. The real conversations either don't happen due to political constraints or because there is not a trusting context in which to raise issues of class, race, inequality, and so on."[205]

To foster community engagement, build trust and facilitate real conversation, it is more productive to tap common values rather than whip up crisis.

Partnerships

Everybody talks about partnerships, but it is hard to build and maintain a successful effort to scale innovation. Greg Butler, founder of Collaborative Impact, learned education technology while leading laptop initiatives in Australia and then in America. He learned how to build partnerships during a decade at Microsoft.

 Greg Butler:
Building Innovation Partnerships

Innovation and partnership are words often used and less often deeply understood. These two competencies are often practiced at a superficial level at best. Education systems can no longer be counted on to "fix" education in isolation or at a superficial level. The challenge requires multiple stakeholders—working across organizational and sectorial boundaries—to collaborate and innovate at a deeper level for continual inquiry-based cycles of improvement.

A transactional form of partnership, such as sponsorship, is common today. Such partnerships may increase access to resources, but in answering questions—such as "How can we fund this new program?"—they are unlikely to support the type of innovation and collaboration that will generate the thinking and learning required to address today's bigger challenges.

Transactional/
Tactical

Innovative/
Transformative

The Collaboration Continuum

Relational partnerships, however, go a step further and require deeper partnering skills. Such partnerships operate with a process focus, with partners working together on how things are done to address such questions as "How might the school integrate visiting experts into the curriculum?" For success at this level, there needs to be a focus on interpersonal issues with the output being relationships that facilitate people working together to achieve new processes.

Type	Transactional	Relational	Transformative
Collaboration Focus	Inputs and outputs	Interpersonal issues	Addressing the "un-discussable"
Outcomes	Tangible resources and actions	Relationships that facilitate working together to achieve new processes	Co-created and implemented innovative and transformative solutions

The deepest level of education transformation requires the most complex partnering skills and requires addressing the "un-discussable" by facilitating people to address core issues of drivers, culture, values and behaviors. Deeper questions—such as "How should we organize curriculum if student learning is our highest priority?"—can be addressed. When you get people working together across boundaries on the "un-discussable," real innovation and lasting transformation can be the output.

Managing partnership processes at the higher relational and transformative levels requires brokering competencies. Just as you wouldn't teach students without tools to measure performance, tools to measure partnership capacity are critical. Deeper innovation partnerships are critical for both innovation and partnership to flourish, at the system, school and classroom levels.[206]

 Greg Butler on Collective Impact

In our Google Hangout with Butler, he cited the Partnership Initiative and the four stages of successful relationships, including scoping and building, maintaining and managing, revising and reviewing, and sustaining outcomes. Education transformation requires complex partnering skills and addressing core issues of culture, values and behaviors.

Partnerships for achievement. Improved student learning at scale is always accompanied by partnerships focused on achievement. Shuttling from London to Punjab, Sir Michael Barber worked with the Chief Minister of Punjab, Pakistan, Shahbaz Sharif and top officials to draft the Punjab Education Reform Roadmap. The plan set targets, initiated a shift to merit-based hiring, supported teacher quality, supported facilities improvement, and promoted public-private partnerships. The result was a dramatic increase in student enrollment and teacher attendance.[207] In a report to the Massachusetts Business Alliance for Education, Barber and colleagues outlined the future of education and the opportunity to lead.

London : A Partnership Approach

London is one of the few capital cities in the world where educational results significantly exceed the national average. Results in national examinations at age 16 are better than any other region in England, and improving faster. In addition, children from low-income and ethnic minority backgrounds do better in London than in any other part of the country. How has London achieved this success? Partly it has been about the U.K. equivalent of charter schools, called academies, but on its own this would not have been enough. One of the most important factors has been stronger school-to-school partnerships created by a government program known as the London Challenge. The Office for Standards in Education (OFSTED), which inspects all schools in England, commented that "pan-London networks of schools allow effective partnerships to be established between schools, enabling needs to be tackled and progress to be accelerated."[208] The partnership approach in London included networks of experienced school leaders and current head teachers, who formed a pool of "system leaders" working with schools across London, as well as "coaching triads" in which lead teachers worked with colleagues from other schools to demonstrate high-quality teaching. London's success over the past decade is now receiving global attention.[209]

"Compact" cities. One barrier to city education partnerships is competition between school districts and charter schools. "For me, the common ground has been a long time coming," said Don Shalvey, adding, "I've lived on both sides. I was a public school teacher and administrator in California and then a district superintendent."[210] Sixteen years ago Shalvey founded Aspire Public Charter Schools, which has grown into a network of 37 schools that have delivered success for California students and expanded into Tennessee last fall. Five years ago, he joined the Bill & Melinda Gates Foundation, which gave him the opportunity to spend time with educators working inside and outside the system with the same goal of providing great learning opportunities for all students. His team has supported the development of 22 Compact Cities, where school districts and public charter schools have structured partnerships around desired outcomes.

Don Shalvey: Choosing Excellent Schools— Not Charter Versus District

Too often these days in schools, if you support charter schools you are seen as against the school district or even against public schools. Or, if you are a supporter of the district, you are often seen as anti-charter and against giving educational choices to parents. For students, education shouldn't be a zero-sum game among adults. It doesn't have to be. Adult labels can be put aside in favor of better schools for students. Some places are doing that. In a score of diverse communities, leaders from local school districts and high-performing charter schools are coming together to put students first.

Not surprisingly, the players from both sectors are realizing they have the same goals, the same challenges and the same respect for the craft of teaching and the joy of learning. They are replacing the charter-district battleground with common ground over excellent schools for students. Instead of choosing sides, they are choosing excellence.

And, if we as a nation truly care about real educational opportunities for all children, this move is necessary. Without charters and districts working cooperatively, we can't produce the quality schools needed for all students to succeed. Excellent charter schools are critical, but we won't collectively succeed without *all* schools becoming academically excellent. We need changed behaviors that produce better results.

It's no longer 1992, when I helped found the first California charter school and the nation's second. The sector is growing up, and the concept has gone from outrageous to ambitious. Consider the crossover effect where former superintendents like me have now formed and joined charter organizations while charter leaders like John King and Stefan Pryor are now the chief schools officers in New York and Connecticut. Things are changing. The lines are appropriately blurred in the service of youth.

Superintendents and charter leaders recognize that there's more common ground than battleground, and mayors are echoing those sentiments as well. For mayors, education is a quality of life issue and it's about all the youth in their cities.[211]

Shalvey finds it promising that districts like Spring Branch (Houston) and Franklin-McKinley (San Jose) are collaborating with charters on facilities. Hartford Public Schools and Achievement First are implementing a Residence Program for School Leadership. Denver Public Schools is working with charters on teacher preparation and special education. Boston and New Orleans each have a common enrollment system.

Shalvey continues, "If all of our neighborhood schools were great, we wouldn't be facing this crisis. But our children need great schools now—whether district-run public schools or public charter schools serving all students—and we shouldn't limit the numbers of one form at the expense of the other. Excellence must be our only criteria for evaluating our schools.'"[212]

There are more than 15,000 school districts and only 22 Compact cities. Shalvey admits that may be a "weak signal," but he is optimistic: "My money is on the collaborators and crossover leaders who see impact from these early adopters."[213]

The bottom line is that innovation at scale requires stakeholders working together to solve problems.

Partnerships for Employability. The survey of chief executives mentioned in the chapter on next gen learning makes clear the need to improve work skills—and work ethic was the clear winner. The next four priorities describe the demands of the new workplace—teamwork, decision-making, critical thinking and computer literacy. The "3 Rs" come next on the priority list.[214,215]

Most family wage jobs require some postsecondary education or training, but a college degree does not guarantee any of the priority work skills employers demand. Parents and politicians have figured out that even college graduates should possess skills and dispositions that make them employable. The need for better employability and the new opportunities of digital learning make it a great time for cities and states to rethink career education. Incentives to do just that were incorporated into the Workforce Innovation and Opportunity Act, signed into law in July 2014. It aims to streamline the federal workforce training system; encourage smaller, nimbler, and more strategic state and local workforce development boards; give schools the opportunity to cater their services to the needs of their region; and empower businesses to identify what skills workers need for success and help workers acquire them.[216]

After years of slow decline in career and technical (CTE) enrollment, there is growing nationwide interest in high-quality job preparation. But there is a persistent myth that CTE is the solution for the lowest-performing kids at the lowest-performing schools. It may be a more focused and accelerated path to employment, but, as high school expert JoEllen Lynch puts it, "CTE is a higher bar—not a lower bar." Lynch suggests that for all students, job number one is to "double down on efforts to engage high-quality literacy and numeracy."[217]

Boosting employability requires education and industry partnerships. For example, along with a "full-court press" on the basics, Houston Independent School District (HISD) set out to reinvent career and technical education in order to feed students into the local workforce. HISD partners with local employers, businesses, and industries—medicine, energy, computer technology, space, arts and humanities, Tier One educational and research institutions—in a reinvention of elementary through secondary education that blends academic rigor with preparation for higher education and career. This goes beyond programs to the development of targeted schools. A partnership with the Baylor College of Medicine, for example, has led to the development of a feeder middle school and DeBakey High School for the Health Professions in order to prepare students for medical and research careers; a partnership with the Independent Petroleum Association of America and Houston-area energy companies led to the creation of Energy Institute High School; and professional partnerships within central Houston support the High School for Law Enforcement and Criminal Justice and High School for the Performing and Visual Arts.

HISD is also addressing the critical need for workers in the middle skills, those skills that require education beyond what high schools traditionally offer but not necessarily a traditional four-year degree.

Encouraging students to consider a variety of pathways means being intentional about providing hands-on experiences in order to provide context and motivation. Michele Cahill notes that in her experience in technical skill pathways in fields like construction and nursing, "Project-based academic work and internships were important as both motivators and potential integrators of knowledge and skills but the underlying academics still needed to be towards high learning standards."[218]

Following are 10 partnership strategies to boost employability, five for all students and five strategies to improve career and technical education.

For all students:

1. **Encourage career awareness** in grades six through twelve. States and/or districts should encourage all secondary schools to incorporate career awareness into advisory curriculum and make career education resources available to all students. (See Core & More: Guiding & Personalizing College & Career Readiness). Starting in middle grades, students should be setting goals and linking job options with educational pathways. Advisers (and advisory systems) should track progress and provide decision-making support (*e.g.*, Summit Public Schools).

2. **Expand course choice** with an emphasis on CTE. Louisiana Course Choice is a great example of a state proactively seeking expanded online CTE courses linked to emerging job clusters.

3. **Expand work-based learning** for all students in grades six through 14. All students should graduate having experienced success in a career setting. Jobs for the Future outlines best practices in work-based learning, including assessment and feedback; work experiences that progress from introductory to advanced; mentoring and leadership development opportunities; and a digital portfolio to capture evidence and artifacts.[219]

4. **Applied learning** experiences ask teams of students to struggle with real-world problems. Examples include Reynoldsburg capstone super blocks; METSA New Tech capstone, presentations of learning at High Tech High,

and intensive, nine-week interdisciplinary courses at NYC iSchool.

5. **Improve work skills.** Most college graduates lack the skills for basic employability—work ethic, business analytics and communication, and design thinking. Programs like General Assembly, Koru and Fullbridge are filling the gaps left by K-16 education.

For Career and Technical Education (CTE):

6. **CTE flex academies** linked to emerging job clusters. GPS Education Partners is a network of manufacturing flex academies in the Upper Midwest. Career Path High near Salt Lake City is an early college flex high school at an applied technology training center.

7. **Grade 9-14 CTE schools** like Pathways to Technology Early College High School (P-TECH) computer science schools in Chicago and New York, where corporations such as IBM have partnered with districts to combine high school, work experiences and an associate's degree—with a good shot at a good job. "The P-TECH model takes the best of these other ideas and then goes a step further by bridging the job divide. I give IBM a lot of credit for that," says Harvard education professor Robert Schwartz.[220]

8. **Making stuff** can get kids excited about careers. There is a growing range of K-12 coding resources, Maker Faire (see a recap of Portland's #iPDX14) and DIY activities. Baltimore's Digital Harbor Foundation is making hands-on learning available after school and during the summer. Project Lead The Way is a great applied high school engineering curriculum. FIRST is a great robotics competition.

9. **Competency-based learning** is expanding in postsecondary and beyond. The more dynamic the job category, the more providers there are and the more alternative market signaling (*i.e.*, badges, alternative

credentials) is evident. Check out P2PU, the "university for the Web."

10. **Lifelong career education** is becoming the norm as obs change as fast as new technologies. Every adult should be part of a lifelong learning network. States could encourage colleges and universities to consider a lead role in lifelong learning. With a small investment and ongoing industry partnerships, it could be a self-sustaining line of business. Udemy for organizations is powering lifelong career learning for thousands of companies and nonprofit associations.[221]

Leaders in every region of the country need to recognize the need to help people skill up fast, not just to promote economic vitality but to address rising inequality, to build the quality of life and to build civic participation.

Partnerships for productivity. Different cities use different launch pads for productive partnerships. Cities and districts can frame opportunities for partners to invest in delivery solutions. In Boston, improvement was driven by the Boston Plan for Excellence and sustained district leadership (in part due to mayoral control). The partnership made Boston the leading urban district in the U.S. in the last decade. In New York, it was Joel Klein's embrace of intermediaries starting with New Visions for Public Schools, which became the most productive intermediary in the country helping to launch over 400 new schools in New York City.

Steven Hodas, former Executive Director at the New York City Department of Education (NYC DOE) Office of Innovation, describes how developing a collective innovative mindset within a city can make a powerful difference, as it has in New York City.

Steven Hodas:
Fostering Innovation in Cities

To create real and lasting change in any large organization, but particularly in government, it's not enough to change policy: you also have to change the daily practice and culture of the organization. Policy changes and headline-grabbing initiatives are always subject to detour and reversal, but changes in the processes for *how* the organization solves its problems are much longer lasting.

It's like a software stack. Policies—the prominent issues like curriculum, accountability, charters, etc., on which candidates for mayor, school boards and superintendencies campaign—are the big software applications, the word processors and spreadsheets that we think of when we go to do work. They're feature-rich and top-of-mind, but they're also easy to replace with other applications if we want to.

Contrast this with the underlying operating system that makes it possible for these applications to run, and the machine language that enables the computer to actually execute the instructions sent by the application. We think about those less often and engage with them less often, but they completely determine what applications can run and how well they run.

In school districts, as in government generally, scant attention is also paid to the organizational equivalents of operating systems and machine languages: functions like procurement, contracting, IT policy and stakeholder engagement. Yet, as with software, these less-visible enabling functions determine how (and how well) the bureaucracy can execute its policy goals, whatever they may be.

In fact, the frustrations that people feel when dealing with school districts often relate more to these underlying systems than to the more visible policy agenda. Since most political leadership doesn't appreciate the role that the "district operating system" (DOS) plays in maintaining the status quo, it tends to remain in place across successive waves of reform. It is supported by long-time managers who continue to operate as they have been trained while waves of policy crusaders come and go.

One of the most promising opportunities for upgrading the DOS has been the rise of "open governance" assumptions and activities. Through alliances of grassroots political activists and civic-data hackers, open governance emphasizes the creation of Application Program Interfaces (APIs) for information that is already nominally public, but not usefully so because it is locked up in PDFs, Word documents and spreadsheets. APIs allow citizens, solvers and advocates outside the agencies to create applications and analysis tools for public data, linking it to other municipal, state and federal data sets in ways that enable new insights and uses that often would not have been anticipated by the agencies themselves.[222]

Inviting people into the guts of a public delivery system requires an unusual degree of openness and transparency, but like pull mechanisms discussed later in this chapter, it allows investors and advocates to contribute better and more directly to public services.

Partnership tools. FrameWorks Institute (featured at the beginning of this chapter) looks "for places where there is incongruity between experts' and the public's conceptualization of the issue."[223] By mapping the gaps in perception, FrameWorks helps leaders reframe their communication and develop useful metaphors.

Joel Gershenfeld of the University of Illinois developed a data visualization scheme to identify differences in opinion on important issues. The color-coded honeycomb measures levels of agreement on various aspects of a proposal, giving leaders details feedback. He contends that "increased visibility of stakeholder interests will accelerate stakeholder dialogue and alignment," and that "a shared vision of success will enable faster formation and more robust forms of stakeholder alignment."[224] He argues that "[s]ustained stakeholder alignment requires leadership based on influence, rather than authority," and that influence requires trust.[225] Shared data and well-specified protocols can build stakeholder trust, encouraging alignment of top-down and bottom-up change initiatives. Gershenfeld's maps have been used to bridge differences in labor-management relationships and in helping communities considering new energy proposals.

Katelyn Donnelly, who runs Pearson's Affordable Learning Fund, gets to observe school communities worldwide. "Taking a deep examination of community culture and the behavior standards is critical to extracting the potential learning achievement gains made possible by new technologies and tools," said Donnelly. "Teachers, parents, students and the community will need to learn to engage each other in a new way and there will be a set of standards, expectations and culture that will guide these interactions."[226]

New tools like FrameWorks "Map the Gap" analysis and Gershenfeld's visualization matrix should help leaders be culturally sensitive, recognize important differences, and build lasting and productive partnerships.

Building Collective Impact

"Collective impact is a wonderful concept that is at the risk of becoming yet another social sector buzz word," said Jeff Edmondson, Managing Director of Strive at KnowledgeWorks, an operating foundation in Cincinnati. "Investors, researchers and practitioners are all confused as they look for solid examples, but instead find cases where the word 'collaboration' seems to have been replaced by 'collective impact.'"[227] Edmondson is a pioneer in the new social impact field, having built the StrivePartnership in Cincinnati and Northern Kentucky.[228] Building on that success, StriveTogether has worked with over 40 communities to offer up an initial definition of what quality collective impact really means.[229] "Leaders in these pioneering communities have been willing to 'fail forward', actively capturing and sharing lessons they are learning along the way," said Edmondson.[230] Their lessons are captured in a theory of action, summarized below, which provides a framework for action and differentiates the work from traditional collaboration.[231]

Collaboration   ## Collective Impact

Convene around
Programs/Initiatives Work Together to
Move Outcomes

Prove Improve

Addition to
What You Do Is What You Do

Advocate for Ideas Advocate for What Works

Chart [232]

Greg Landsman runs the StrivePartnership in Cincinnati. Edmondson and Landsman boil down the key differentiator between collaboration and collective impact to the use of data "to *improve*, not just prove, what works over the long-term."[233]

Landsman and Edmondson: Quality Collective Impact = Impactful Innovation

In the social sector, we most often think of data as a punitive, not constructive, tool. This is understandable since the most common use for data is in long-term evaluations that often culminate in hasty and dramatic decisions. The work of collective impact requires communities to use data all the time, as often as it is available, to improve and refine how we work each and every day. As an example, StrivePartnership is learning from lessons in the health sector, which is decades ahead of the education sector in the use of data, to improve teaching and learning inside and outside the classroom. Executive-level leaders and practitioners alike are learning the skills needed to set concrete targets for improvement together, capture programmatic and service delivery data on an ongoing basis, and then use this data to inform their work in areas such as providing quality preschool instruction, tutoring students who need to catch up to peers, and easing the college enrollment process for first-generation college students.

It is worth noting that some say the disciplined use of data that collective impact requires could actually work against innovation by limiting creativity. This could not be further from the truth. One could actually argue that the social sector is rife with *too much* innovation. Every day a new "silver bullet" seems to emerge that will somehow solve all our challenges. What we really need is to be more informed about where we innovate and to what end. By taking the time to bring partners with diverse experiences and perspectives together to agree on the outcomes everyone hopes to accomplish together—and work purposefully to build on existing assets and strengths—we can do two things: identify where we have outages that require new and creative solutions and make more informed decisions about what innovation could really have impact over the long-term.

Collective impact, done well and with rigor, can help us form smarter cities. It can do this by helping us continue to iterate on what already works, while focusing efforts to innovate on where communities actually face clear gaps. This may sound restrictive in some ways. But in the end, if what we hope to achieve is impact at the population level on a specific set of outcomes—not just creating the "latest, greatest idea"—we can move beyond traditional collaboration and prove to ourselves and the world that seemingly intractable problems can be overcome, and the lives of millions can be improved as a result.[234]

The most recent Collective Impact Forum brought over 200 funders from across the country to learn how to move their own work forward. "Over the past several years, we have rolled up our sleeves to support efforts in Texas and believe the collective impact framework will become a foundational structure to advancing our goals for student success," said George Tang, Educate Texas COO[235]. He outlines three reasons why collective impact is here for good.

George Tang:
Three Reasons Collective Impact Is Here to Stay

1. **Helping everyone know where and how to focus.** In today's rapidly changing environment, understanding a community's progress on the education-to-workforce pathway (positive, flat, or negative) is critical for determining where to focus resources, seek innovation

and make investments. In Dallas, a simple, digestible scorecard has been developed to show how 800,000+ students are progressing toward key indicators. This easy-to-consume annual scorecard is shared publicly across the city so the mayor, businesses, philanthropy, community-based organizations, parents, and institutions serving students all know how we, as a city, are benefiting or failing our students. This has led to healthy competition, the identification of areas to target for new investments, and a better lens for understanding the overall health of our educational ecosystem.

2. **Accelerating the replication of effective strategies.** Despite having identified so many different "evidence-based" initiatives and approaches, education reformers have long struggled to achieve change at scale. Breakthrough programs and approaches (*e.g.*, charters, early college high schools, Project-Based Learning) have yielded powerful results for students, but combined they have had limited reach and impact on the student population as a whole. The goal for collective impact initiatives is to create a network of partners who are committed to identifying local strategies that are working for students and then promoting and directing resources to help lower-performing institutions replicate these efforts. (See the strategy pioneered in Pharr and outlined at the beginning of the chapter.)

3. **Building a robust partnership focused on continuous improvement.** With the new normal being some level of a postsecondary credential (technical, two-year, four-year), our historical focus on improving a single organization or designing an innovative solution is not realistic to create the step-function change required for our most underserved students to succeed. Further, with the constant shifts in policy and funding, a concerted focus on aligning partners to manage the education-to-workforce transition is required. Collective impact enables communities to more quickly recognize and adapt to changes and new conditions. For example, the Rio Grande Valley responded to new legislation requiring school districts to partner with higher education to develop college prep courses in math and English. A collaborative task force quickly designed and developed two courses that could be replicated across the region and accepted by all five institutions of higher education.[236]

Smart Cities

The Educate Texas team believes that collective impact is a "critical component for strengthening the public and higher education system so that all students can succeed."[237] It is one of the best regional examples of collective impact. A national example is Digital Promise, an independent, bipartisan nonprofit authorized by Congress to improve the opportunity to learn for all Americans through technology and research. Launched in 2011 as an engine of excellence and innovation, Digital Promise set out to link the public sector, the private sector, the research community and the startup scene. CEO Karen Cator said, "We believe that innovation is not only aided by, but dependent upon, stakeholders working together to solve problems."[238]

Digital Promise launched the League of Innovative Schools, which represents 46 members in 25 states, collectively representing nearly 3 million students. Cator describes the key elements of the League partnerships.

 Karen Cator:
Building a National Innovation Partnership

We formed the League of Innovative Schools (League), a national network of school districts and superintendents who collaborate with developers, researchers and one another to improve the education technology ecosystem. Here are the methods we use for establishing this partnership:

Start smart. Through the guidance of the U.S. Department of Education, thought leaders and practitioners, we selected the first cohort of League members. Some had a proven track record of improving student achievement through technology; others were in the early stages of forward-thinking, outcome-driven initiatives. In all cases, we looked for school leaders willing to try new things, share ideas with others, and partner to solve common and complex problems. They also reflected the national scope and diversity of public education in the U.S.—rural and urban schools, low-income and middle-class, high-minority and English language learners. Since its inception, for the League to work, it's been important that we highlight innovations that can occur *anywhere*.

Create incentives. With any partnership, it's important to create incentive for participation. Because League members were selected by a group of respected peers and leading thinkers, our initial cohort of superintendents, led by Mark Edwards of the renowned Mooresville Graded School District, were important early advocates. Membership meant more than a line on the resume; it meant collaboration with thought leaders in the field. By partnering with developers and researchers, we offer opportunities that many districts cannot access in their local communities—curated product pilots, invitations to participate in potentially groundbreaking research, and information about grants and competitions that can accelerate their work.

Eliminate "us vs. them." In all cases, we aim for our partners to benefit *mutually* from solving real problems for real schools. We've heard from stakeholders that it's nice to not feel as though it's "us vs. them"—that there is a venue where educators and non-educators can collaborate around a shared set of priorities and interests. In this respect, Digital Promise's role is that of convener and, in some cases, a "matchmaker," finding the right stakeholders for the right need.

Blended participation. In partnerships, just as in classrooms, online and face-to-face interaction are important in sparking collaboration. Twice per year, we convene our stakeholders for a collaborative workshop, co-hosted by one of our League member districts. In between meetings, members participate in research studies, visit each other's districts, organize around common areas of interest, and generally share knowledge. We are also re-launching DigitalPromise.org as a place for educators to share ideas and successes, challenges and strategies.[239]

The League has uncovered several challenges that it is well suited to address, including competency-based education, aggregated purchasing and research. Cator said, "Our theory of change is that a stronger ecosystem will lead to better decision-making, which in turn will produce better results for students. If the giants within communities of educators, entrepreneurs, and researchers stand together, we will all be better informed and equipped to solve shared problems."[240]

Harbormasters help. Having spent a decade building charter school networks, Kristoffer Haines gained an appreciation for the role of a lead partner in a city, what CEE-Trust calls harbormasters. While working as a trailblazer for the KIPP Foundation in the spring of 2006, Haines visited Gary, Indiana, a city that was now mostly forgotten, and sitting at or near the bottom of all economic and educational indicators. "We were committed to opening a high-quality KIPP Middle School off Gary's main street," said Haines.[241]

 Kristoffer Haines:
Why Harbormasters Are Critical to a City's Ecosystem

Navigating Gary, Indiana, to build broad community support for high-quality schools eight years ago was an effort in mastering the door-to-door salesman technique, hopping library to city hall to community center to YMCA to McDonald's to neighborhood park. We listened, shared information and began a dialogue to build a coalition of supporters.

We did this day-in and day-out, for months. It was, at times, fruitless. It was always incredibly slow moving. After all, it's difficult to coalesce a true movement in any meaningful way, for most agendas. But pulling together the disparate threads from those committed to great educational options across any city is an art—and it's nearly impossible to do so from without. It requires a local gravity from within.

What I know now is that it requires a harbormaster: an individual, organization or coalition of champions who take it upon themselves to ensure their city has excellent school options for all children and families.

KIPP LEAD College Prep opened in a church, and ultimately educated five cohorts of KIPPsters, as the highest-performing middle school in Gary, Indiana. Sadly, the lack of momentum and cohesion within the city, coupled with the inability of the city politicians and special interests to acknowledge the need for true educational reform, led to KIPP LEAD College Prep closing.

The unfortunate truth is that Gary needs a lot more decision-making adults acting on behalf of non-decision-making children—a reality too many of our cities face. There were no harbormasters eight years ago, and without them, cities like Gary cannot prove what's possible. The same gravity that gave rise to a great manufacturing and steel economy is equally required to create a first-rate educational ecosystem.[242]

Over the last five years, "the idea of the harbormaster has taken shape in a variety of forms, in a few pockets of our country," said Haines.[192] "In some places, harbormasters were born of natural disaster, as with New Schools for New Orleans; elsewhere, it was a response to a generation of declining results, as with Schools That Can Milwaukee; or sheer volition, as with San Antonio's Choose to Succeed; or the sound execution of a strategy, as with the DC Fund of NewSchools in collaboration with the CityBridge Foundation." Haines said top networks like Rocketship will not consider a city without a group like these playing harbormaster role.

There are other nonprofits and foundations strengthening their coordination, funding and support role. "There is no greater lift a city will realize for its children than the moment its harbormaster sets out to be the gravity for the creation of high-quality options," said Haines. He predicts that "the next five years will produce the next cohort of harbormasters, each more sophisticated and organized than the last, garnering unapologetic collaborative support from grasstops to grassbottoms; at which point the very mass of our collective work will finally begin to influence the system as a whole."

Whether engaging and partnering with students, parents, business leaders, harbormasters, policy makers, or others, the potential to positively impact learning and employability outcomes improves exponentially with common goals.

Smart Cities

Chapter Summary

- Family engagement starts with a relationship; supporting high expectations is key.

- It is more productive to tap common values in community engagement rather than whip up crisis.

- Education transformation requires complex partnering skills and addressing core issues of culture, values and behaviors.

- Innovation at scale requires stakeholders working together to solve problems.

- Boosting employability requires industry partnerships.

- Cities and districts can frame opportunities for partners to invest in delivery solutions.

- Collective impact requires a common agenda, shared measurement systems, mutually reinforcing activities, continuous communication and a backbone organization.

5: Aligned Investment

Investing in Learning:
Oakland

The Rogers Family Foundation is supporting blended learning pilots in eight Oakland public schools. Blended learning director Greg Klein is observing and reporting important lessons learned.[244] The foundation brings leading-edge expertise in addition to well-structured grants. The model work and reported lessons are an example of a productive local investment partnership of national importance.

Oakland is also home to Kapor Capital and NewSchools Venture Fund, making 94612 one of the best ZIP codes in the world for EdTech seed capital. Both funds are active early investors; they are both return-seeking and impact-focused, but NewSchools is structured as a tax-exempt nonprofit. The two have invested in dozens of local startups, often together, spurring the global learning revolution.[245] From 2011 to 2014, Oakland investment partnerships have improved local and global learning opportunities.

"Internet access, inexpensive devices, open content and mobile applications are changing learning on planet Earth, said the authors of a recent paper on impact investing. "The two-decades-old learning revolution has been fully incorporated into the business sector, partially incorporated into consumer offerings, and is beginning to transform the elementary, secondary and postsecondary landscape."[246]

Smart cities are developed by leaders with a vision of how invite investors to join them in addressing problems and capitalizing on opportunities; they frame markets, create incentives, and align public and private investment.

Investing to Grow an Ecosystem

Matt Greenfield, partner at venture capital firm Rethink Education, focuses on innovative technology for learning. Rethink has thoughtful impact criteria, as well as market return expectations. Four foundations have invested in the Rethink fund , and they often co-invest with nonprofit investors like NewSchools Venture Fund. Early lessons taught Matt Greenfield that specific pieces of an ecosystem can either help, or hinder, growth.

Matt Greenfield:
The Role of Impact Investing in Innovation Ecoystems

Looking back to the '80s, the Research Triangle in North Carolina had more serious talent than Silicon Valley. The triangle is formed by Duke University, North Carolina State University and the University of North Carolina at Chapel Hill. In addition to being home to these universities, the Triangle also included substantial corporate research and development organizations such as those from Glaxo, ITT, ATT and IBM. While there were several exciting investment opportunities, none of them ever took venture funding and there was something missing from the entrepreneurial ecosystem.

Today, Research Triangle, like much of the country, does have a thriving, innovative entrepreneurial ecosystem. It took a lot of pain and sweat to get there. By looking at what might explain the lack of startup growth in the Research Triangle in the 1980s, we can gain glimpses of what is required to grow and sustain a healthy ecosystem. The first explanation is that back in the late '80s, engineers in Research Triangle could feel relatively secure in their jobs. Those jobs allowed them to live a pretty nice life and build toward a secure retirement. The second explanation is that there was not a huge number of new job options: the list of potential employers in the region was not unlimited. One of the greatest strengths of the Silicon Valley corporate ecosystem is that it continually generates exciting new employment opportunities. The dynamism and diversity of Silicon Valley opportunities make it a lot easier to take risks. And the cost of living makes it much more urgent to try for a big win. Moreover, in Silicon Valley staying at one company for a long period can also be quite risky.

Attitudes toward failure, risk and entrepreneurship have changed across the nation. But making Research Triangle safe for entrepreneurs also required a long, patient collaboration between local angels and other stakeholders, including real estate owners, lawyers, accountants, university administrators and politicians. Research Triangle needed civic boosters willing to make financial investments with multiple non-financial goals.

Every region needs similar boosters in order to thrive. And every industrial sector within an entrepreneurial ecosystem must be nurtured separately. Even if a region has a thriving biotech ecosystem, its software ecosystem could still be stunted. Each sector's ecosystem must be considered.[247]

Private investors follow momentum; impact investors create momentum. Building an ecosystem, in either a category or geography, takes brave early investors that spot a gap or opportunity and can take a long-term view. Learn Capital (where the author is a partner) was the first learning-focused venture fund. Launched in 2008 after a seven-year drought of EdTech investment, the fund laid the groundwork for funds like Greenfield's Rethink Education and the $559 million invested in the first quarter of 2014.[248]

Examples of philanthropic organizations investing locally include the Abell Foundation, which supports the Baltimore EdTech ecosystem, Silicon Schools, which supports Bay Area blended learning models, and a group of local and national funders that launched The Mind Trust in Indianapolis. Foundation support for the national innovation ecosystem includes Gates Foundation funding for Next Generation Learning Challenges, Dell Foundation support for data tools and new schools, and Hume Foundation support for blended learning.

Funders as Leaders
Frustrated by incremental change, the Denver-based Donnell-Kay Foundation launched an ambitious initiative, ReSchool Colorado, "to design and implement a new

statewide public education system that pushes the boundaries of current thought and practice to provide an exceptional education for students living in this century, not the 20th century for which our current system was largely designed."[249] As their website states, goals of the foundation are to:

- Ignite a love of learning through mastery of academic, personal and professional competencies measured against international benchmarks.
- Encourage a marketplace of dynamic educational opportunities that provide families and educators with more customized options.
- Exist free from burdensome and layered statutes, rules, policies, and regulations that plague our existing education systems.
- Be designed for today, adaptable to tomorrow, and never "finished." The system will evolve to meet societal demands and changes. It will nurture what works and discard what does not.
- Minimize barriers to entry and enable diverse people to benefit. To ensure active participation and ownership, the new system will be co-designed with citizens and leaders who will be a part of it.
- Be funded through a mix of private and public resources at no additional cost to taxpayers.[250]

"What sets ReSchool Colorado apart from these other important efforts is our commitment to rethinking learning in a new system, as compared to trying to retrofit new learning into existing systems," said project lead Amy Anderson. "Smart policies and a solid implementation plan will drive this effort."[251] Launching in 2016, ReSchool Colorado will start small and operate in parallel with existing education options.

Responsiveness. Donnell-Kay's ReSchool initiative is an aggressive effort to fund a theory of change. It is part of a shift from responsive to strategic philanthropy. Twenty years ago, most foundations had a few donation categories, but they relied heavily on requests from the community. That began to change a decade ago as tech executives formed new foundations and sought more active investing. The big consulting companies started selling to foundations expensive planning projects that resulted in comprehensive plans. The increased focus on strategic planning made foundations more outcome-focused and data-driven, but it made most of them less capable of responding to a good idea coming from outside the foundation; if it does not fit the plan, it does not get funded. Developing a vision, demanding metrics and creating an aligned portfolio of grants is an improvement over the sloppy relationship-based philanthropy of the past, but it is also creating more missed opportunities and, in some categories and areas, making it harder to launch innovative new programs.[252] Supporting collective impact, as described in the previous chapter, requires more responsiveness and flexibility than is common today among national funders.

Effective funders create their focus based on donor intent and their distinctive competence. Sometimes they lead by providing the vision and building the investment framework; sometimes they support local leaders and important partnerships. They balance strategic and responsive philanthropy. They leverage their endowments by investing in impact-focused funds.[253] They often invest in funding alliances with other public and private investors.

Funding Alliances
Building productive philanthropic funding alliances is hard work. Steve Seleznow of the Arizona Community Foundation, Ana Tilton of Grantmakers for Education and Ingrid Ellerbe of MIND Research Institute collaborated on 10 tips for forming funding alliances:

10 Tips for Forming Funding Alliances
1. Interest-based conversations are held up front;
2. Project viability is assessed up front through site visits, audits and interviews;
3. There is clear mission and goal alignment around desired impact, most often a replicable, scalable program that positively affects multiple constituents;
4. Challenges, barriers and risks are identified;
5. Clear plans are developed to accomplish goals and mitigate risk;
6. There is ownership and engagement of all partners, funders, supporters and implementers;
7. Project governance respects roles and boundaries;
8. There are regular project reports with full transparency;
9. There is flexibility to adjust plans, timelines and resource allocations; and
10. There are celebrations of progress and recognition of people contributing to impact.[254]

Tilton said, "Complex problems, like those our members and their partners are working to address, often require them to abandon or compromise single focused agendas in favor of a collective approach."[255] Like any good marriage, partners must find common ground and do best when they "don't go it alone." When funders collaborate with people and organizations that share their objectives, they are able to leverage individual expertise to do more together than they ever could have done alone.

One "complex problem" that foundations have created for themselves is that they all have smart staffs that have built their own frameworks for describing desired learning outcomes—all competing pictures of what "good" looks like (as evidenced by the introductions to this book). This adds confusion and inefficiency to the field and may reduce collective impact. Another self-inflicted barrier to collaboration is that every big foundation has an elaborate strategic plan (as discussed in the last section of this chapter) that reduces their flexibility.

There are advantages to contributing to a single grantmaking fund, but such a fund requires strong goal agreement and a capable lead grantmaker. It may produce unanticipated consequences like jeopardizing the tax status of a nonprofit or shutting out potential partners.[256] The alternative to investing from one pot is coordinated grantmaking; MIND Research Institute has used this strategy to build a dozen citywide math initiatives. Coordinated funding allows foundations to take on unique aspects of a project (*e.g.*, hardware, capacity building, advocacy) aligned with their mission. An experienced lead partner with a regional leadership role, a harbormaster, can be very helpful. However, this partner comes with an agenda that will include some actors and exclude others, so it is important for investors to know what they are getting into.

There are many reasons that partnerships fail. Most common reasons include different agendas, power imbalances, leadership changes and partners that over-promise and continually under-deliver on resources or commitment. On the contrary, when philanthropic funding alliances are built around shared goals, they can change the skyline of a city and the landscape of opportunity.

Investment and Incentives
Leading venture investor Marc Andreessen said, "My personal view is that Silicon Valley will continue to take a disproportionate share of the No. 1 positions in great new markets, and I think that's just a reflection that the fact that the valley works as well as it does."[257]

What about other cities striving to build an innovation ecosystem? Andreessen does not think there should be 50 Silicon Valleys, but he thinks there is room for niche ecosystems, such as a "Biotech Valley, a Stem Cell Valley, a 3-D Printing Valley or a Drone Valley" (or an EdTech Valley). To spur innovation,

Andreessen thinks starting with barrier reduction is the first step. As he noted, there are huge regulatory hurdles in many of these fields.

Can government aid business formation? The short answer is that the blocking and tackling issues that affect business climate are more important than "sexy" initiatives, investments and incubators.[258] While perhaps suffering from being trendy, incubators serve a critical role.

Startup support. Leading the incubator frenzy is New York City, with more than 100 incubators, accelerators and co-working spaces. Joining the party every week is another city, ranging from urban centers like Fort Worth to Westminster, a small town 30 miles northwest of Baltimore. Universities are all jumping in. Not to be left behind, companies are launching new business support initiatives. Thirty years ago there were a couple dozen incubators, and now there are a couple thousand; there is even the National Business Incubation Association. A dated survey suggests about one-third of business incubation programs are sponsored by economic development organizations, one fifth by cities or counties, and another fifth by higher education.[259]

There are three types:

- **Co-working space:** Companies pay to be there; some become more resource-heavy; some offer learning experiences (*e.g.*, General Assembly, 1776).
- **Incubators:** Offer more resources than co-working space; often run by nonprofits focused on a sector or a city; companies usually get in free but they may pay rent (*e.g.*, 4.0 Schools).
- **Accelerators:** Companies are selected and are residents for a defined period of time; they receive some funding and services in return for an equity stake (*e.g.*, ImagineK12, LearnLaunch, 500 Startups, and TechStars).

It is clear that some incubators work and some do not. Robert Litan, Bloomberg Government's Director of Research, thinks good successful incubators grow organically where it make sense; that is, incubators fighting trends will struggle and require subsidy.[260] Some college incubators are among the most successful. Well-run incubators hold tough admissions standards and manage for results; others do not. The bottom line is that it is hard to start a successful business, and most will fail—that includes incubators.

Government investment. Does it make sense for governments to make direct investments in startups? There is no evidence of that being done successfully at scale. Many projects funded by the National Science Foundation and Small Business Innovation Research, especially game-based learning, may have some sector-advancement benefit but are not commercially viable and do not result in scaled organizational capacity. Weak results from direct investment are primarily a function of poorly written grant criteria and reviewers with little or no venture investing experience.

Foundations are also getting into the direct investment business and falling prey to some of the same problems. For example, a program officer falls in love with a literacy deal and sells the idea of an investment without the benefit of seeing the other dozen deals just like it and an attorney with no venture experience signs off on the paperwork. A recent paper on Boosting Impact recommended that foundations should invest in venture funds as a better alternative.[261] Public-private investment partnerships, as opposed to direct investment, also make more sense for state and federal agencies.

"Government should stick to basic R&D," according to Litan, and "at the commercial end, the market should be funding new companies."[262] While intent behind local and state governments funding incubators and direct startup investments may well-intentioned, most are not successful. If a city is going to get into the business formation space, it should be done with capable partners and treated like a business—not a charity.

Business climate. Stephen Adams, President of the American Institute for Economic Research agrees that climate is key. In fact, he is skeptical of public investment in incubators and enterprise zones and thinks what really matters is low taxes, quick permits, and lightweight compliance.[263]

The most important thing that local, state and federal governments can do to promote business formation is to promote next gen learning and job training and a pro-business climate: rational taxes, easy licensing and efficient workers' compensation systems.

1. **Risk-friendly climate.** One way to influence climate is by creating a risk-friendly (or at least not risk-averse) climate. David Kautter, American University, said it is the "culture of try, fail, try again" that made America the world's business engine. Kautter said the opportunity to declare bankruptcy rather than going to prison is an example of a legal framework that underpins a culture of risk taking and is another example of how the government can create a risk-friendly culture.[264]

2. **New business-friendly climate.** Another way to influence climate to create a new business-friendly culture. Frederic Meunier, member of the "Doing Business" team at the World Bank, highlights the need to create a new business-friendly culture. He noted that it is a lot easier to start a new business in Singapore than in the U.S.

3. **Low red-tape climate.** New York is advertising tax-free zones—a great start, but it is still tough to get licenses and deal with payroll tax and workers' compensation in the Empire state. Fixing the compliance environment,

according to Adams, is not sexy, but it can be the most cost-effective path to job creation.

4. **Pro-education climate.** Governments can also help the new business culture by improving education. New business formation was about 600,000 annually but dropped to 400,000 during the Great Recession, according to Litan.[265] It has only recovered to about 420,000 starts, and many ask, "What can government do?" Litan says the percentage of college-educated people is a key economic development statistic, so governments should try to improve education.[266]

Prizes and pull mechanisms. In healthy markets, participants respond to incentives, invest in research and development (R&D) and produce new innovations. Capital investments bring productivity to scale. In underdeveloped or inefficient markets, customers have few choices, often controlled by bureaucratic mechanisms rather than market mechanisms, and there is little investment in R&D. Underdeveloped markets suffering from a lack of investment and innovation can be addressed through direct investment (return-seeking or philanthropic), by advocating for better policies, or through pull mechanisms, which include:

- **Market development.** Aggregated demand and advance market commitments;
- **Fast-track policies.** Cutting through the bureaucracy with accelerated approvals and proactive incentives;
- **Inducement prizes.** Rewards for successfully meeting a breakthrough challenge or outcome; and
- **Leveling the playing field.** Creation of a level regulatory space that invites non-traditional players to participate and offer solutions.

The following table summarizes the difference between direct investment ("push") and pull mechanisms.[267]

	Push	Pull
Investment	Up front	On success
Common Mechanism	Grant	Inducement prize
Solution	Defined up front	Determined/created by participants
Mobilization	Low: only selected participants	High: participants respond to incentives
Leverage	Little; secondary outcome	Significant investment by participants
Advocacy	Traditional PR	Competition drama with potential breakthrough

Market development. The most common pull mechanism is the broad category of efforts to improve market efficiency by organizing buyers or addressing blockages. By aggregating demand, market facilitators seek better access to inexpensive supply. Aggregated purchasing is one example, discussed in a recent paper, Smart Series Guide to EdTech Procurement, in which the authors describe how aggregated purchasing saves time and money for school districts.[268]

Another example can be seen in the area of global health, where advance market commitments (AMCs) guarantee purchase commitments for drugs over a period of time. The increased certainty enables drug manufacturers to make investments to deliver drugs or even develop new ones. As noted by the Global Health Technologies Coalition, "Pull mechanisms help overcome this barrier by creating or securing a market" and "are more appropriate for use in the later stages of R&D. The pull often provides the incentive to get products over the finish line."[269]

Until June 2014, Stacey Childress led the education innovation team at the Gates Foundation, where she observed pull mechanisms at work in the area of global health and applied those lessons in education. Childress said pull mechanisms increase the chances of finding solutions by getting lots of innovators working on the same problems, in different ways, at the same time.[270]

Stacey Childress: Connect What Students Need and What Entrepreneurs Create

The most promising example from the Gates team so far is the Literacy Courseware Challenge. Working closely with English Language Arts (ELA) teachers, literacy experts and cutting edge school leaders, we put out a call to innovators to show up with products or product roadmaps to meet the needs of students and teachers in real classrooms.

The challenge received 151 entries, and four external selection panels narrowed the group to 29 finalists who then each received smallish grants totaling $6 million. These instructional supports are being tested in classrooms by teachers with their students over an 18-month period. And, since being named as finalists, nine of the companies have collectively raised nearly $40 million in private capital to accelerate their development efforts. SRI International is running an implementation and outcomes study during the life of the challenge, and all the information will be made public next year.

Some promising local efforts are emerging, including LEAP Innovations in Chicago, which is supporting local schools, teacher networks and product developers and is committed to making connections among them. 4.0 Schools in New Orleans is ramping up its efforts to connect its product and services entrepreneurs with innovative school designers. NewSchools Venture Fund has a City Fund in Washington, D.C., that supports both school designers and EdTech innovations like LearnZillion, but NewSchools could do much more to connect the work of its robust national networks of EdTech and school entrepreneurs. Digital Promise is a national organization with 46 member districts in its League of Innovative Schools; it has a Marketplace project focused on the intersection between supply and demand, and the team is thinking hard about how best to make connections across its networks and projects.

All of this activity in cities and across national networks is creating glimpses of what a more connected innovation ecosystem of local and national players might look like, one that can help create incentives and supports for innovations that more effectively meet the needs of students and teachers. There is still room for city-based and national leadership in this area. I am optimistic that over the next two years, the picture will come into much clearer focus.[271]

Childress notes that the challenges of running multiple challenge grants include connecting the voice of users with product developers, recruiting test bed schools, managing relationships and logistics, and producing useful information about the trials. She recommends that foundations work with local and national implementation partners with a commitment to the needs of teachers and students, an understanding of market dynamics, and capacity to implement complex projects with an improvement mindset.[272]

Incentives. Inducement (or incentive) prizes are routinely used to promote private and public benefit. Awards recognize prior achievement, while prizes induce future actions. Grants sponsor identified work by a named beneficiary, while prizes have the potential to mobilize an army of experts to work on a problem—and they only get paid if they achieve the goal.

Prizes can also be effective mechanisms to cultivate innovations by creating the financial incentives needed to attract a broad array of competing innovators. They can also be more efficient in the sense that the prize funding is only awarded when certain criteria are met. So the funders pay only for the output, not the inputs with the hope of a breakthrough.

There are no silver bullets in education, but targeted incentives for innovation, like the Hewlett-sponsored essay scoring competitions, can mobilize talent and resources to improve access and quality. Prizes could be used to boost literacy, middle grade math achievement and language acquisition. Prizes could also be used to analyze big data sets and produce useful algorithms. While not an exhaustive list, there are four types of prizes that could prove to be useful in education.

- **Design prizes.** Small prizes could be used to incentivize innovative designs for new schools, new school facilities or new systems of education.

- **Intervention challenges.** Products, services and strategies could be tested in comparable short cycle trials.
- **Data competitions.** Invite data scientists globally to work on well-defined problems.
- **Geo-Competitions.** Invite districts, cities or regions to compete on specific challenges over a specific period of time or to achieve a certain outcome.[273]

A successful prize draws attention to a problem or opportunity, mobilizes significant resources (perhaps 10 times the prize purse), and solves the problem—or at least illustrates the path forward.

Community investment. Imagine 200 families with children in a park on a Saturday morning. Now imagine that park lined with old shipping containers and located on the north end of the Vegas Strip. The Downtown Project in Las Vegas is an interesting mixture of smart real estate investment, philanthropy and venture investment, all within a vibrant cultural context.

 Katie Vander Ark:
Transforming Downtown Las Vegas

Education is the bedrock on which a truly great city is built," according to Tony Hsieh and the Downtown Project—his $350 million investment fund. The CEO of shopping giant Zappos is leading efforts to help reimagine the old city center north of the Las Vegas Strip. It's one of several promising efforts to reverse the economic free fall that started in 2008 and create a vibrant, dense urban core and, as the project's website states, "the most community-focused large city in the world."

Edward Glaeser's Triumph of the City inspired Hsieh to found Downtown Project to help transform downtown Las Vegas into a dynamic urban center. Downtown Project's website declares its goal and purpose: "to help make downtown Las Vegas a place of Inspiration, Entrepreneurial Energy, Creativity, Innovation, Upward Mobility, and Discovery, through the 3 C's of Collisions, Co-learning, and Connectedness in a long-term, sustainable way."

An explosion of activity encompassing art, culture, business formation, and a new school development are now part of a $350 million, five-year project. Of that initial investment, funds have been allocated to a $50 million fund to invest in small businesses; $50 million for the VegasTechFund to invest in tech startups; $50 million for arts, education and culture, including the monthly First Friday arts festival, and a private school focused on brain-based education, social-emotional learning and entrepreneurship; and $200 million for real estate and development.

The Downtown Project encourages learning by hosting a monthly speaker series focused on tech and fashion, along with Catalyst Week and Creative Week, an exploration of strategic partnerships in philanthropy, wellness, music, fashion, education and technology.[274]

Investing in Public and Education

For smart cities, the most important investment issue is how public education is funded from early learning to graduate school and job training.

Early learning. The belief in the importance of early learning shared by President Obama and U.S. Secretary of Education Arne Duncan is homegrown. "Chicago is the leader in early childhood education—no contest," said Ryan Blitstein of Change Illinois.[275] But even if Chicago is the leader in this area, there are many other organizations and initiatives making strides in the area of early learning. For example, Ounce of Prevention Fund advocates locally and supports Educare centers nationwide. First Five Years Fund is a new breed of data-driven advocates for integrated early learning services for low-income children backed by Buffett, Gates, Harris, Kaiser and Pritzker. McCormick Foundation advocates for public policy that improves birth to three learning opportunities in Illinois.[276] The City of Chicago's Early Learning Portal makes it easy for parents to find and compare early learning options.

Some states have taken an active role in expanding access to preschool, including Oklahoma, where 70 percent of students attend public pre-K programs. The federal government has rewarded leading states; more than $1 billion in federal grants has been awarded to 20 states under the Race to the Top–Early Learning Challenge.[277] States were encouraged to promote quality and access, improve the early learning workforce, and measure outcomes.

The opening of a <u>New America Education Policy Brief</u> describes the importance of intentional investments for children: "Each year of their lives, children and their families should have the benefit of ascending a sturdy, well-lit staircase of development and learning rather than navigating disconnected and uneven platforms where they can easily fall through the cracks."[278] The report recommends guaranteed experiences from birth to primary grades:

- Home visits and high-quality child care with public support prioritized for low-income families;
- Well-prepared and well-compensated teachers/ caregivers with deep understanding of early learning;
- Language-rich, stimulating environments to build content knowledge;
- Development of social-cognitive skills to smooth transitions from between pre-K and primary grades and cooperating providers;
- P-3 data-driven collaboration to meet the needs of struggling and excelling children; and
- Families welcomed into each classroom with connected and positive home learning experiences.[279]

K-12. The patchwork of local, state and federal elementary and secondary education funding typically focuses on institutions rather than learners, advantages wealthy communities rather than promoting equitable outcomes, and stifles innovation.

Next gen learning requires a student-centered finance system that recognizes diverse student needs, allows dollars to follow students to high-quality online and blended learning options, creates mechanisms for ensuring quality, and fosters educational innovation. Authors of Funding Students, Options, and Achievement recommend four design principles of a student-based funding system, saying that systems should be:

- **Weighted.** Funding should reflect individual student needs by attaching "weights" to student funding amounts based on factors that affect the cost of educating certain students, such as poverty, special needs and English language learner status.
- **Flexible.** A flexible finance system does not restrict funds or designate them for particular uses and thus creates greater school-level autonomy.
- **Portable.** The principle of portability ensures that dollars can follow students to the school or course that best suits their individual needs—including fractional funding for full-time or part-time options.
- **Performance-based.** To ensure quality, a performance-based system creates incentives tied to student outcomes that reward performance and completion.[280]

The authors contend that there is enough money funding K-12 education in the U.S, but that the system is inequitable and funds are inefficiently spent. The solution is a full system redesign that funds students according to these four design principles.

Funding the shift. Next gen learning requires new tools, updated learning environments, and lots of training. Navigating the Digital Shift from Digital Learning Now recommends that states boost access to online learning, help districts and networks improve broadband connectivity and the purchase of student access devices, and invest in teacher development.[281]

The Bellwether Education Partners "A Policy Playbook for Personalized Learning" argues that investment is required on the supply and demand side of next gen learning, for development of new tools as well as adoption and implementation in schools.[282] The "Playbook" recommends that state policy makers create innovation funds "that support the development, testing, and implementation of innovative models." By funding districts and networks ready to move, the "Playbook" argues, "states can also foster the development of personalized learning 'proof points,' which can spur increased demand among other schools and districts in the state." The report argues that if several more states created innovation funds like the Ohio Straight A Fund, it would "also build the supply of effective personalized learning models to meet growing demand."

Higher education. Smart cities and states expand affordable access to higher education. Emerging trends include performance-based funding and competency-based learning.

In 2010, Tennessee implemented an aggressive performance-based funding model that controls state funding for higher education. Its formula allocates funds based on a series of outcomes related to student persistence and graduation, weighted for low-income and adult students. The formula also considers institutional mission, recognizing that outcomes will look different for a community college than a four-year research university.[283]

Cost pressure on higher education is yielding more competency-based models. Western Governors University (WGU) is an online competency-based university founded by 19 governors in 1997. WGU enrolls 43,000 students and boasts over 30,000 graduates, according to its website. Growth has been fueled by affordable pricing (about $6,000 per year), the ability to test out of subjects where students have experience, and self-paced learning.[284] WGU has a performance-based relationship with some of its vendors, in which vendors pay for content when it boosts achievement. As mentioned in an earlier chapter, College for America is a great example of a low-cost, high-outcome degree by providing a bachelor's degree program that costs $2,500 per year.[285]

Smart Cities

Aligning and blending secondary and postsecondary education can also save families and states money. If 11th and 12th graders are well prepared and have access to college courses, they can leave high school with up to an associate's degree. Texas requires that all students have a graduation plan with pathways that include college credit opportunities.

Smart cities and states are creating learner-centered, performance-based learning opportunities. Weighted funding systems match budgets and challenges. Portable funding creates options for learners and incentives for innovative providers.

Chapter Summary

- Public education funding from early learning to higher education should be weighted, flexible, portable and performance-based.

- Foundations should balance strategic and responsive investment.

- Funding alliances can leverage investment and build impact but must be built around shared goals.

- The block and tackling issue of business climate beats sexy initiatives, investments and incubators.

- Efficient market development strategies include prizes, demand aggregation and grants for pilot projects.

- States and cities should make investments to help schools make the shift to next gen learning.

For more information on this topic:

 Michael Staton on Investment and Incentives

6: New Tools and Schools

 Taking Quality to Scale:
Indianapolis

Bart Peterson took office as mayor of Indianapolis in 2000 and quickly won the right to authorize charter schools—the first mayor in the country with that authority. David Harris ran the mayor's charter school office, which won Harvard's Innovations in American Government Award. Unlike the charter free-for-all in some states, Harris moved carefully to ensure quality. They approved a few schools and saw favorable early results. But he recognized the need to build and import talent and school models to bring quality to scale. To pull that off, Harris launched The Mind Trust in 2006 with Mayor Peterson as board chair.[286]

Inspired by talent development shops like Teach For America (TFA) and charter networks like KIPP, Harris deployed his core insights in a way that has become a national model. Just as the Bay Area had become an ecosystem of innovation, The Mind Trust's founders wanted to cultivate in Indianapolis a similar climate of talent, creativity and boldness—one focused on improving education.

The Mind Trust has found success in five strategies:

1. **Recruiting top national organizations.** TFA, The New Teacher Project, and College Summit;
2. **Launching new initiatives.** Eleven homegrown and six recruited organizations have transformed Indianapolis into a national hub of education innovation;
3. **Incubating world-class schools.** KIPP and the George and Veronica Phalen Leadership Academy, a startup blended learning school based in Indianapolis;
4. **Scaling up the highest-impact efforts.** An $18 million Grow What Works campaign;
5. **Developing and advancing bold policies.** Creating Opportunity Schools plan for Indianapolis Public Schools.

Since The Mind Trust's launch seven years ago, their relentless focus on empowering talented people to transform their city's public education system has established The Mind Trust as the driving force for improvement and innovation in Indianapolis.

Smart Cities

The *Star* has described The Mind Trust as being "at the center of the reform movement in Indianapolis" and credits the nonprofit for "single handedly changing the tenor of the debate surrounding the city's schools and [bringing] an army of education talent to Indianapolis."[287] Largely built from scratch over the last decade, the Indianapolis improvement and innovation ecosystem is a great example of sustained leadership. It is such a good example that the *Chicago Tribune* ran an opinion piece touting the Mind Trust's Innovation School Fellowship and urging Chicago leaders to embrace a similar effort, saying "Chicago, give it a try."[288] Like Indianapolis, smart cities incubate talent, tools and schools.

New Schools

In 2003, Diane Tavenner launched Summit Prep, a college preparatory high school for diverse students in Redwood City, California. After almost a decade of sending nearly 100 percent of her diverse graduates to college, Tavenner began innovating on the school model to further improve college and career readiness of graduates. The network, Summit Public Schools, opened two high schools in San Jose that featured a math program developed in partnership with Khan Academy. A grant from the Girard Education Foundation allowed Tavenner's team to work with Illuminate Education to develop ActivateInstruction, an open platform that delivers playlists of content linked to learning standards. In 2013, Summit opened Summit Denali, the Sunnyvale secondary school that may be the best example of an innovation school model built around a custom-developed learning platform.

Three lessons can be drawn from one of the most important innovation engines in education. First, Summit's commitment to hiring and developing extraordinary educators is unparalleled. Second, bringing innovation to scale almost always requires a partnership, particularly in the public sector; for Summit that included a software developer and a foundation. And third, innovation may start with an individual, but it is more often the product of years of struggle than a bolt from the blue; it typically builds on the work of others—and not always from the same field. The Summit team benefits from the most innovative ecosystem in the world, and they exhibit remarkable openness about learning from others.

New school development, particularly in managed networks, is one of the most important developments of the last 20 years in American education. New schools contributed to improved graduation rates and have proven to be a "sticky" reform. Autonomous new schools quickly develop a constituency that makes them resilient to change forces. Compared to the challenges of dramatically improving struggling schools, there is a reliable track record and knowledge base associated with new school development. Since 2010, new school designs have incorporated new tools blending online learning and face-to-face instruction. New school development is a reliable improvement strategy and an opportunity to pilot innovation. Designing and opening new schools, particularly next generation models, requires a web of support. New Orleans is the best example of a new school ecosystem.

NOLA rising. "Soon there will be zero failing schools in NOLA," said Neerav Kingsland, former CEO of New Schools for New Orleans (NSNO).[289] The same could not be said for any other urban center in the country. The devastation of Hurricane Katrina in 2005 created an opportunity for the community to rethink the education system. Of the 112 failing schools in Louisiana, only nine are in New Orleans—and they will be improved or closed. Compared to the old system, the new schools in New Orleans have learning gains equivalent to five months of extra learning. New Orleans has nearly caught the state average in proficiency and college readiness and has passed the state average graduation rate. African American students have gone from lowest performing in the state to five percentage points above the state average for African American students. That is "improved but not excellent," said Kingsland. "New Orleans needs 50,000 high-quality seats to provide every child with an excellent education," and he estimated that they were halfway there.

Key to progress in New Orleans was the development of new schools, many of which were incubated at NSNO, a best-in-class operation led at the time by Matt Candler and supported by an amazing confluence of talent assembled at a converted retail center. The center, purchased by Tulane and home of the Cowen Institute, is also home to Teach for America, New Leaders, The New Teacher Project, the Louisiana Association of Public Charter Schools and NSNO. For local and recruited leaders who wanted to build a great network of schools, the converted mall at 200 Broadway was a turbocharged incubator.

Matt Candler on New Tools and Schools

As a member of the Louisiana Board of Elementary and Secondary Education (BESE), Leslie Jacobs was a primary architect of the Recovery School District (RSD), a statewide school improvement zone, in 2003. The RSD took over a failing school in the fall of 2004 and gained control over four more in the spring of 2005. Hurricane Katrina ripped through New Orleans in August of 2005, devastating most school buildings and displacing many families. After the hurricane, the state board placed most of the New Orleans public schools into the RSD. Jacobs and her colleagues began recruiting partners and high-quality charter operators including KIPP, which made an early commitment to being part of the new system. (Today they operate nine schools). The fact that BESE and the legislature addressed chronic failure, developed a solution and built capacity pre-Katrina is a critically important to the educational success evident today.

In 2008, Jacobs launched nonprofit Educate Now! to make reform effective and sustainable. In the last few years, that has meant supporting the growth of blended learning in New Orleans schools. In addition to assembling and coordinating $3 million in local funding to assist schools in exploring, planning for and implementing blending learning models, Educate Now! supports programs to foster broad engagement, including a Community of Practice for blended learning leads, and the New Orleans Blended Learning Fellowship for teachers interested in converting to a blended model.

Today, new school development in NOLA is also supported by Leading Educators Education Pioneers and the innovative competency-based Relay Graduate School of Education. Candler's 4.0 Schools is training future Edupreneurs, incubating EdTech startups and helping teams conceptualize schools. Given the policy set, philanthropic support and the amazing supporting cast, New Orleans is the best place in the world to start an innovative new school.

Miami flexing. With online core instruction and onsite academic support and guidance, flex model high schools are gaining popularity because they are easy to open, very scalable and extremely flexible.[290] Students in flex schools progress as they demonstrate mastery in most courses. In some courses, particularly those with teachers at a distance, they may remain part of a virtual cohort. Some flex schools add projects, some add internships, some add teacher-led workshops. The flex name comes from San Francisco Flex and Silicon Valley Flex, two new schools that combine the K12 online public schools' core curriculum with a full day of academic support, clubs and activities.

Miami Dade County Public Schools Superintendent Alberto Carvalho spotted the flex trend and opened one in the central office in 2010. The following year the district opened seven more iPrep Academies in comprehensive high schools. Powered by Florida Virtual School and other providers, the iPrep Academies offer accelerated course options, internships and community-based projects. For the 2013-2014 school year, Miami Dade introduced 36 new magnet and choice programs including science and mathematics, legal studies, IT and coding, international studies and the arts.

Other flex examples include Connections Learning, which is supporting development in the Midwest of a flex network called Nexus Academy. These double-shifted high schools serve about 250 students who benefit from a Success Coach and personal trainer. GPS Education Partners operates flex academies at manufacturing sites in Wisconsin, where students benefit from internships.[291] Career Path High students take online high school courses and onsite vocational training classes and leave with college credit and job certificates.[292]

Supporting new schools. Since 2002, more than 400 new schools have been created in New York City with a variety of intermediaries and networks, leading to improved graduation rates and expanded learning options.[293] On a relevant scale and leveraging local assets, every major metro area should be supporting the development of new and transformed schools with grants and support services.

Replicating the success of the national education innovation accelerator Next Generation Learning Challenges (NGLC), Chicago and the District of Columbia launched new school grant programs using the same framework. "This metro-regional strategy will rest a lot more than the national one on close, intensive incubation of promising applicants and planning grantees," said NGLC's Andy Calkins. "These metro incubator programs will be working much more intensively with a smaller, local pool of potential applicants."[294] These city grant programs will rely on local ability to identify and nurture teams from planning to school launch.

Supporting new school development requires a local or regional funder like NSNO, New Schools for Chicago or Silicon Schools in the Bay Area; it also takes incubatory capacity like that of 4.0 Schools to take full advantage of new tools.

Partnering for new schools. College Park Academy partners with Maryland-based Connections Education for its digital curriculum and platform. Connections Co-founder and Executive Vice President Mickey Revenaugh sees the school as a vibrant example of purpose-driven innovation. "College Park Academy is using blended learning as a means to an end—a rigorous early college experience for all. The flexibility and personalization of blended learning make that goal possible."[295]

The city of College Park, also in Maryland, has opened this new school through a city-university partnership between the University of Maryland, College Park Academy and the city in which it resides. Education, and the resulting new school, is just one facet of the broader College Park City-University Partnership (CPCUP), which also has goals in the areas of housing and development, sustainability and transportation, evidence that smart cities partner on high-leverage outcomes. In addition to increasing educational options for students in the area, College Park Academy is a model for blended learning and is getting results. According to Donna Wiseman, Dean of the UMD College of Education, "We have data now that shows that when we started the Academy, 70 percent of kids were passing most of their courses. Now that number is between 85-90 percent, so we think there's plenty of opportunity to impact educational outcomes for students."[296]

Re-engaging. There are 5.8 million disengaged young adults who are neither in school nor working. According to Elisabeth Jacobs at the Washington Center for Equitable Growth, "We risk really having this lost generation of workers, and what that means in terms of the economy's ability to innovate and compete, when you've kind of wasted the talents of some substantial portion of a generation, is really, it's alarming."[297] Networks in the Association for High School Innovation operate over 275 schools and programs in 35 states and 170 cities nationwide.[298] Their work makes clear the potential for new schools to re-engage disenfranchised youth.

New blended and competency-based options improve engagement and speed completion. Early college options that combine high school, college credit and job credentials provide rapid pathways to employment.

Connecting Teachers and Tools

In April of 2014, Phyllis Lockett made a job change symbolic of the new opportunity set. As CEO of New Schools for Chicago, Lockett spent the last decade leading the most powerful intervention strategy possible—new school development. Spotting the potential of new learning tools but also the lack of a test bed to demonstrate and iterate, she incubated and then launched LEAP Innovations, an education technology hub in Chicago connecting educators and tech companies from across the nation. LEAP researches, pilots and scales instructional technology solutions that advance teaching and learning from early childhood through early college. As CEO of the new organization, she is attacking the new tools agenda with the same vigor that she approached the new schools agenda.

By connecting teachers and technology in new and powerful ways, Lockett sees the potential for system transformation in

---

 Phyllis Lockett:
Our Kids Can't Wait

In certain struggling communities in Chicago, unless you are lucky enough to get into a magnet, selective enrollment or charter school, you have a 60 percent chance of graduating from high school. If you drop out, you have a 75 percent chance of being unemployed, and a very high risk of being incarcerated. Of the 30,000 freshmen who enter Chicago Public Schools high schools, only eight percent will earn a college degree.

Yet I have seen firsthand the power of next generation personalized learning models that accelerate student achievement and increase student engagement while improving teacher satisfaction. These are schools where teachers pinpoint each student's needs, fast track remediation and exponentially advance students to the next level. I have also seen the potential cost savings that these models can deliver, a concern in cities across the country, including Chicago,

---

where the school system faces a $1 billion deficit each year. Impossible? Visit Chavez Elementary, a traditional public school in Chicago's Back of the Yards neighborhood, where seventh graders take algebra and advance to geometry as soon as they are ready. Or look at KIPP Create in our Austin community, and see how they achieved the greatest literacy gains among all KIPP campuses nationwide.

Education technology is a $1 billion industry in America, with accelerators and incubators popping up on both coasts. It has caught the attention of policy makers, districts, educators and families nationally and right here in Chicago. Yet little is known about what tech tools actually work. Plus, educators are often on their own to integrate stuff developed far away from experts in teaching and learning.

That is why I started LEAP Innovations, to hasten the introduction of the next generation of teaching and learning. The LEAP Innovation Hub offers a new and systematic approach to evaluating what works in the EdTech marketplace. We will advance personalized learning to prepare Americans for 21st century skills by supporting pilot studies of instructional technology in schools and other learning environments, conducting research, and providing training space and programs to connect educators, entrepreneurs, tech companies, learning scientists and students to create next gen learning school designs, share ideas and co-develop solutions for critical learning gaps.

Across the country, we can no longer wait for innovative models of teaching and learning to pop up in isolation. We have to work together across all school models and learning environments to blend the best of what we have with the education technology innovations that are expanding rapidly across the globe. Our kids can't wait.[299]

the nation's third largest public school district—and beyond. Like LEAP Innovations, data analytics startup BrightBytes benefited from a Gates Foundation grant for short cycle efficacy trials connecting teachers and tools.[300] The three goals of the work are to 1) empower students to provide learning-experience data to teachers and school administrators; 2) enable teachers to access outcome-based application feedback from students and other teachers in order to make better choices when selecting learning applications; and 3) establish a feedback channel between the teachers/students and vendors, enabling quicker and constant improvement throughout the system and its constituents. The BrightBytes Clarity platform is now used by more than 12 percent of U.S. schools to provide better feedback to teachers so they can improve student learning outcomes.

New Tools

Innovation is coming to every aspect of learning from early learning to K-12, higher education, professional learning and informal interest-driven investigations. Recent market research suggests that provoking deeper learning, assessing and tracking student progress are areas of opportunity for innovation.[301] Academic systems, including instructional content, classroom management, and productivity tools, have received far more attention in the last few years than they had previously. Content is quickly shifting from flat and sequential courseware to engaging, mobile, modular playlists.

The chart below outlines the major categories of systems used by educational institutions and the categories where new tools

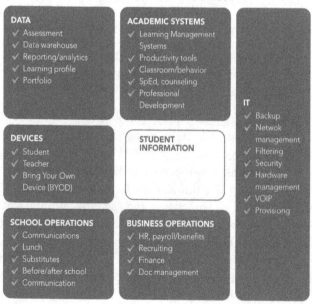

NEW TOOLS BY FUNCTION

DATA
- ✓ Assessment
- ✓ Data warehouse
- ✓ Reporting/analytics
- ✓ Learning profile
- ✓ Portfolio

ACADEMIC SYSTEMS
- ✓ Learning Management Systems
- ✓ Productivity tools
- ✓ Classroom/behavior
- ✓ SpEd, counseling
- ✓ Professional Development

DEVICES
- ✓ Student
- ✓ Teacher
- ✓ Bring Your Own Device (BYOD)

STUDENT INFORMATION

IT
- ✓ Backup
- ✓ Netwok management
- ✓ Filtering
- ✓ Security
- ✓ Hardware management
- ✓ VOIP
- ✓ Provisiong

SCHOOL OPERATIONS
- ✓ Communications
- ✓ Lunch
- ✓ Substitutes
- ✓ Before/after school
- ✓ Communication

BUSINESS OPERATIONS
- ✓ HR, payroll/benefits
- ✓ Recruiting
- ✓ Finance
- ✓ Doc management

-Adapted from Christensen Institute[302]

are being developed.

The chart shows separate categories for the various systems, but in an ideal environment, new tools would enable elements of systems to be linked. For example, data stored in a student information system, where basic enrollment data are captured, could be linked to a gradebook and a transcript of courses taken. Likewise, the chart shows assessment as a separate category from content, but increasingly assessment is embedded in learning experiences with real-time performance feedback to students and background data collection. Big advances have been made in adaptive learning systems that quickly assess learning levels and deliver targeted tutoring. Examples include i-Ready from Curriculum Associates (K-12 diagnostic, K-8 reading and math), DreamBox Learning (K-8 math), and ALEKS from McGraw Hill (secondary and postsecondary math). Engaging game-based products like ST Math from MIND Research Institute have produced impressive results at scale when used several times weekly in elementary grades.

Platforms that support individual learning progressions are the most interesting development and the area of greatest opportunity. The Buzz platform from Agilix (introduced in the chapter on leadership) and the platform developed by Summit Public schools (discussed above) are the best examples of platforms that support an individualized course of study combining digital content and projects. Other platforms adding next gen capabilities include Compass Learning, Canvas by Instructure and social learning platform Edmodo. Higher education platforms like NovoEd and Echo360 are boosting engagement and extending faculty reach. Graduate schools are launching next gen programs with 2U, one of the few EdTech companies to sell shares to the public in recent years.

Edupreneurs are attacking back-office and recruiting challenges, improving communication capabilities, and making networks more robust and secure. Professional development platforms Bloomboard, LearnZillion and PD360 bring the benefits of personalized learning to teachers. Career advancement sites General Assembly, Udemy, Lynda.com and a host of online code academies are boosting employability. Active learning startups include DIY, TackTile and Imagination Foundation. Every aspect of learning and every challenge associated with managing educational delivery is being reinvented by new tools.

The next big opportunity is a comprehensive learner profile that goes beyond standard achievement data to include student goal statements, badges and other recognitions, and a college and career readiness tracker. The parent-managed profile would include a full portfolio of work, complemented by teacher narratives on student assets and challenges. The profile could also include non-cognitive variables that impact achievements, as well as an "early warning system," self-management skills, behavior/character education, and a record of community service.[303] Learner profiles—powered by achievement and keystroke data—will unlock secrets about the kinds of experiences that inspire persistence and performance for each student.

Special needs. New tools and new school models are creating the opportunity to better serve all students—including those with special needs. "Blended learning has been a big help to our special needs students because it gives us a wider range of content and strategies to meet them at their level," said Doug Haynes, CEO at Rocky Mount Prep, a K-12 charter school in North Carolina. "They especially enjoy adaptive programs and virtual services such as speech therapy."[304]

Developing school models that blend the best of online and face-to-face learning holds real promise for better meeting special needs for five reasons outlined below.

Inclusion. "At Rocketship Education," said Genevieve Thomas,

"We start with the assumption that all of our kids can be in their general education classroom for the entire day. Then, students are brought out for specialized instruction when their unique learning needs require it. Technology, specifically what is used in our widely-recognized blended learning model, helps make this possible. Based on a student's individual needs, we may pull them out for targeted support for short periods of time or use a special app on an iPad to address a specific Individualized Education Plan (IEP) goal. This means each student's day is customized to fit their needs and abilities."[305] Lab rotation models can provide more time with specialists, while class rotation models may provide inclusion and fewer transitions between rooms. "Blended learning models have allowed special needs to students to be present and fully connected to the classroom community throughout the day, instead of spending large amounts of time removed from their classmates," said Robin Wise, special service manager for blended schools at K12.[306]

Differentiation. "We are implementing a program called eSpark," Thomas continues. "Each of our schools has iPads that are assigned to students with IEPs in Kindergarten through third grade. The iPads are programmed with a suite of apps that are customized based on the student's unique needs. Individual playlists are automatically created for students, so they go into different apps every day based on their playlist. While eSpark wasn't designed specifically for special education students, we're finding that it works well with this student population."[307] Game-based learning has the potential to boost persistence. Instructional flexibility that provides accommodations for all students is key—and blended environments often afford more opportunities for customization. School culture may be the most important ingredient—a fortified environment of high expectations and strong supports.

Better tools. New tools are helping teachers better address special needs:

- Adaptive learning products. Rocketship uses i-Ready, DreamBox and ST Math.
- Augmentative and alternative communication (AAC) include amplification and speech-to-text for hearing impaired students and magnification and text-to- speech for visually impaired students.
- The iPad and apps like LAMP Words For Life, a vocabulary app with touch controls, are transforming learning for students on the autism spectrum. A $299 app replaces a $7,000 device and helps thousands of children communicate.
- Social-emotional learning. A variety of applications help students on the autism spectrum learn how to manage social situations.

Matchmaking. Distributed workforce strategies can better match specialists and special needs—any service, anytime, anywhere. During the 2013-2014 school year, PresenceLearning conducted more than 200,000 live, online therapy sessions in public district and charter schools. They even offer online occupational therapy.

Personalized pathways. Blended learning can increase chances for inclusion and more dynamic (and possibly shorter duration) IEPs for special needs students. It also makes it possible to create an individual plan and pathway for all students.

Continued progress from primary research combined with the potential of customized learning appears to have transformative potential for special education and signals opportunity for a special education app fund. Some learning disability categories are small, but low-cost mobile apps make it much easier to aggregate global demand. The combination of higher cost and niche segments has slowed innovation. A fund that combined philanthropic and venture capital could be just the ticket—and an important niche opportunity for a city ecosystem to take on.

The customized learning revolution is clearly benefiting high achievers, but the biggest impact may be in the learning opportunities created for students with special needs. It is finally becoming possible to fine tune learning experiences, build resilience and self-reliance and power effective communication.

Engagement Tools

When Preston Smith co-founded Rocketship Education nine years ago with John Danner, he was excited about building a network with a strong relationship between teachers and parents. "Preston built an incredibly deep culture of parent engagement at Rocketship with home visits to every family, monthly community meetings, and volunteer time in every classroom," said Danner.[308] Great teachers, an innovative blended school model, and the involvement of parents make Rocketship schools among the best in California. When Danner realized that most of the low-income Rocketship parents had smart phones, he launched Zeal, a mobile learning and relationship system.

 John Danner:
Tools for Connecting With Parents

Zeal is an online learning system that makes it as easy for teachers to provide differentiated and personalized instruction as it is to provide whole-class instruction. We know that if there are no separate lesson plans, no extra assessments, etc., that many teachers will do it. Teachers feel tremendous guilt that they can only teach so many different things at once. Zeal helps them solve that problem, and reach their high- and low-performing students easily, by managing the tactics of what each student learns while the teacher focuses on the goal and coaching students who need extra help.

When we were designing Zeal, we thought a lot about parents. One thing that I learned from Rocketship is that if you can get parents engaged with their children, you can make a lot more progress. One of the things I learned as a parent of two children is that you are in the dark almost all year long. Once a year you get a report card and have a teacher conference and feel really good about your ability to help your child for about a week.

Other than that, staying informed takes a lot of work. So one of the things we are working on at Zeal is allowing parents to see exactly how their children are doing academically, whenever they want to know. And then, when they have questions or want to know how to help, we are making it easy for them to be able to message the teacher within our app. Likewise, if the teacher feels a child needs extra help on something, they can message the parent to work with them on their phone that night.

These simple ideas of transparency and convenient communication are crucial, because parents are extremely busy, and if engagement takes too much work, many parents won't have the time to do it. I believe what we are doing at Zeal will be the norm in the future. Many more parents will be fully informed and engaged because of apps like Zeal they can use on their smartphones. In effect, we will be opening the virtual doors to our school so that parents can observe and participate with their child and the teacher in a way that they could never do in the physical world. That engagement will translate into a lot more support for students at home.[309]

Efficacy

In November 2012, Pearson released a report outlining an approach to improve the efficacy of education products and services, and they committed to using the framework to drive better learner outcomes. CEO John Fallon said, "Our aim is to ensure that every action, every decision, every process, and every investment we make will be driven by a clear sense and understanding of how it will make a measurable impact on learning outcomes."[310]

Pearson's efficacy framework asks that reviewers ask tough questions meant to assess a product or strategy along four areas and a dozen points considered essential for determining if a tool can achieve its intended learning results:

- Outcomes and impact. Intended outcomes, overall design and value for money;
- Strength of evidence base. Comprehensiveness, quality and application of evidence;

- Quality of planning and implementation. Action plan, governance, monitoring and reporting; and
- Capacity to Deliver: Internal capacity and culture, user capacity and culture, and stakeholder relationships.[311]

Once the review process is done, the focus shifts to developing action steps that can be completed to improve learning outcomes, no matter what the purpose and goal of the tool may be. It is a set of questions that allows stakeholders to truly think about how lives can be improved by learning what we do on a daily basis.

Bror Saxberg, Kaplan's chief academic officer, thinks Pearson's efficacy framework is an important contribution because the lack of an evidence frame is holding back the sector. "In the long term, mediocre education will be free," said Saxberg. "[T]he only sustainable value for a learning organization is helping people develop valuable skills," he said, adding, "Companies will need to be good to charge a fee."[312]

Cumulative benefit. Teams incubating new tools and developing new schools benefit from an ecosystem that shares an innovation mindset, is rich with talent development initiatives, and is supported by partnerships and aligned investment.

Not every city needs an EdTech venture fund, but every city needs an incubator like 4.0 Schools because they understand next gen learning and can support teams in organizational design and tech integration; they are focused on impact and take a longer view than accelerators; they help educators develop an innovation mindset. They are the one organization that a superintendent, charter executive, chamber executive, and foundation executive could all get behind.[313]

Smart Cities

A city with a harbormaster will gradually increase the number of high-quality traditional schools. A city with a harbormaster, an incubator, a talent development strategy and collective impact funding alliance will see transformational results.

Chapter Summary

- New school development is a reliable improvement strategy and an opportunity to pilot innovation.

- Cities should support the development of new and transformed schools with grants and incubatory capacity; having an ecosystem of capable partners helps.

- Connecting teachers and technology in short cycle trials could prove transformational.

- New tools hold the promise of engaging parents, partners and community.

- The development of new tools and schools benefits from an innovation mindset, robust talent development and collective impact funding alliances.

7: Advocacy & Policy

 Community Leaders Advocating for Better Options: Denver, Colorado

Barbara O'Brien kicked the Colorado Children's Campaign (CCC) into high gear in the early 1990s. Using Kids Count data to drive change, CCC helped win improved access to early learning and expanded access to quality K-12 options. CCC inspired many of the solid charter networks and reform groups in Denver including DSST, Democrats for Education Reform (DFER), Get Smart Schools, TFA, Colorado Succeeds, A+ Denver, and many community organizations active in education. Active advocates have supported and help sustain a reform-minded Denver Public Schools board.

Denver has an active group of local philanthropists advocating for better educational options. The Donnell-Kay Foundation has emerged as a national leader in next gen models. After a stint with the state as Assistant Commissioner of Education, Amy Berk Anderson returned to lead ReSchool Colorado, a multi-year effort to create a new state public education system. While working for the commissioner, Amy launched a number of projects funded by the Colorado Education Initiative led by Yee-Ann Cho.[314]

Denver advocates and philanthropists form partnerships that benefit families and create community assets. While some long-sought gains were reversed by a combination of the Great Recession and anti-tax measures, Denver remains an example of why advocacy matters.

"Over a long period of time, the main force in favor of greater equality has been the diffusion of knowledge and skills," said Thomas Piketty, author of *Capital in the Twenty-First Century*. He added, "The principal force for convergence [of wealth]—

the diffusion of knowledge—is only partly natural and spontaneous. It also depends in large part on educational policies."[315] While federal policy gained relevance in the last decade, it is state education policy that matters most in America. Measured against a forward-leaning policy platform like Digital Learning Now, most states get a grade of D or F for lack of equity and opportunity.

Equity and innovation have two things in common—they are advanced by advocates and opposed by the status quo. Advocates, particularly those with funding, help education leaders create momentum toward an equitable next gen vision. Aligned advocates add political capital and increase the change capacity of policymakers and system heads. Scaling and sustaining learning innovations is aided by hospitable local and state policy.

Comprehensive policy redesign takes significant political capital and sustained advocacy. The policy frame for next gen learning focuses more on learning than on institutions, and on outcomes more than input. Next gen policies promote equity, achievement and innovation. This new frame starts with an innovation mindset.

Bringing an Innovation Mindset to Policy

After almost a decade as COO at NewSchools Venture Fund, Joanne Weiss went to Washington to run the new Race to the Top program in 2009. She was warned about "bad actors." She came to learn that bad actors are "incompetent, inefficient, or ill-intentioned state or district bureaucrats or administrators—people who might use the 'freedoms' granted in policy in ways that harm students, waste government funds, result in scandalous acts of favoritism, or worse."[316] She found that the perceived need to prevent this type of behavior has dominated policy thinking for decades. Her challenge was to spur innovation with appropriate risk mitigation.

Joanne Weiss:
Bringing an Innovation Mindset to Public Policy

I had come to D.C. after spending decades in the entrepreneurial and nonprofit worlds. There, my focus had been on supporting strong leaders as they created organizations capable of driving ever-improving educational outcomes for each of their students. And to me, the Race to the Top's theory of change was consistent with this work. Across states, we needed to spur excellence; identify and fund it; then support it, highlight it and help disseminate nationwide the lessons learned through early successes.

I had come face-to-face with competing policy mindsets: one focused on ensuring compliance, and the other on spurring improvement through innovation. The job, I quickly realized, was to do both. There was no question that "bad actors" (and bad systems) needed to be prevented from doing harm; but there were also a lot of "good actors" and smart innovators whose ideas could help lift students' outcomes, if given the opportunity. The challenge, then, was to introduce innovation as a policy goal while preventing (and not unintentionally enabling) abuse. A few principles stand out as critical; let me list five.

1. Be clear who owns the levers and put them in the driver's seat.
2. Grant competitions and prizes can channel innovation if they're pointed in the right directions and supported in the right ways.
3. Be tight on the goals but loose on the means to encourage a diversity of solutions.
4. Risk taking is critical to innovation but failure is the nemesis of compliance so evidence-based decision-making is critical to implementation.
5. Transparency drives up quality and accelerates learning.

A policy environment that treats compliance as the "floor" below which we must not fall, but that sets its sights on enabling innovation to lift the "ceiling" for every student—that's the "holy grail" of education policy. It's complex and requires cultural and behavioral changes for both policymakers and grantees, so incentives and consequences have to be carefully thought through. But it's the right work to be doing if the U.S. wants to reclaim its position as a global leader in educating its people.[317]

Race to the Top put governors, state chief school officers and state education boards—together with their willing districts—-in the driver's seat. It set a high bar for success with a lot of funding behind a small number of winners. Applications "were judged on the likelihood of implementation as much as the quality of the concepts, since ideas without execution don't drive outcomes," said Weiss.[318] Evidence-based decision making proved critical to implementation. "By keeping the goals constant but allowing changes in how to get there, the government could ensure that taxpayer resources were being well deployed—and states were properly incented to innovate and improve rather than blindly comply," she added. The open process allowed grantees to review each other's work, develop a clear and shared understanding of what "good" looks like and allow a marketplace for ideas and a shared vocabulary to emerge.

Cities that work for everyone have high-quality and equitably distributed learning opportunities from preschool to grad school. Weiss's five principles apply an innovation mindset to policy in ways that are likely to boost achievement and innovation.

Policies that Boost Achievement, Innovation and Employability
To create widespread access to next gen learning opportunities that result in high rates of employability, it takes sustained leadership that promotes an innovation mindset, fosters aligned investment, produces collective impact through aligned efforts, supports talent development, incubates new tools and schools, and facilitates productive local and state policies. Rather than launching expensive advertising campaigns and chasing big corporate factory jobs with lucrative incentives that erode funding for schools, local and state policy makers should enact policies that are pro-growth, pro-achievement, pro-employability, pro-innovation and pro-productivity.

Pro-growth. More important than marketing branded initiatives, prioritizing the creation of pro-growth policies is critical to creating an innovation ecosystem. Local and state policies should include competitive business tax rates, streamlined business formation and lightweight compliance, according to Stephen Adams, President of the American Institute for Economic Research.[319]

The fastest growing cities in the country are in Texas, owing to pro-growth policies as well as an oil boom caused by new drilling technology.[320] CNBC named Texas the second-best state in which to do business, just behind Georgia, which jumped from eighth place to first[321] (although both lag in measures of child well-being[322]).

While Adams (as described in the chapter on investment) is skeptical of public investment in incubators and enterprise zones, city and state investment in EdTech incubators may prove to be an exception. Not every city will become an EdTech hotspot but, as discussed in the last chapter, a good incubator like 4.0 in New Orleans can change the mindset, talent pipeline and learning landscape. Connecting teacher-leaders to new tools and helping them design new learning environments are two of the best and most efficient investments cities can make.

Pro-achievement. State education policy is critically important to creating a high-skill, high-innovation workforce.

The percentage of adults with postsecondary degrees has traditionally been the best workforce metric. In the competency-based future of stackable credentials, more robust measures will be used, including the percentage of college- and career-ready high school graduates, job certificate holders, and people receiving post-baccalaureate training. State policy should embrace career readiness skills, as well as high common standards in the basics.

Policies should follow forward-leaning K-12 frameworks, such as that of Digital Learning Now, including:

- Local and statewide providers providing full- and part-time access to online and blended learning with equitable access to quality options;
- Strong outcome-based accountability that ensures that every neighborhood has access to good schools;
- Weighted, flexible, portable funding that reflects challenges;
- Competency-based educator preparation and development; and
- Support for learning infrastructure including facilities, broadband and devices.

Because high school and college are becoming a blend of onsite and online learning from multiple providers, states should ensure that every student has access to an adviser that monitors their progress and provides guidance on course selection.[323]

Pro-employability. To dramatically increase the percentage of adults with postsecondary credentials, states should support inexpensive community college and job training, and it should be free for low-income individuals. Business advisory groups should help set employability objectives.

Support for public baccalaureate institutions should be provided via performance contracts with a focus on outcomes, including completion rates weighted toward priority degrees and value added as measured by Collegiate Learning Assessment.[324]

High school and college students should have access to coaching on habits of success—the personal management and social skills to succeed in a dynamic work setting. Students should experience success in college, work, service, and the arts *before* graduating from high school.

The National Governors Association (NGA) recognizes that more highly educated and trained workers typically are more productive than those who have less education and training.

In the 2013-2014 Chair's Initiative report, "America Works: The Benefit of a More Educated Workforce to Individuals and the Economy," the NGA emphasizes building partnerships to get results, including:

1. **Provide state support for cross-system partnerships tied to the vision.** Governors can strengthen state partnerships to launch new or improve existing initiatives that support more precise alignment between their state education and workforce training systems and the needs of their economy. Such partnerships may include preschool to grade 20 (P-20) councils and state workforce investment boards (WIBs).
2. **Identify and promote effective regional or local partnerships.** Governors can identify and promote active and emerging regional partnerships that connect education and training pipelines to high-wage, high-demand careers within key industries in their state's economies.[325]

Pro-innovation. To kickstart innovation and expand access to next gen learning, states and cities should also support:

- New/transformed school development with a Next Generation Learning Challenge-like grant program;[326]
- Collaborative projects focused on innovation and sustainability like Ohio Straight A Fund;
- In- and out-of-school maker, DIY, robotics and coding opportunities;
- Greenfield projects like Donnell-Kay Foundation-sponsored ReSchool Colorado; and
- Low-cost, competency-based higher education alternatives like Western Governor's University or Relay Graduate School of Education.

Regardless of the focus of policy, improvements are made better when done together. Policy Innovators in Education (PIE) Network is breaking new ground regarding what is possible for moving ideas and information across state lines. According to PIE Network CEO Suzanne Tacheny Kubach, "For too long, we've approached the task of influencing education policy at the state level as if states coexist in a national, top-down institution. In reality, when it comes to influencing state-level policy, information and ideas move in multiple directions, defying traditional notions of orderly coordination. Information moves differently through networks, which create a whole new world for strategy."[327] Kubach continues, "Really, PIE and other key connector organizations like New Schools Venture Fund, Excel in Ed and CEE-Trust provide the 'keg presence' (*i.e.*, convening partner) of education reform. They create places where leaders bump into each other, which fosters brain-bending idea exchanges. Because networks spread ideas and resources further and more efficiently, funders no longer need narrow their focus on just a handful of possible state partners. Networks often surface 'up and comers' from surprising places, which is really exciting."[328]

Advocacy

The basic philanthropic change strategy is: proof points lead to positive public relations, which builds public support for policy changes.[329] The last chapter focused on strategies for developing and introducing new tools and schools to improve learning options and create proof points for system change. Each of the seven keys produces important advocacy benefits:

1. **Innovation mindset.** A culture of innovation results in increased demand for high-quality learning options and powerful learning experiences.
2. **Sustained leadership.** A distributed network of leaders that share a common vision, share the leadership load and make the case for change.
3. **Talent development.** Teacher-leaders develop proof points and support the professional learning of others.
4. **Collective impact.** Aligned and activated partners work toward common goals.
5. **Aligned investment.** Funding for pilots and change levers ensures needed support is present.

6. **New tools and schools.** These create proof points of learning experiences and environments that work better for students and teachers.

7. **Policy.** Good policy reduces barriers to change and improves incentives for action.

ADVOCACY ROLE BY KEY

Campaign thinking. The shift to next gen learning requires three coordinated campaigns targeting three stakeholder groups:

- **Internal.** System heads lead an employee campaign to build support for next gen environments and the new staffing roles and relationships that come with them.

- **Learners.** System heads campaign to build learner and family demand for next gen environments and learning progressions. Environments may have unique themes or connections to job clusters. Competency-based progressions may use different grouping and reporting strategies than traditional schools.

- **Policy makers**. Advocates campaign for local and state policy change that reduces barriers and improves incentives for next gen learning.

Before launching a campaign, leaders should identify the decision makers and key influencers for specific decisions—district superintendent, state board or the legislature, for example. While the appearance of broad-based support may be useful, for many decisions there are one or two key decision makers and a couple of key influencers, which is a case where strategic advocacy is more efficient than a public campaign.

Campaigns require specific time-bound objectives. They usually start by building awareness, then creating alignment and building engagement, and finally a call to action. Campaigns lower the barriers against action and increase the incentives to take action.

Successful change efforts often leverage current trends. Leaders should start by analyzing change forces and asking, "What's heading in the right direction?" They should also identify allies, and consider the point of view of opponents.

Leaders should make their case, keep it simple and use a simple, unambiguous call to action. They should do research and find out what people think. Campaigns are more about motivation than education—the desired outcome is action. Leaders should communicate the plan and lay out a path a better future. They should not show stakeholders a problem, but rather show them an opportunity to implement a solution.

Environmentalist Chris Rose suggests, "Don't argue, do."[330] Campaigns are about verbs: starting, publishing, petitioning, demonstrating, improving. Campaigns seek to change to the status quo; that may involve conflict, and conflict makes news.

Leaders should create symbolic acts and communicate in pictures. They should be direct and use straightforward language. Leaders should remember that they are not just persuading that they are right, but that they are right and that the audience needs to take action.

Simplexity. When the author was a public school superintendent, his team introduced standards-based grading the year after Washington state introduced new learning expectations. Teachers revolted, not because of the concept of providing more specific feedback, but because of the 26-page report card, which was hard to fill out and a nightmare to print.

In the leadership chapter, Michael Barber made the case for "whole-system reform, an innovation agenda, and a focus on implementation." The Washington report card initiative probably rated a B for system reform, a C for innovation, and an F for implementation. A campaign must be proportional to the difficulty of the change; if the change can be made easy and appealing, it will not require much of a campaign.

"Change really isn't as hard as we thought if we capture people's interest and give them enjoyable, worthwhile experiences," said Canadian education expert Michael Fullan. "We are learning more about large-scale change, making it less complicated by focusing on a small number of ambitious goals with a coherent strategy that attends in concert to half a dozen or so key factors: intrinsic motivation, capacity building, transparency of results and practice, leadership at all levels, and a positive but assertive stance on progress." [331] Fullan calls this "simplexity"—a small number of key factors that must be made to gel with large groups of people.

Next gen learning is promising but challenging to pull off at scale because the tool set is a few years behind and training needs are daunting. Fullan challenges leaders to build partnerships simply; he suggests that "new developments must be 1) irresistibly engaging for students and for teachers; 2) elegantly efficient and easy to use; 3) technologically ubiquitous 24/7; and 4) steeped in real-life problem solving."

Big levers. As Fullan suggests, irresistibly powerful tools are one big lever. As suggested in the investment chapter, boosting access to broadband is critical.[332] States and urban districts should also adopt weighted funding to create stronger incentives to develop new strategies to meet the needs of historically underserved student groups.

"Governments can increase the ability of online learning innovators by releasing them from regulatory requirements that unnecessarily restrict innovation," said Tom Arnett of the Christensen Institute. "In general, regulations applied to online and blended learning should move away from input requirements, such as class size limits, staffing requirements, and instructional hours, and instead focus on outcomes such as student mastery of competencies."[333]

Week-long, end-of-year state testing locks in the traditional age cohort model. States have the opportunity to encourage next gen learning by adopting on demand (or frequently scheduled) end-of-course exams.

Improving access to college credit opportunities (often called "dual credit") in high school boosts graduation, college enrollment and completion. Given the challenges of working across institutional boundaries, a mixture of carrots and sticks will be required to make early college opportunities widely available.

Coordinated advocacy and policy efforts are enhanced by leveraging mindset, leadership, talent, investment and new tools. Advocacy and policy can also bring improvements to each of the keys to education and employment.

Chapter Summary

- Some change takes strategic advocacy focusing on a small number of decision makers, while some requires a broad-based campaign.

- An aggressive change agenda requires a campaign inside educational institutions, with learners and families, and targeting policy makers.

- The seven key strategies produce important campaign assets including education leaders, proof points, activated partners and focused investment.

- Enhancing and simplifying next gen learning solutions will speed adoption.

- Big change levers include weighted funding, online learning, better assessment and dual enrollment opportunities.

For further information on this topic:

 Michael Horn on Advocacy and Policy

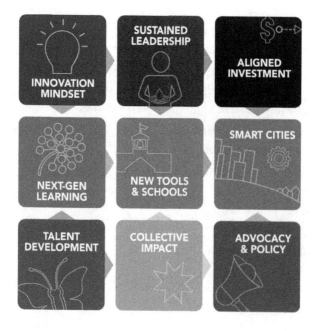

Next Steps

Alex Hernandez:
Creating Innovative Ecosystems

When it comes to education innovation, all cities are not created equal. San Jose is the Mesopotamia of blended learning with Summit Public Schools, Rocketship Education, Alpha Public Schools, KIPP Bay Area, and Milpitas Unified School District all within a few miles of a bustling coffeehouse where new education ideas are brewed and served daily. Khan Academy and EdSurge are headquartered a few miles north on the 101 Highway. And the Silicon Schools Fund provides early-stage philanthropy for new breakthrough school models.

New Orleans is home to 4.0 Schools, an incubator that brings together communities of educators to prototype new solutions to real problems. New Schools for New Orleans provides capital, coaching and startup support for educators launching high-quality new schools. And Teach for America (TFA) fuels the Crescent City's entrepreneurial spirit with over 1,200 mission-driven corps members and alumni.

Innovative cities tend to have some common characteristics:

Courageous, early-stage capital. Education entrepreneurs need money to pursue their bold ideas, and innovative ecosystems have philanthropists and for-profit investors with an appetite for investing at the earliest stages.

Places to tinker, prototype and meet other education innovators. Organizations like 4.0 Schools, the Digital Harbor Foundation and Startup Weekend EDU provide safe spaces for educators to lean into new ideas and meet other like-minded innovators.

People, people, people. Innovative ecosystems are home to organizations that attract talent and develop tomorrow's leaders.

> For example, Dan Carroll, co-founder of the successful EdTech startup Clever, began his career as a TFA member and was a teacher at STRIVE Prep, a successful charter school network. Organizations like TFA and STRIVE are magnets for talent and set the foundation for future innovation.
>
> **Support to launch new ventures.** Innovative ecosystems are places where educators see a path to bring their ideas to life. This means access to capital, talent, advisers and other supports that make the difference between success and failure.
>
> There has never been a better time to be an education entrepreneur. And whether they know it or not, cities compete to attract our best talent. The good news: cities can significantly increase education innovation through targeted, strategic investment.[334]

World-class cities provide safe and secure living conditions, a social safety net, transportation and trade infrastructure, and an opportunity platform that connects people to the innovation economy. First and foremost, that means quality learning opportunities. And, as Hernandez suggests, there has never been a better time for cities to take the lead in education entrepreneurship.

The new global priority for individuals, organizations and cities is getting smart. We named our first book and organization for this priority, embracing the mindset of effort and action rather than status and pedigree. In the innovation economy, nobody cares where you came from, only what you can do to add value—and that demands an innovation mindset that embraces the act of becoming—learning, creating, making—rather than a state of being.

"Economic growth flows only from reforms that bring actual improvements in cognitive skills," said Eric Hanushek. "If we are to remain economically competitive, we need to solve the puzzle of our schools."[335] New tools and transformed schools hold the promise of solving Hanushek's puzzle. Online resources and better access to broadband are making learning possible everywhere.

Innovative learning options occur anywhere there is leadership, but often—in ecosystems where talent is developed—tools are incubated, and new schools are encouraged. These environments begin with an innovation mindset—one that can be replicated in every classroom and every city.

"The success or failure of the human species will be determined in cities," says Yuwa Hedrick-Wong, of the Center for Inclusive Growth.[336] Now is the time for cities to take action.

Action Steps for Smart Cities
There are seven keys to education and employment. This concluding chapter outlines suggested next steps in each category.

Innovation Mindset
- Model openness and inquiry.
- Encourage an innovation mindset and powerful learning experiences in every classroom with every student.
- Provide summer and extracurricular opportunities that grow an innovation mindset.
- Recognize and reward student and educator innovation.

Sustained Leadership
- Create shared future dialogues: what should grads know and be able to do? What learning opportunities should our community have access to?
- Build a city innovation agenda with learning at the core. Students deserve the opportunity to work with adults who expect them to participate in an innovation economy.
- Ensure stable and effective governance to give innovation a place to grow.
- Build partnerships to expand equitable access to quality options.

Talent Development

- Provide learning experiences to develop innovation mindset.
- Identify and support teacher-leaders (*e.g.*, CityBridge Fellowship).
- Share leadership competencies with multiple partner providers (higher ed and alternative) and only hire/promote leaders who have met these competencies.
- Model active learning with leadership dialogues, community conversations and site visits.

Collective Impact

- Schools should build action-oriented partnerships around shared vision and values with clarity around goals, responsibilities, timelines and resources.
- Cities and educational institutions should set up a change management office to coordinate partnerships, monitor progress and adjust plans.
- Cities/districts should signal aggregated demand for better engagement apps and should use mobile technology to connect with learners and families.
- Cities and philanthropies should support an urban "harbormaster" who coordinates an improvement and innovation agenda.

Aligned Investment

- Raise/align funds and make a few smart investments.
- Invest in a talent pipeline of teachers, leaders and Edupreneurs.
- Invest in new tools and schools (below).
- Invest in advocacy to build public support for next gen learning environments and policies (below).

New Tools and Schools

- Proactively address issues of youth disengagement and unemployment through quality schools that lead to viable career pathways.

- Create or recruit an incubating capacity for new tools and schools.
- Create or recruit short cycle trial capacity to connect teachers and technology.
- Create a new and transformed school grant program (*e.g.*, NGLC Chicago and D.C.).

Policy and Advocacy
- States should sunset their education code and rewrite their policies around next gen learning opportunities (see 10 Elements of High-Quality Digital Learning).
- States and districts should adopt weighted student funding to improve services to underserved learners.
- States and districts should expand full- and part-time access to online learning while ensuring that students have quality guidance.

Do Now! 10 (or more) Things You Can Do to Contribute to Your Smart City

10 Things Mayors Should Do Now
1. Expand access to high-quality early learning experiences.
2. Help create or appoint a "harbormaster" to coordinate and support metro educational improvement and innovation.
3. Work with providers to increase broadband access for low-income families.
4. Encourage businesses to provide work-based learning experiences.
5. Encourage an innovation mindset at city hall and in city partnerships.
6. Host community conversations about workforce requirements and new learning options.
7. Encourage providers to use a single application (like New Orleans); encourage colleges to offer dual enrollment courses; encourage expanded access to job training.

8. Sponsor youth entrepreneurship programs in school, after school, and during the summer.
9. Sponsor a community leadership development program.
10. Work with the state to ease barriers to business formation.

10 Things Learning Professionals Should Do
1. Focus your learning: pick a topic to learn about, build a learning plan, read a few education bloggers every day
2. Broaden your learning: pick something new to learn about every year.
3. Blend your learning: encourage your school to use a platform like Bloomboard to connect you to online professional development opportunities.
4. Do some hands-on learning: sign up for or create a maker experience (see 4 steps from Gayle Allen).
5. Do some work-based learning: visit and, if possible, work in a few different work environments, particularly places that embrace an innovation mindset.
6. Reflect on your learning: join online professional learning communities and learn with and from others. See if you can write 50 probing questions (or read John Hardison's).
7. Portfolio your learning: chronicle your professional development (see Vanderbilt summary).
8. Share your learning: write a weekly blog about what you are learning, and share your portfolio artifacts.
9. Support peer learning: sign up to mentor a new teacher.
10. Extend your impact: lead a grade span team, teach a class online, or pilot another extended reach strategy (see OpportunityCulture).

10 Things Business Leaders Should Do Now
1. Make learning a priority for your employees.
2. Encourage employees to make learning a priority for their families; give parents flexibility to be involved in their children's education.

3. Help sponsor the transition to next gen learning in your community with a donation, project management support, advocacy or training.
4. Sponsor and lead a community leader field trip to innovative schools (see 35 High Schools Worth Visiting and 38 K-8 Schools Worth Visiting).
5. Provide work-based learning experiences including projects, job shadows and internships.
6. Help parents and students understand the new world of work by hosting or supporting community conversations about workforce requirements.
7. Use your position to advance next gen learning in your community and state.
8. Mentor and tutor students who need extra help.
9. Help kids do some hands-on learning by sponsoring maker, robotics, coding, DIY or scouting activities.
10. Become an adviser for a community college degree program.

10 Things Superintendents Should Do Now

1. Start a community conversation about what graduates should know and be able to do; pay attention to career readiness skills and dispositions; express new learning goals. (See Summit's readiness indicators.)
2. Encourage Deeper Learning and writing across the curriculum with challenging writing prompts and useful teacher resources. (See feature on Literacy Design Collaborative.)
3. Plan the shift to next gen learning in three phases over the next three years. Pick a strategy that makes sense for your district, then consider school models, platform and content, devices, staffing and staff development. (See Blended Learning Implementation Guide.)
4. Expand student options with online learning. Shift most Advanced Placement courses online and offer all 34; you will save money and boost options. Expand world language offerings K-12, starting with high school. For the course you can enroll 200 students in, use your own staff.

For lower-enrollment courses, use a partner.

5. Open flex academies that combine online learning with onsite support in every high school to serve students way behind, way ahead, and/or interested in a theme (*e.g.*, global studies, performing arts, manufacturing).

6. Incorporate adaptive learning K-8 using a lab or classroom rotation model (depending on the software you choose and the number and type of devices you have).

7. Encourage maker, coding, DIY, work-based learning, and other active explorations with an expedition unit every eight weeks. Hold a science fair every year.

8. Transform special education with new tools and online learning. (See 5 Ways New Tools & Schools are Transforming Special Education.)

9. Work with employee groups on staffing and development plans that anticipate new roles and relationships. (Study OpportunityCulture.)

10. Listen hard and communicate clearly with staff and community members about the intent, the goals and the process. Communicate twice as much as you think you need to in person and using social media. (Also see The 10 Questions Every Superintendent Needs to Answer and 10 Entry Points.)

10 Things Parents/Guardians Should Do

1. Manage student time online; some recreation is great (especially if they are playing something like Minecraft) but they have work to do, and it is your job to keep them safe and productive. Turn off the devices and have dinner together every day.

2. Boost student career awareness with visits to a variety of work environments. Take your kids (and other people's kids) to work, and other work settings, as often as possible. Talk about what you see.

3. Tell your eighth graders that they'll be doing college-level work in two years. Help make high school choices that facilitate that—Advanced Placement, International

Baccalaureate or dual enrollment courses. Make sure high schoolers take a few online classes.

4. Build a family learning plan. Pick a topic and learn together. Build a learning objective into your next vacation—make a game of it.
5. Set aside a monthly Saturday maker morning and build, code or post something.
6. Know your options and choose wisely. The options are ever-expanding—public schools, neighborhood schools, charters, magnets, online, early college and more.
7. Make service part of your family routine, and talk about what your family is learning through service. Support student leadership experiences through faith congregations, sports and clubs.
8. Encourage students to start a business in high school. Let them know by high school graduation they should have an LLC, a website and a mobile app.
9. Review your student's digital portfolio at least quarterly, and help him or her build a positive social media presence that incorporates a collection of personal bests.
10. Help your student figure out how he or she learns best. What promotes curiosity and persistence? What promotes understanding? Help your student do more of what works in and out of school.

20 Things States Should Do Now
1. Fund universal access to preschool and full-day Kindergarten.
2. Embrace Core & More. Common Core State Standards are internationally benchmarked, college-ready expectations in reading, writing and math. With online networks, they represent a platform for innovation allowing teachers to share tools, resources and strategies across state lines.
3. Like the 19 states that have joined the Partnership for 21st Century Skills, states should encourage a broad view of career and civic readiness incorporating an innovation mindset.
4. Support competency-based preparation of educators

(see Preparing Teachers For Deeper Learning) and expand alternative preparation pathways, especially those linked to high-performing school districts/networks.

5. Support an incubator like 4.0 Schools to encourage and prepare Edupreneurs and incubate new learning environments. (See 4 reasons every city needs an incubator.)

6. Ensure that high school students receive informed guidance, academic support and access to youth/family services. (See Core & More.)

7. Support new/transformed school grants modeled after Next Generation Learning Challenges grants. (See feature on CityBridge and NGLC in Washington, D.C.). Grants could also be used to encourage schools to work in networks and use smart procurement to adopt one of several EdTech clusters. (See Smart Series Guide to EdTech Procurement and Schools and Software from Christensen Institute.)

8. Support improved broadband access to schools and homes with public-private partnerships.

9. Provide matching grants to districts and networks with a good plan to boost student access to take-home technology like laptops and tablets.

10. Expand part time online course access: full- and part-time access to online and blended options from multiple providers. (See Louisiana students gained online options, and 10 Strategies States & Districts Can Use to Boost AP.)

11. Encourage secondary schools to provide coding and computer science options, and support adoption of nationally recognized information technology industry certifications. (See advice from the experts.)

12. Encourage competency-based student progressions by requiring students to show what they know and making end of course exams available on demand. (See DLN section on Advancement; for more see CompetencyWorks.)

13. Enable data backpacks, gradebooks of data that follow each student from grade to grade and school to school. Encourage use of parent-managed comprehensive learner profiles. As recommended by the U.S. Department of Education, parents should have the ability to download a learner profile and share it with multiple providers. Give every student a digital portfolio. (See features on EduClipper and Pathbrite.)
14. Power equitable options with funding that is weighted, flexible and portable.
15. Support short cycle trials of promising tools and strategies and Proposals for Better Growth Measures.
16. Set a timeline for the digital conversion. State leaders should frame compelling goals and encourage proactive planning around a specific timeline. (See Blended Learning Implementation Guide 2.0.)
17. Adopt the 5 Game Changers from Complete College America: supported college preparatory curriculum in high schools, performance funding for higher education with 15 credits as the baseline for full-time enrollment with access to structured schedules and guided pathways to success.
18. Encourage dual enrollment in high school and keep community and technical college affordable for all.
19. Improve ranking on competitiveness by streamlining business formation, cost of doing business and compliance.
20. Invest in infrastructure and transportation, and expand equitable access to learning options.

10 School Partnerships to Start Now

1. **Change Management Partnership.** Actively seek out targeted skills for your school leadership team. For example, there likely are parents in your school who work as project managers or specialize in change management and can turn your team's ideas into results by outlining deadlines, responsibilities and tracking systems to make things happen.
2. **Career Guidance Partnership.** This can be as simple as inviting guest speakers into the classroom to draw connections

between the subject at hand and their daily work, or it could be as involved as a job shadow program or career day. Do not be afraid to start small and expand as opportunities arise.

3. **Community Service Partnership.** The possibilities are endless and typical examples bountiful. Write or send gifts to those serving in the military; personalize these by targeting relatives of students and staff. Collect food for the local food shelf/pantry, raise money for a local cancer research fund, or visit a nursing home and play games. Almost any activity can be connected to language arts (*e.g.*, writing letters to the military) or math goals (*e.g.*, tracking money raised).

4. **STEM Partnership.** Partner with local STEM specialists. In South Washington County Schools in Minnesota, 3M employees serve as science fair moderators and regularly conduct "Science Wizard" presentations. Not every district has a 3M in their backyard, but most have access to a variety of STEM-focused businesses or organizations.

5. **Digital Partnership.** Know a teacher or parent in a different part of the county or world? Create virtual classroom "Skype pals." Have students correspond with each other and periodically connect classroom to classroom using Google Hangout or Skype.

6. **Youth and Family Services Partnership.** School counselors are a great resource to help initiate youth and family service partnerships to ensure that students are referred to community agencies that provide critical services for students. Conduct site visits and build awareness campaigns.

7. **Facility partnership.** Many schools are sharing indoor and outdoor space with community centers, churches, parks and recreation departments. A school that rented its facility to a local church ended up being a recipient of a $50,000 service project grant. What started as a facility partnership evolved into both community service and grant partnerships.

8. **College or University Partnerships**. Contact someone at your local college or university to initiate a classroom-level partnership. If local options are not available, initiate contact with one of many virtual programs.

9. **Grant Partnerships**. Just as every senior in high school should be encouraged to apply for scholarships, every classroom teacher would benefit from applying for grants. While some grants are awarded on a school or system level, many are awarded to local community organizations.

10. **Advocacy Partnership.** If you have policy initiatives or legislation you would like to influence, partner with a local communications or public relations firm or department. They may be able to help with your messaging.

As Hernandez noted in his opening to this concluding chapter, "not all cities are created equal." The Bay Area, New York and Chicago are clear leaders when it comes to innovations in learning—and that is beginning to translate into learning opportunities for citizens of those great cities. But what is new and exciting is that, as Hernandez notes, "New education ideas are flourishing in places like Baltimore, Boise and Memphis, cities with relatively little activity just a few short years ago."[337] Among the common characteristics of innovative cities, Hernandez notes investment, incubation capacity and talent development. This book has suggested that the smart cities agenda start with an innovation mindset and, to Hernandez's list, added partnerships and policy as key to scaling innovation and opportunity.

There truly has never been a better time to be an education entrepreneur. The opportunity to help people learn improves every month as new tools are incorporated into new schools and as new apps become available to more learners. The good news for cities that incorporate the seven keys to education and employment is that they can help diverse populations skill up fast for a better future for everyone.

Smart Cities

Appendix A: Contributor Bios, Posts, and Videos

Joe Ableidinger is the Executive Director of World Class Schools, an NGLC grant winner. Joe was previously a Senior Consultant with Public Impact.
Blog Post: Innovative Models Pave the Way for Changes in Policy and Practice

Amy Anderson is Senior Director at the Donnell-Kay Foundation (DK) and Director of ReSchool Colorado.
Blog Post: What's Next in Education? A New Education System

Abby Andrietsch is Co-Founder and Executive Director of Schools That Can Milwaukee.
Blog Post: Cross Pollinating Education Ideas in Milwaukee

Sir Michael Barber is Chief Education Advisor to Pearson. Formerly he led the education practice at McKinsey and advised Prime Minister Tony Blair.
Blog Post: The Path to Systemic Innovation
The views expressed in the article are his personal views and do not represent the views of Pearson or any of the organisations he has worked for past or present

Greg Butler is founder and partner of Collaborative Impact, a social innovation partnership.
Blog Post: Building Innovation Partnerships
Hangout: Greg Butler on Collective Impact

Michele Cahill is Vice President for National Programs at Carnegie Corporation. Previously she was senior counselor to the chancellor in New York City.
Blog Post: Leadership for Education Innovation
Hangout: Michele Cahill on Smart Cities

Andy Calkins is Deputy Director of Next Generation Learning Challenges, an initiative managed by EDUCAUSE.
Blog Post: Moving Towards Next Generation Learning

Smart Cities

Matt Candler is CEO of 4.0 Schools, an early-stage incubator. Previously he developed new charters at New Schools for New Orleans and KIPP.
Blog Post: An Educator's Lean Startup Mindset
Hangout: Matt Candler on New Tools and Schools

Karen Cator is President and CEO of Digital Promise. From 2009-2013, Karen was Director of the Office of Educational Technology at the U.S. Department of Education.
Blog Post: Building a National Innovation Partnership

Stacey Childress is CEO of NewSchools Venture Fund. Formerly she led innovation at the Gates Foundation and was a business professor at Harvard.
Blog Post: It's Time: Connecting What Students Need & What Entrepreneurs Create

David Conley is CEO of the Educational Policy Improvement Center (EPIC) and a professor at the University of Oregon.
Blog Post: Q&A: David Conley on College & Career Readiness

John Danner is CEO of mobile learning startup Zeal. Previously he was co-founder and CEO of Rocketship Education.
Blog Post: What Would Real Engagement Look Like

Isral DeBruin is Schools That Can Milwaukee's Manager of Communications & Development.
Blog Post: Cross Pollinating Education Ideas in Milwaukee

Katelyn Donnelly is Managing Director of the Pearson Affordable Learning Fund.
Blog Post: The Importance of Culture

Nick Donohue is President and CEO of the Nellie Mae Education Foundation and former state chief in New Hampshire.
Blog Post: What Would Real Engagement Look Like?
Hangout: Nick Donohue on Collective Impact

Jeff Edmondson is Managing Director of StriveTogether, a national cradle-to-career initiative that brings together leaders committed to helping children succeed from birth through careers.
Blog Post: Quality Collective Impact = Impactful Innovation

Adrian Fenty is a Special Advisor at Andreessen Horowitz, Business Development Manager at Perkins Coie, and former Mayor of the District of Columbia.

Ethan Gray is founder and CEO of CEE-Trust, a national non-profit that works with cities to ensure all children have access to high quality public schools.
Hangout: Ethan Gray on Talent Development

Matt Greenfield is a partner at Rethink Education, a venture capital firm focused on innovative technology for learning.
Blog Post: Innovation Ecosystems: The Role of Impact Investing

Dr. Terry B. Grier is Superintendent of the Houston Independent School District, the first district to win the Broad Prize twice.
Blog Post: For Houston ISD, The Talent Pipeline Flows Both Ways

Kristoffer Haines is the former Senior Vice President of Growth, Development & Policy at Rocketship Education.
Blog Post: Why Harbormasters are Critical to a City's Ecosystem

Alex Hernandez is a partner at the Charter School Growth Fund and leads their next generation schools practice.
Blog Post: Creating Innovative Ecosystems

Frederick Hess is an educator, political scientist and author who serves as Director of Education Policy Studies at the American Enterprise Institute.
Blog Post: Cage-Busting for Smart Cities
Hangout: Rick Hess on Sustained Leadership

Tim Hilborn is Chief Instructional Officer at TRECA Educational Solutions and runs a high engagement learning network for Superintendents.
Hangout: Tim Hilborn on Talent Development

Renee Hill is Assistant Superintendent in Riverside Unified School District.
Blog Post: Talent is UNDERrated

Steven Hodas is an edu policy advisor and entrepreneur and former Executive Director at the New York City Department of Education (NYC DOE) Office of Innovation
Blog Post: Fostering Innovation in Cities

Michael B. Horn is co-founder and Executive Director of Education Practice at the Clayton Christensen Institute, a nonprofit think tank. He is also the co-author of *Disrupting Class*.
Blog Post: Why Public Schools Struggle to Innovate
Hangout: Michael Horn on Advocacy and Policy

Smart Cities

Kevin Johnson is Mayor of Sacramento and a former NBA player.

Neerav Kingsland is the former CEO of New Schools for New Orleans.
Blog Post: Smart Cities/Humble Cities

Lyle Kirtman is CEO of Future Management Systems, a leadership development organization.
Blog Post: Innovation Leadership
Hangout: Lyle Kirtman on Sustained Leadership

Greg Landsman is Executive Director of StrivePartnership, a consortium working together to improve academic achievement in Cincinnati and Northern Kentucky.
Blog Post: Quality Collective Impact = Impactful Innovation

Jason Lange is co-founder and CEO of BloomBoard, an online development platform to ignite growth and personalized professional development for K-12 educators.
Blog Post: New Study Reveals Trends in Professional Learning
Hangout: Jason Lange on Talent Development

Tina Law is an Associate at Social Policy Research Associates where she engages in studies related to education reform, youth development and community-based advocacy.
Blog Post: Building a "Smart" Talent Pipeline

Sengsouvanh Leshnick is Director of Education Research at Social Policy Research Associates where she focuses on education reform and workforce development.
Blog Post: Building a "Smart" Talent Pipeline

Phyllis Lockett is CEO of LEAP Innovations, an education technology hub in Chicago connecting educators and tech companies.
Blog Post: Our Kids Can't Wait

JoEllen Lynch is Executive Director of Springpoint, a national organization that partners with school districts and networks to establish new, innovative high schools.
Blog Post: The Job Good Schools Fulfill

Michael Matsuda is the Superintendent of Anaheim Union High School District.
Hangout: Mayor Tait and Superintendent Matsuda on Innovation Mindset

Scott McLeod is the Director of Innovation at Prairie Lakes Area Education Agency.

Christopher Nyren is founder of Educelerate and Educated Ventures and organizer of Chicago Startup Weekend EDU.
Blog Post: Innovation Leadership: Spurring & Supporting Entrepreneurship

Ryan S. Olson is Team Leader for K-12 Education at The Kern Family Foundation and is a Center for Hellenic Studies (CHS) Fellow at Harvard University.
Blog Post: Forming an Entrepreneurial Mindset in K-12 Students

Susan Patrick is the President and CEO of the International Association for K-12 Online Learning (iNACOL).
Blog Post: Fostering Next-Gen Learning: A Q&A with iNACOL's Susan Patrick

Shawn Rubin is the Director of Blended Learning at the Highlander Institute.
Blog Post: Providence Picking Up The Pace

Carri Schneider is Director of Policy & Research at Getting Smart, an education advocacy firm.

Don Shalvey is Deputy Director of Bill & Melinda Gates Foundation. Prior to working with Gates, Shalvey founded and led Aspire Public Schools
Blog Post: Choosing Excellent Schools - Not Charter Versus District

Andy Smarick is a Partner at Bellwether Education Partners, a nonprofit organization working to improve educational outcomes for low-income students.
Blog Post: The Urban Schools System of the Future

Preston Smith co-founded Rocketship Education in San Jose with John Danner in 2006. Formerly, Smith was founder and Principal of L.U.C.H.A. Elementary in Alum Rock.
Blog Post: What Would Real Community Engagement Look Like?

Sandy Speicher is an Associate Partner at the global design and innovation firm, IDEO and Managing Director of IDEO's Education practice.
Blog Post: Design Thinking: A Human-Centered Approach to Innovation in Education
Hangout: Sandy Speicher on Innovation Mindset

Smart Cities

Michael Staton is a partner at Learn Capital, an education venture capital firm.
Blog Post: Rebundling Education: Emerging Business Models
Hangout: Michael Staton on Investment and Incentives

Chris Sturgis is CEO of MetisNet and co-founder of CompetencyWorks.org.

Suzanne Tacheny Kubach is Executive Director at Policy Innovators in Education Network (PIE Network), which supports and promotes a network of education advocacy organizations working to improve K-12 education in their states

Tom Tait is the mayor of Anaheim, California.

George Tang is the Chief Operating Officer Educate Texas, whose mission is increasing postsecondary readiness, access, and success for all Texas students.
Blog Post: Collective Impact - Creating a Self-Sharpening Education System

Caroline Vander Ark is COO of Getting Smart, an education advocacy firm, and board member for Advancing Leadership.

Katie Vander Ark is a Community Manager at CatalytCreativ.
Blog Post: Las Vegas: Downtown Project, Blended Progress

Joanne Weiss is an independent consultant on education programs, technologies, and policy. She was formerly Chief of Staff to U.S. Secretary of Education Arne Duncan, Director of the federal Race to the Top program, and a partner and COO at NewSchools Venture Fund.
Blog Post: Policymaking and Innovation Mindsets

Jessie Woolley Wilson is CEO of DreamBox Learning, a K-8 adaptive learning math curriculum.

Esther Wojcicki is an American journalist, educator and vice chair of the Creative Commons board of directors.
Blog Post: Student Entrepreneurship in Action

Appendix B: City Blog Posts

Austin
gettingsmart.com/2014/06/smart-cities-austin/

Baltimore
gettingsmart.com/2014/06/incubating-edtech-revolution-baltimores-digital-harbor/

Boise
gettingsmart.com/2014/06/boise-emerging-ecosystem-education-innovation/

Boston
gettingsmart.com/2014/08/smart-cities-boston/

Chicago
gettingsmart.com/2014/04/smart-cities-chicago/

Denver
gettingsmart.com/2014/05/smart-cities-denver-advocates-partnerships-making-impact/

Detroit
gettingsmart.com/2014/04/smart-cities-detroit/

Houston
gettingsmart.com/2014/07/smart-cities-houston-weve-got-an-opportunity-here/

Indianapolis
gettingsmart.com/2013/04/mind-trust-develops-the-smart-cities-formula/

Kansas City
gettingsmart.com/2013/06/smart-cities-kansas-city/

Las Vegas
gettingsmart.com/2014/07/smart-cities-viva-las-vegas/

Los Angeles
gettingsmart.com/2013/12/smart-cities-los-angeles-startup-weekend-edu-124/

Smart Cities

Miami
gettingsmart.com/2014/01/smart-cities-miami-move/

Milwaukee
gettingsmart.com/2014/05/smart-cities-milwaukee-schools-can/

Minneapolis/St Paul
gettingsmart.com/2013/02/smart-cities-twin-cities-is-no-wobegon-but-on-the-rise/

New Orleans
gettingsmart.com/2014/04/smart-cities-new-orleans/

New York City
gettingsmart.com/2014/07/smart-cities-new-york/

Oakland
gettingsmart.com/2014/06/oakland-social-justice-meets-edtech/

Phoenix
gettingsmart.com/2014/04/smart-cities-phoenix/

Pittsburgh
gettingsmart.com/2014/05/pittsburgh-an-edtech-hive/

Portland
gettingsmart.com/2014/05/smart-cities-portland-countercultural-interesting/

Providence
gettingsmart.com/2014/05/smart-cities-providence-ri/

Raleigh/Durham
gettingsmart.com/2013/04/smart-cities-raleighdurham/

San Diego
gettingsmart.com/2013/02/smart-cities-san-diego/

San Francisco gettingsmart.com/2014/06/san-francisco-powering-global-learning-revolution/

Silicon Valley
gettingsmart.com/2014/06/creative-cluster-silicon-valley/

Tampa
gettingsmart.com/2014/07/smart-cities-lessons-from-tampa-part-2/

Washington D.C.
gettingsmart.com/2014/07/smart-cities-washington-d-c/

Appendix C: Organizations Referenced in Book

4.0 Schools - www.4pt0.org
500 Startups - www.500.co
1776 - www.1776dc.com
A+ Denver - www.aplusdenver.org
The Abell Foundation - www.abell.org
Achievement First - www.achievementfirst.org
Agilix - www. agilix.com
Alverno College - www.alverno.edu
J.A. and Kathryn Albertson Foundation - www.jkaf.org
Alliance for Excellent Education - www. all4ed.org
American Association of Colleges for Teacher Education (AACTE) - www.aacte.org
American Enterprise Institute - www.aei.org
American Institute for Economic Research (AIER) - www.aier.org
Arizona Community Foundation - www.azfoundation.org
Arizona State University - www.asu.edu
Aspire Public Schools - www. aspirepublicschools.org
Bellwether Education Partners - www. bellwethereducation.org
Bill & Melinda Gates Foundation - www.gatesfoundation.org
Bloomboard - www.bloomboard.com
Boston Public Schools - www.bostonpublicschools.org
Eli & Edyth Broad Foundation - www.broadfoundation.org
Boston Plan for Excellence (BPE) - www.bpe.org
Boston Public Schools - www.bostonpublicschools.org
BrightBytes - www.brightbytes.net
Canvas by Instructure - www.instructure.com
Carnegie Corporation - www.carnegie.org
Carnegie Foundation for the Advancement of Teaching - www.carnegiefoundation.org
Carnegie Mellon University - www.cmu.edu
Carpe Diem Learning Systems - www.carpediemschools.com
CEE-Trust - www.cee-trust.org
Center for Reinventing Public Education - www.crpe.org

Smart Cities

Change Illinois - www.changeil.org
Chicago Public Schools (CPS) - www.cps.edu/Pages/home.aspx
Chiefs for Change - www.chiefsforchange.org
Chicago Public Schools - www.cps.edu
Christensen Institute - www.christenseninstitute.org
CityBridge Foundation - www.citybridgefoundation.org/
Collaboration/Foundation
Collaborative Impact - www.collaborativeimpact.net
Collective Impact Forum - www.collectiveimpactforum.org
College Board - www.collegeboard.org
College for America - www.collegeforamerica.org
College Park Academy - www.collegeparkacademy.com
College Summit - www.collegesummit.org
Colorado Children's Campaign - www.coloradokids.org
Colorado Education Initiative - www.coloradoedinitiative.org
Colorado Succeeds - www.coloradosucceeds.org
Common Core State Standards - www.corestandards.org
Compass Learning - www.compasslearning.com
Connections Education - www.connectionseducation.com
Consortium on Chicago School Research - www.ccsr.uchicago.edu
Cowen Institute For Education Initiatives - www.coweninstitute.com
Curriculum Associates - www.curriculumassociates.com
Denver Public Schools - www.dpsk12.org
Digital Learning Now - www.digitallearningnow.com
Digital Promise - www.digitalpromise.org
DIY - www.diy.org
Donnell-Kay Foundation - www.dkfoundation.org
Dreambox Learning - www.dreambox.com
DSST Public Schools - www.dsstpublicschools.org
Echo360 - www.echo360.com
Edmodo - www.edmodo.com
edTPA - www.edtpa.aacte.org
Education Achievement Authority - www.michigan.gov/eaa
Educate Texas - www.edtx.org
Educate Now! - www.educatenow.net
Education Week - www.edweek.org
EduClipper - www.educlipper.com
eSpark - www.esparklearning.com
Expeditionary Learning - www.elschools.org
Foundation for Excellence in Education(Excel in Ed) - www.excelined.org
FSG - www.fsg.org

First Five Years Fund - www.ffyf.org

Florida Virtual School - www.flvs.net

Frameworks Institute - www.frameworksinstitute.org

Franklin-McKinley School District - www.fmsd.org

Fullbridge - www.fullbridge.com

General Assembly - www.generalassemb.ly

Getting Smart - www.gettingsmart.com

Global Health Technologies Coalition - www.ghtcoalition.org/incentives-pull.php

GPS Education Partners - www.gpsed.org

Grantmakers for Education (GFE) - www.edfunders.org

Hartford Public Schools - www.hartfordschools.org

Heritage Foundation - www.heritage.org

High Tech Middle Chula Vista (HTMCV) - www.hightechhigh.org/schools/HTMCV

Jaquelin Hume Foundation - www.philanthropyroundtable.org/topic/excellence_in_philanthropy/jaquelin_hume_foundation

IDEO - www.ideo.com

International Association for K-12 Online Learning (iNACOL) - www.inacol.org

Interstate Teachers Assessment and Support Consortium - www.ccsso.org/Resources/Programs/Interstate_Teacher_Assessment_Consortium_(InTASC).html

ImagineK12 - www.imaginek12.com

Harvard University - www.harvard.edu

William & Flora Hewlett Foundation - www.hewlett.org

Houston Independent School District - www.houstonisd.org

Imagination Foundation - www.imagination.is

Junior Achievement - www.juniorachievement.org

K12 - www.k12.com

Kapor Capital - www.kaporcapital.com

Kern Family Foundation - www.kffdn.org

KIPP - www.kipp.org

Koru - www.joinkoru.com

League of Innovative Schools - www.digitalpromise.org/league

LEAP Innovations - www.leapinnovations.org

Lean Enterprise Institute - www.lean.org

Learn Capital - www.learncapital.com

LearnLaunch - www.learnlaunch.com

LearnZillion - www.learnzillion.com

Louisiana Association of Public Charter Schools - www. lacharterschools.org

Louisiana Recovery School District - www.rsdla.net
Lynda.com - www.lynda.com
Miami Dade County Public Schools - www.dadeschools.net
Massachusetts Business Alliance for Education - www.mbae.org
McCormick Foundation - www.mccormickfoundation.org
McGraw Hill Education - www.mheducation.com
Michael & Susan Dell Foundation - www.msdf.org
MIND Research Institute - www.mindresearch.net
Mindset Works - www.mindsetworks.com
MIT - www.mit.edu
Mooresville Graded School District - www.mgsd.k12.nc.us
National Business Incubation Association - www.nbia.orgabout_nbia#
National Council on Teacher Quality - www.nctq.org
National Science Foundation - www.nsf.gov
Nellie Mae Education Foundation - www.nmefoundation.org
Next Generation Learning Challenge - www.nextgenlearning.org
Network for Teaching Entrepreneurship - www.nfte.com
New Leaders - www.newleaders.org
New Schools for Chicago - www.newschoolsnow.org
New Schools for New Orleans - www.newschoolsforneworleans.org
NewSchools Venture Fund - www.newschools.org
New Visions for Public Schools - www.newvisions.org
New York City Department of Education - www.schools.nyc.gov
Northwest Nazarene University - www.nnu.edu
NovoEd - www. novoed.com
The Office for Standards in Education (OFSTED) - www.ofsted.gov.uk
Organisation for Economic Cooperation and Development -
    www.oecd.org
Ounce of Prevention Fund - www.ounceofprevention.org
Partnership for 21st Century Schools - www.p21.org
Pathbrite - www.pathbrite.com
PD360 - www.pd360.com
Pearson - www.pearson.com
Policy Innovators in Education (PIE) Network - www.pie-network.org
Race to the Top - www2.ed.gov/programs/racetothetop
Relay Graduate School of Education - www.relay.edu
Reynoldsburg City Schools - www.reyn.org
ReSchool Colorado - www.dkfoundation.org/our-work/reschool-
    colorado/reschool-colorado
Rethink Education - www.rteducation.com
Riverside Unified School District - www.rusdlink.org

Rocketship Education - www.rsed.org
Rocky Mount Prep - www.rmprep.org
Rogers Family Foundation - www.rogersfoundation.org
Schools That Can Milwaukee - www.stcmilwaukee.org
Silicon Schools - www.siliconschools.com
Spring Branch Independent School District - www.springbranchisd.com
Springpoint - www.springpointschools.org
SRI International - www.sri.com
Stand for Children - www.stand.org
Stanford University - www.stanford.edu
Stanford University's Stanford Center for Assessment, Learning and Equity - www.scale.stanford.edu
Straighter Line - www.straighterline.com
Summit Public Schools - www.summitps.org
TackTile - www.tacktile.org
Teach For America - www.teachforamerica.org
TechStars - www.techstars.com
Time to Succeed - www.timetosucceed.com
The New Teacher Project - www.tntp.org
Turnaround for Children - www.turnaroundusa.org
Udemy - www.udemy.com
University of Chicago Urban Education Institute - www.uei.uchicago.edu
University of Idaho - www.uidaho.edu
University Now - www.unow.com
Washington Center for Equitable Growth - www. equitablegrowth.org
Western Governors University - www.wgu.edu
World Bank - www.worldbank.org
Zappos - www.zappos.com

Smart Cities

Appendix D: Smart Cities Asset Mapping

The Smart Cities project began with the construction of an index to rate the quality of urban learning assets across a dozen metrics. Organized and updated for the seven keys to education and employment, the following framework is recommended for asset mapping.

Innovation Mindset
- Schools develop a growth mindset and support habits of success
- Out of school coding/maker/DIY/robotics learning opportunities
- Support for career awareness, internships, work and service opportunities

Sustained Leadership
- School districts have strong/sustained improvement, new schools, and innovation agenda
- Civic leaders prioritize education and support quality options
- R1 university contributes to intellectual life of the community

Talent Development
- National organizations are active (TFA, NTP, New Leaders, Education Pioneers)
- Local initiatives are attracting and developing talent P-20
- Vibrant career education sector connected to emerging job clusters

Smart Cities

Collective Impact
- Strong presence of reform and support organizations
- Metrowide initiative to boost quality and access to early learning
- Evidence of P-20 partnerships

Aligned Investment
- Local funders are aligned and active
- National funders find ecosystem investment worthy
- Active early stage investors

New Tools and Schools
- High-performing charter school networks are active
- Venture funded EdTech startups
- Incubators support startups and connect teachers and EdTech

Advocacy and Policy
- Weighted, flexible, portable, performance-based funding
- Multiple full- and part-time online learning providers
- State policy context promotes quality with low barriers to innovation (see 10 Elements of High Quality Digital Learning)

Appendix E: Resources

Next Generation Learning
- Digital Learning Now, Navigating the Digital Shift
- Christensen Institute, Schools and software: What's now and what's next
- MIND Research Institute, Better Blends With Visual Game-Based Math
- iNACOL, Mean What You Say: Defining and Integrating Personalized, Blended and Competency Education
- Rosetta Stone, The Next Generation of World Language Learning
- DreamBox Learning, Making Math Work
- EdFuel, Fueling A Revolution

School Profiles
- Christensen Institute Blended Learning Universe
- Next Generation Learning Challenges: K-12 breakthrough school models
- Next Generation Learning Challenges: Higher education breakthrough models
- Getting Smart, Deeper Learning for Every Student Every Day

Competency-Based Learning
- Digital Learning Now, The Shift from Cohorts to Competency
- iNACOL, Necessary for Success: A State Policymaker's Guide to Competency Education
- iNACOL, A K-12 Federal Policy Framework for Competency Education: Building Capacity for Systems Change

Smart Cities

Shaping Markets
- Getting Smart, Boosting Impact: Why Foundations Should Invest In EdTech Venture Funds
- Digital Learning Now, Using Prizes & Pull Mechanisms to Boost Learning

Hot Topics
- Digital Learning Now, Core & More: Guiding and Personalizing College & Career Readiness
- Getting Smart, Preparing Teachers For Deeper Learning
- Getting Smart, Assessing Deeper Learning: A Survey of Performance Assessment and Master-Tracking Tools

Appendix F: Disclosures

The author has a relationship with some of the organizations mentioned as shown below.

Getting Smart Advocacy Partners
- Agilix
- Connections Education
- Curriculum Associates
- DreamBox Learning
- Educause, Next Generation Learning Challenges
- Foundation for Excellence in Education, Digital Learning Now
- Instructure
- K12
- The Learning Accelerator
- Literacy Design Collaborative
- MIND Research Institute
- Pearson
- Scholastic

Organizations where Tom Serves as a Director
- International Association for K-12 Online Learning (iNACOL)
- Imagination Foundation

Learn Capital Portfolio Companies
- Bloomboard
- BrightBytes
- Coursera
- DIY
- Edmodo
- General Assembly
- LearnZillion
- NovoEd
- Udemy

Smart Cities

Endnotes

1. Simon, D. "David Simon: 'There are now two Americas. My country is a horror show.'" *The Guardian.* December 7, 2013. www. theguardian.com/world/2013/dec/08/david-simon-capitalism-marx-two-americas-wire

2. Schmidt, E. and Cohen J. *The New Digital Age.* New York: Knopf. 2013. www.amazon.com/The-New-Digital-Age-Reshaping/dp/0307957136

3. www.edtech.md

4. "Urban population growth." World Health Organization www. who.int/gho/urban_health/situation_trends/urban_population_growth_ text/en/

5. Glaeser, E. Interview with Fareed Zakaria. Global Public Square. June 15, 2014. transcripts.cnn.com/TRANSCRIPTS/1406/15/fzgps.01.html

6. Florida, R. "What If Mayors Ruled the World?" City Lab. June 13, 2012. www.citylab.com/politics/2012/06/what-if-mayors-ruled-world/1505/

7. Kotkin, J. "Richard Florida Concedes the Limits of the Creative Class." *The Daily Beast.* March 20, 2013. www.thedailybeast.com/ articles/2013/03/20/richard-florida-concedes-the-limits-of-the-creative-class.html

8. Porter, M. and Stern, S. "Social Progress Index 2014." *Social Progress Imperative.* March 2014. tinyurl.com/ socialprogressimperativeindex2

9. Ibid.

10. Hanushek, E. "Education quality and economic growth." In *The 4 percent solution: Unleashing the economic growth America needs,* edited by Miniter, B. New York: Crown Business. 2012. hanushek.stanford.edu/ publications/education-quality-and-economic-growth-0

11. Hanushek, E., Jamison, D., Jamison, A. and Woessmann, L. "Education and Economic Growth." *Education Next* 8 no. 2. Spring 2008. educationnext.org/education-and-economic-growth/

12. Ibid.

13. Ibid.

14. Grier, T. "For Houston ISD, The Talent Pipeline Flows Both Ways." Getting Smart blog. May 2014. gettingsmart.com/2014/05/ houston-isd-talent-pipeline-flows-ways/

15. Vander Ark, T. "Short Cycle Efficacy Trials Key to Personalized Learning." Getting Smart blog. December 2013. gettingsmart. com/2013/12/short-cycle-efficacy-trials-key-personalized-learning/

16. Ableidinger, J. "Innovative Models Pave the Way for Changes in Policy and Practice." Getting Smart blog. May 2014. gettingsmart. com/2014/05/innovative-models-pave-way-changes-policy-practice/

17. Lewin, T. "Educator Has Accomplishments and Enemies." New York Times. August 31, 2002. www.nytimes.com/2002/08/31/ nyregion/educator-has-accomplishments-and-enemies.html

18. To see data about these and other districts, visit nces.ed.gov/ nationsreportcard/subject/publications/dst2013/pdf/2014468XW8.pdf.

19. See the time series improvement in your state on the chart at www.americashealthrankings.org/all/graduation.

20. To learn more about what is possible, see Bonk, C. The World Is Open: How Web Technology is Revolutionizing Education. San Francisco: Jossey-Bass. 2009. www.amazon.com/World-Open-Technology-Revolutionizing-Education-ebook/dp/B002JMV6KK/ref=sr_1 _7?ie=UTF8&qid=1394316430&sr=8-7&keywords=bonk

21. Carolan, J. and Murali, V. "A closer look at K12 edtech venture funding in 2013." New Schools Venture Fund blog. December 2013. www.newschools.org/blog/closer-look-2013

22. "Blended Learning Model Definitions." Clayton Christensen Institute for Disruptive Innovation. www.christenseninstitute. org/?s=blended+learning

23. See Opportunity Culture from Public Impact for more on school models that leverage great teaching with technology at opportunityculture.org.

24. Moe, M., Hanson, M., Jiang, L., and Pampoulov, L. "American Revolution 2.0: How Education Innovation is Going to Revitalize America and Transform the U.S. Economy." GSV Asset Management. July 2012. gsvadvisors.com/wordpress/wp-content/themes/gsvadvisors/ American%20Revolution%202.0.pdf

25. Florida, R. Who's Your City? How the Creative Economy Is Making Where to Live the Most Important Decision of Your Life. New York: Basic Books. 2008.

26. For a summary, see Educational Research and Innovation's "Measuring Innovation in Education" at www.keepeek.com/Digital-Asset-Management/oecd/education/measuring-innovation-in-education_9789264215696-en#page18.

27. Read an interview with Weinman at gettingsmart. com/2013/04/what-could-lynda-com-do-for-your-school.

28. Nagel, D. "One-Seventh of the World's Population Got a Smart Phone Last Year." *THE Journal.* January 2014. thejournal.com/articles/2014/01/28/one-seventh-of-the-worlds-population-got-a-smart-phone-last-year.aspx

29. Ibid.

30. Horn, M. "Why Public Schools Struggle to Innovate." *Getting Smart* blog. July 2014. gettingsmart.com/2014/07/public-schools-struggle-innovate

31. All quotes and attributions in this paragraph appeared originally at gettingsmart.com/2014/07/public-schools-struggle-innovate.

32. Horn, M. "Why Public Schools Struggle to Innovate." *Getting Smart* blog. July 2014. gettingsmart.com/2014/07/public-schools-struggle-innovate

33. Hess, F. *Cage-Busting Leadership.* Cambridge: Harvard Education Press. 2013. www.amazon.com/Cage-Busting-Leadership-Educational-Innovations-Frederick/dp/1612505066

34. Moe, M., Hanson, M., Jiang, L., and Pampoulov, L. "American Revolution 2.0: How Education Innovation is Going to Revitalize America and Transform the U.S. Economy." GSV Asset Management. July 2012. gsvadvisors.com/wordpress/wp-content/themes/gsvadvisors/American%20Revolution%202.0.pdf

35. Ibid.

36. Ibid.

37. Andreitsch, A. and DeBruin, I. "Cross Pollinating Education Ideas in Milwaukee." *Getting Smart* blog. May 2014. gettingsmart.com/2014/05/cross-pollinating-education-ideas-milwaukee. All quotes and attributions in this paragraph originally appeared at gettingsmart.com/2014/05/cross-pollinating-education-ideas-milwaukee.

38. Jacobs, J. *Systems of Survival.* New York: Random House. 1992. www.amazon.com/Systems-Survival-Dialogue-Foundations-Commerce/dp/0679748164

39. Conley, D. *Getting Ready for College, Careers, and the Common Core: What Every Educator Needs to Know.* San Francisco: Jossey-Bass. 2014. www.amazon.com/Getting-Ready-College-Careers-Common/dp/1118551141

40. All quotes and attributions in this paragraph originally appeared at gettingsmart.com/2014/07/smart-cities-qa-jessie-woolley-wilson.

41. See more of Eliana's story at cdno3.gettingsmart.com/wp-content/uploads/2014/02/Deeper-Learning-For-Every-Student-FINAL-.pdf.

42. For a summary, see Educational Research and Innovation's "Measuring Innovation in Education" at www.keepeek.com/Digital-Asset-Management/oecd/education/measuring-innovation-in-education_9789264215696-en#page23.

43. Vander Ark, T. "Smart Cities: Providence Picking Up The Pace." Getting Smart blog. May 2014. gettingsmart.com/2014/05/smart-cities-providence-ri/

44. Elliott, P. "ACT: Third of High School Grads Not College Ready." 21 Aug 2013. bigstory.ap.org/article/act-only-quarter-grads-ready-all-subjects

45. Vander Ark, T. "Managed Instruction or Digital Learning?" Getting Smart blog. March 2014. gettingsmart.com/2014/03/managed-instruction-digital-learning/

46. The Business Council. "CEO Survey Results." February 2013. www.thebusinesscouncil.org/assets/TCB_BCS_FEB_2013.pdf

47. Vander Ark, T. "CEOs Want Hard-Working Decision-Making Team Players." Getting Smart blog. May 2013. gettingsmart.com/2013/05/ceos-want-hard-working-decision-making-team-players/

48. Wagner, T. *Creating Innovators: The Making of Young People Who Will Change the World*. New York: Scribner. 2012. www.amazon.com/exec/obidos/ASIN/1451611498

49. McLeod, S. "Which vision are you selling?" Dangerously Irrelevant blog. April 2014. dangerouslyirrelevant.org/2014/04/which-vision-are-you-selling.html

50. McLeod, S. "3 big shifts." Dangerously Irrelevant blog. September 2013. dangerouslyirrelevant.org/2013/09/3-big-shifts.html

51. Calkins, A. "Moving Towards Next Generation Learning." Getting Smart blog. June 2014. gettingsmart.com/2014/06/moving-towards-next-generation-learning/

52. "Deeper Learning Defined." The William and Flora Hewlett Foundation. April 2013. www.hewlett.org/uploads/documents/Deeper_Learning_Defined__April_2013.pdf

53. Vander Ark, T. and Schneider, C. "Deeper Learning For Every Student Every Day." Getting Smart. January 2014. cdno3.gettingsmart.com/wp-content/uploads/2014/02/Deeper-Learning-For-Every-Student-FINAL-.pdf

54. See profiles of the 20 Deeper Learning schools, including Springfield Renaissance on page 64, at cdno3.gettingsmart.com/wp-content/uploads/2014/02/Deeper-Learning-For-Every-Student-FINAL-.pdf.

55. Vander Ark, T. "Mooresville Adopts Gateway Projects in 4 Grades." Getting Smart blog. March 2014. gettingsmart.com/2014/03/mooresville-adopts-gateway-projects-4-grades/

56. Learn more about Expeditionary Learning's approach at_ gettingsmart.com/2013/12/expeditionary-assessment.

57. Extensive resources on next gen learning are available at nextgenlearning.org/topics/next-gen-learning.

58. Ravitch, D. "Petrilli: Schools Are Best Way to End Poverty." Dian Ravitch's blog. October 2013. dianeravitch.net/2013/10/10/petrilli-schools-are-best-way-to-end-poverty/

59. Turnaround for Children, Inc. "Poverty, Stress, Schools: Implications for Research, Practice, and Assessment." December 2013. turnaroundusa.org/wp-content/uploads/2013/12/Turnaround-for-Children-Briefing-Dec-2013.pdf

60. Vander Ark, T. "Fortified Environments Turnaround Impacts of Poverty." Getting Smart blog. August 2013. gettingsmart.com/2013/08/fortified-environments-turnaround-impacts-of-poverty/

61. Turnaround for Children, Inc. "Poverty, Stress, Schools: Implications for Research, Practice, and Assessment." December 2013. turnaroundusa.org/wp-content/uploads/2013/12/Turnaround-for-Children-Briefing-Dec-2013.pdf

62. The Alliance for Excellent Education. "A Time for Deeper Learning: Preparing Students for a Changing World." May 2011. www.all4ed.org/files/DeeperLearning.pdf

63. Vander Ark, T. "Carnegie Supports New High Schools that Recuperate & Accelerate." Getting Smart blog. March 2013. gettingsmart.com/2013/03/carnegie-supports-new-high-schools-that-recuperate-accelerate/

64. Stone, W. "A 'Lost Generation Of Workers': The Cost of Youth Unemployment." NPR. www.npr.org/2014/07/02/327058018/a-lost-generation-of-workers-the-cost-of-youth-unemployment

65. Hamilton, L. and Mackinnon, A. "Opportunity by Design: New High School Models for Student Success." Carnegie Corporation. Spring 2013. carnegie.org/fileadmin/Media/Programs/Opportunity_by_design/Opportunity_By_Design_FINAL.pdf

66. Lynch, J. "The Job Good Schools Fulfill." Getting Smart blog. June 2014. gettingsmart.com/2014/06/job-good-schools-fulfill/

67. Gronberg, R. "Bell: City needs to attack poverty." *The Herald Sun* (North Carolina). February 3, 2014. www.heraldsun.com/news/localnews/x1385734119/Bell-City-needs-to-attack-poverty

68. Richwine, J. "Study: Charter Schools Raise Nearby Home Values by Thousands of Dollars." *National Review Online*. January 2014. www.nationalreview.com/corner/368980/study-charter-schools-raise-nearby-home-values-thousands-dollars-jason-richwine

69. Vander Ark, T. *Getting Smart: How Digital Learning Is Changing the World*. 2012. San Francisco: Jossey-Bass. www. amazon.com/Getting-Smart-Digital-Learning-Changing-ebook/ dp/B005OVZ99C/ref=sr_1_1?ie=UTF8&qid=1402605483&sr=8- 1&keywords=getting+smart

70. "Next Gen Learning." Next Generation Learning Challenges. nextgenlearning.org/topics/next-gen-learning

71. Holly, C., Dean, S., Hassel, E.A., and Hassel, B. "Projected Statewide Impact of 'Opportunity Culture' School Models." Public Impact. 2014. opportunityculture.org/wp-content/uploads/2014/05/ Projected_Statewide_Impact_of_Opportunity_Culture_School_Models-Public_Impact.pdf

72. Learn more about Rocketship and other schools at gettingsmart.com/2014/03/how-digital-learning-is-boosting-achievement.

73. Learn more about ST Math and other programs recognized by the Business Roundtable at businessroundtable.org/media/news-releases/business-roundtable-recognizes-five-programs-for-outstanding-work-i.

74. Scholastic. "Compendium of READ 180 Research." January 2011.

75. Vander Ark, T. "Blended Speech Therapy: Q&A with Clay Whitehead." Getting Smart blog. September 2012. gettingsmart. com/2012/09/blended-speech-therapy-qa-clay-whitehead/

76. Barber, M., Donnelly, K. and Rizvi, S. "An Avalanche Is Coming: Higher Education and the Revolution Ahead." Institute for Public Policy Research. March 2013. www.pearson.com/avalanche/

77. Vander Ark, T. "Experts Weigh in on K-12 Coding & CS Resources." Getting Smart blog. July 2013. gettingsmart.com/2013/07/ experts-weigh-in-on-k-12-coding-cs-resources/

78. See a summary of trends affecting digital learning at gettingsmart.com/2013/02/12-trends-transforming-the-post-sec-landscape.

79. Ryerse, M., Schneider, C. and Vander Ark, T. "Core & More: Guiding and Personalizing College & Career Readiness." Digital Learning Now. May 2014. digitallearningnow.com/site/uploads/2014/05/FINAL-Smart-Series-Core-and-More-Guidance.pdf

80. Vander Ark, T. "How Will Universities Flip, Blend And Go Online?" Getting Smart blog. February 2014. gettingsmart. com/2014/02/will-universities-flip-blend-go-online/

81. Staton, M. "Rebundling Education: Emerging Business Models." Learn Capital. December 2013. learncapital.com/rebundling-education-emerging-business-models/

82. According to Hess, leadership always entails two complementary roles. One is coaching, mentoring, nurturing, and

inspiring others to forge dynamic, professional cultures. This half often absorbs the whole attention of those who tackle educational leadership. Lost in the discussion is the second half of leadership—the *cage-busting* half, in which leaders upend stifling rules, policies, and routines to make it easier for successful professional cultures to thrive. Read more at www.ascd.org/publications/educational_leadership/apr13/vol70/num07/Be_a_Cage-Buster.aspx.

83. Vander Ark, T. "Barber on the Future of Education." Getting Smart blog. March 2014. gettingsmart.com/2014/03/barber-future-education/

84. Barber, M. "The Path to Systemic Innovation." Getting Smart blog. June 2014. gettingsmart.com/2014/06/path-systemic-innovation/

85. See Boosting Impact for a longer discussion of impact investing trends.

86. Vander Ark, T. "Smart Cities: Providence Picking Up The Pace." Getting Smart blog. May 2014. gettingsmart.com/2014/05/smart-cities-providence-ri/

87. Vander Ark, T. "Smart Cities: Baltimore's Digital Harbor." Getting Smart blog. January 2013. gettingsmart.com/2013/01/smart-cities-baltimores-digital-harbor/

88. Wojcicki, E. "Student Entrepreneurship in Action." Getting Smart blog. July 2014. gettingsmart.com/2014/07/student-entrepreneurship-action/

89. Ibid.

90. Agrawal, S. "Six Reasons Millennials Are Actually the Best Workers." *Forbes* Leadership Forum. May 2014. www.forbes.com/sites/forbesleadershipforum/2014/05/16/six-reasons-millennials-are-actually-the-best-workers/

91. Duckworth, A. "Our Work." The Duckworth Lab. sites.sas.upenn.edu/duckworth

92. Dweck, C. "What is Mindset." mindsetonline.com/whatisit/about/

93. Farrington, C. Roderick, M., Allensworth, E., Nagoka, J., Keyes, T., Johnson, D. and Beechum, N. "Teaching Adolescents To Become Learners." *The University of Chicago Consortium on Chicago School Research*. June 2012. ccsr.uchicago.edu/sites/default/files/publications/Noncognitive%20Report.pdf

94. "Deeper Learning Competencies." The Hewlett Foundation. April 2013. www.hewlett.org/uploads/documents/Deeper_Learning_Defined__April_2013.pdf

95. Ibid.

96. Vander Ark. T. "8 Principles of Productive Gamification."

Getting Smart blog. February 2014. gettingsmart.com/2014/02/8-principles-productive-gamification/

97. Read the full study at deloitte.wsj.com/cfo/files/2013/03/Why_entrepreneurs_matter.pdf.

98. Vander Ark, T. "Fostering an Entrepreneurial Mindset in Engineers." *The Huffington Post*. April 2013. www.huffingtonpost.com/tom-vander-ark/fostering-an-entrepreneur_b_3074089.html

99. Vander Ark, T. "Building an Entrepreneurial Mindset." Getting Smart blog. March 2014. gettingsmart.com/2014/03/building-entrepreneurial-mindset-classroom-community/

100. Ellerbe, I. Personal communication. July, 2014.

101. See a summary and access the full report at www-03.ibm.com/press/us/en/pressrelease/31670.wss.

102. Read more from Dockterman and see his follow-up comments at gettingsmart.com/2014/07/david-dockterman-4-belief-statements-underlying-student-performance/#comment-164712.

103. Ibid.

104. Vander Ark, T. "Measuring Mindset in Math 180." Getting Smart blog. October 2013. gettingsmart.com/2013/10/measuring-mindset-math-180/

105. Vander Ark, T. "David Dockterman on 4 Belief Statements Underlying Student Performance." Getting Smart blog. July 2014. gettingsmart.com/2014/07/david-dockterman-4-belief-statements-underlying-student-performance/#comment-164712

106. Ibid.

107. All quotes in this paragraph originally appeared at gettingsmart.com/2014/06/building-innovation-mindset-growth-maker-team-experiences.

108. See the full Lean Startup methodology at theleanstartup.com/principles.

109. Find full degree information at collegeforamerica.org/about/entry/approach#sthash.u1N9Hx8A.6pDGi4pw.dpbs.

110. See the framework at www.p21.org/storage/documents/P21_Framework.pdf.

111. The Hewlett Foundation. "Deeper Learning Competencies." April 2013. www.hewlett.org/uploads/documents/Deeper_Learning_Defined__April_2013.pdf

112. Vander Ark, T. "Innovation Mindset = Growth + Maker + Team Experiences." Getting Smart blog. June 2014. gettingsmart.com/2014/06/building-innovation-mindset-growth-maker-team-experiences/

113. Unless otherwise noted, quotes in the following three paragraphs first appeared at gettingsmart.com/2013/10/measuring-mindset-math-180.

114. Vander Ark, T. "David Dockterman on 4 Belief Statements Underlying Student Performance." Getting Smart blog. July 2014. gettingsmart.com/2014/07/david-dockterman-4-belief-statements-underlying-student-performance/

115. Olson, R. "Forming an Entrepreneurial Mindset in K-12 Students." Getting Smart blog. July 2014. gettingsmart.com/2014/07/forming-entrepreneurial-mindset-k12-students/

116. Vander Ark, T. "Expeditionary Assessment: PBL Lessons from Ron Berger." Getting Smart blog. December 2013. gettingsmart.com/2013/12/expeditionary-assessment/

117. All quotes in this and the following paragraph first appeared at cdno3.gettingsmart.com/wp-content/uploads/2014/02/Deeper-Learning-For-Every-Student-FINAL-.pdf. DSST is profiled on page 43.

118. "NFTE summer BizCamps unlock entrepreneurial mindset in youth." NFTE blog. June 2014. www.nfte.com/why/blog/nfte-summer-bizcamps-unlock-entrepreneurial-mindset-in-youth

119. Candler, M. "An Educator's Lean Startup Mindset." Getting Smart blog. June 2014. gettingsmart.com/2014/06/educators-lean-startup-mindset/

120. Ibid.

121. Candler, M. "A Skunkworks for Schools." Getting Smart blog. February 2014. gettingsmart.com/2014/02/skunkworks-schools/

122. Candler, M. "An Educator's Lean Startup Mindset." Getting Smart blog. June 2014. gettingsmart.com/2014/06/educators-lean-startup-mindset/

123. Sturgis, C. Personal communication. June 2014.

124. Learn more about Pesce at www.ozy.com/rising-stars-and-provocateurs/bel-pesce-how-entrepreneurship-can-change-lives/3345.article.

125. Ibid.

126. Ibid.

127. Vander Ark, T. "Smart Cities: Detroit." Getting Smart blog. April 2014. gettingsmart.com/2014/04/smart-cities-detroit/

128. Kirtman, L. "Innovation Leadership." Vander Ark on Innovation blog. Education Week. May 2014. blogs.edweek.org/edweek/on_innovation/2014/05/innovation_leadership.html

129. Vander Ark, T. "Shifting Superintendents Stuck in a Compliance World." Getting Smart blog. November 2013. gettingsmart.com/2013/11/shifting-superintendents-stuck-compliance-world/

130. Kirtman, L. "Innovation Leadership." Getting Smart blog. May 2011. gettingsmart.com/2014/05/innovation-leadership/

131. All quotes in this paragraph originally appeared at gettingsmart.com/2013/11/shifting-superintendents-stuck-compliance-world/.

132. Vander Ark, T. "Shifting Superintendents Stuck in a Compliance World." Getting Smart blog. November 2013. gettingsmart.com/2013/11/shifting-superintendents-stuck-compliance-world/

133. Horn, M. "Areas of nonconsumption." Clayton Christensen Institute for Disruptive Innovation blog. February 2010. www.christenseninstitute.org/areas-of-nonconsumption/

134. Vander Ark, T. "Improvement vs. Innovation." Getting Smart blog. May 2014. gettingsmart.com/2014/05/improvement-vs-innovation/

135. Read more about the summer institute at gettingsmart.com/2014/03/mooresville-adopts-gateway-projects-4-grades.

136. Vander Ark, T. "Mooresville Adopts Gateway Projects in 4 Grades." Getting Smart blog. March 2014. gettingsmart.com/2014/03/mooresville-adopts-gateway-projects-4-grades/

137. All of Kurtz's comments in this and the following paragraph originally appeared in cdno3.gettingsmart.com/wp-content/uploads/2014/02/Deeper-Learning-For-Every-Student-FINAL-.pdf.

138. Vander Ark, T. "Smart Cities: New Orleans." Getting Smart blog. April 2014. gettingsmart.com/2014/04/smart-cities-new-orleans/

139. Kingsland, N. "Smart Cities/Humble Cities." Getting Smart blog. May 2014. gettingsmart.com/2014/05/smart-cities-humble-cities/

140. Vander Ark, T. "Smart Cities: New Orleans." Getting Smart blog. April 2014. gettingsmart.com/2014/04/smart-cities-new-orleans/

141. Ikemoto, G., Taliaferro, L., Fenton, B. and Davis, J. "Great Principals at Scale: Creating District Conditions that Enable All Principals To Be Effective." New Leaders and George W. Bush Institute. June 2014. www.bushcenter.org/sites/default/files/gwbi-greatprincipalsatscale.pdf

142. See Margaret Spellings' take on the subject at www.realcleareducation.com/articles/2014/06/18/school_districts_must_create_the_right_conditions_for_great_principals_to_excel_1020.html.

143. Hess, F. "Cage-Busting for Smart Cities." Getting Smart blog. June 2014. gettingsmart.com/2014/06/cage-busting-smart-cities/

144. Learn more about the portfolio strategy at docs.gatesfoundation.org/documents/districtwhitepaper.pdf.

145. Access CRPE's full portfolio strategy at crpe.org/research/portfolio-strategy/seven-components.

146. All quotes in this paragraph first appeared at gettingsmart. com/2014/04/urban-school-system-future, where a link to Smarick's book also appears.

147. Statistics cited in this paragraph first appeared at gettingsmart.com/2013/07/smart-cities-where-districts-charters-are-partners.

148. Andrietsch, A. and DeBruin, I. "Cross Pollinating Education Ideas in Milwaukee." Getting Smart blog. May 2014. gettingsmart. com/2014/05/cross-pollinating-education-ideas-milwaukee/

149. Vander Ark, T. "NGLC Grants Sponsor Innovative New Schools in DC & Chicago." Getting Smart blog. September 2013. gettingsmart. com/2013/09/nglc-grants-sponsor-innovative-new-schools-in-dc-chicago/

150. Vander Ark, T. "CityBridge is Changing the School Landscape in DC." Getting Smart blog. October 2013. gettingsmart.com/2013/10/citybridge-changing-school-landscape-dc/

151. "Update on Summit—Denali and Beyond." Getting Smart blog. April 2014. gettingsmart.com/2014/04/update-summit-denali-beyond/

152. Speicher, S. "Design Thinking: A Human-Centered Approach to Innovation in Education." Getting Smart blog. July 2014. gettingsmart.com/2014/07/design-thinking-human-centered-approach-innovation-education/

153. Ibid.

154. Learn more about Boston's approach from the Workforce Strategy Center's briefing paper on Mayors and Workforce Development at collegeforamerica.org/reports/mayors_and_workforce_development_2012-08.pdf.

155. Vander Ark, T. "Personalized Learning Demands Lean, Blended, Iterative Approach." Getting Smart blog. February 2014. gettingsmart.com/2014/02/personalized-learning-demands-lean-blended-iterative-approach/

156. For details on Public Impact's definition of Opportunity Culture, see opportunityculture.org/opportunity-culture.

157. "What is Lean?" Lean Enterprise Institute. www.lean.org/whatslean/

158. For examples, see 10 ways students could co-create customized learning pathways at gettingsmart.com/2014/02/kids-co-created-customized-learning-pathways.

159. Hill, R. "Talent Is Underrated." Getting Smart blog. July 2014. gettingsmart.com/2014/07/talent-underrated/

160. Glaeser, E. *Triumph of the City: How Our Greatest Invention Makes Us Richer, Smarter, Greener, Healthier, and Happier.* London: Macmillan. 2011. www.amazon.com/Triumph-City-Greatest-Invention-Healthier/dp/0143120549

161. Access the full report at www.ceosforcities.org/city-vitals/research/city-vitals-i/.

162. Walker, Aaron, Personal communication. May 2014.

163. See the full fact sheet about Houston from the Broad Foundation at www.broadprize.org/asset/houstonfacts.pdf.

164. Vander Ark, T. "Smart Cities: Houston, We've Got an Opportunity Here." Getting Smart blog. December 2012. gettingsmart.com/2012/12/smart-cities-houston-weve-got-an-opportunity-here/

165. Grier, T. "For Houston ISD, The Talent Pipeline Flows Both Ways." Getting Smart blog. May 2014. gettingsmart.com/2014/05/houston-isd-talent-pipeline-flows-ways/

166. See the full fact sheet about Houston from the Broad Foundation at www.broadprize.org/asset/houstonfacts.pdf.

167. See The Learning Accelerator's fact sheet on EdTech procurement in HISD at learningaccelerator.org/media/fc2ec2cf/EdTechPurchasingSnapshot-FINAL-June2014.pdf.

168. Leshnick, S. and Law, T. "Building a 'Smart' Talent Pipeline." Getting Smart blog. June 2014. gettingsmart.com/2014/06/building-smart-talent-pipeline

169. Cator, K., Schneider, C. and Vander Ark, T. "Preparing Teachers for Deeper Learning." Digital Promise and Getting Smart. April 2014. cdno.gettingsmart.com/wp-content/uploads/2014/06/FINAL-Printable-DeeperLearningTeacherPrep.pdf

170. Vander Ark, C., Personal communication. July 2014.

171. Moe, M., Pampoulov, L, Jiang, L. and Franco, N. "The Next Silicon Valley?" GSV Media. May 2014. gallery.mailchimp.com/1b706b2cf8f39c9d033cc39b8/files/593880fc-9797-4ae8-b5b0-11e79258d887.pdf

172. Learn more about the Prime Minister and his leadership at gallery.mailchimp.com/1b706b2cf8f39c9d033cc39b8/files/593880fc-9797-4ae8-b5b0-11e79258d887.pdf.

173. Moe, M., Pampoulov, L, Jiang, L. and Franco, N. "The Next Silicon Valley?" GSV Media. May 2014. gallery.mailchimp.com/1b706b2cf8f39c9d033cc39b8/files/593880fc-9797-4ae8-b5b0-11e79258d887.pdf

174. EdFuel. "Map the Gap: Confronting The Leadership Talent Gap in The New Urban Education Ecosystem." 2014. edfuel.org/wp-content/uploads/2014/04/EdFuel-Map-the-Gap-final-report-29Apr2014.pdf

175. Lange, J. "New Study Reveals Trends in Professional Learning." Getting Smart blog. July 2014. gettingsmart.com/2014/07/new-study-reveals-trends-professional-learning/

176. Ibid.

177. Read about the current status of educator preparation and new approaches in "Preparing Teachers for Deeper Learning" at cdno.gettingsmart.com/wp-content/uploads/2014/06/FINAL-Printable-DeeperLearningTeacherPrep.pdf.

178. Burke, L. and Butler, S. "Accreditation: Removing the Barrier to Higher Education Reform." The Heritage Foundation. September 2012. www.heritage.org/research/reports/2012/09/accreditation-removing-the-barrier-to-higher-education-reform

179. Greenberg, J., McKee, A. and Walsh, K. "Teacher Prep Review." National Council on Teacher Quality. December 2013. www.nctq.org/dmsStage/Teacher_Prep_Review_2013_Report

180. "Chiefs for Change Statement on NCTQ Teacher Prep Review." Chiefs for Change. June 2014. chiefsforchange.org/chiefs-for-change-statement-on-nctq-teacher-prep-review-2/

181. Schneider, C. and Vander Ark, T. "Preparing Teachers for Deeper Learning." Getting Smart blog. May 2014. gettingsmart.com/2014/05/preparing-teachers-deeper-learning-3/

182. Vander Ark, T. "Fostering Next Gen Learning: a Q&A with INACOL's Susan Patrick." Getting Smart blog. July 2014.

183. Learn more about the partnership and $5 million grant at www.jkaf.org/5-million-grant-announced-for-doceo-centers-for-innovation-learning.

184. Read about the partnership to grow the STEM teaching force at www.wgu.edu/about_WGU/100Kin10_partnership_1-31-14.

185. Cator, K., Schneider, C. and Vander Ark, T. "Preparing Teachers for Deeper Learning." Digital Promise and Getting Smart. April 2014. cdno.gettingsmart.com/wp-content/uploads/2014/06/FINAL-Printable-DeeperLearningTeacherPrep.pdf

186. Nyren, C. "Innovation Leadership: Spurring & Supporting Entrepreneurship." Getting Smart blog. May 2014. gettingsmart.com/2014/05/smart-cities-innovation-leadership-spurring-supporting-entrepreneurship/

187. Ibid.

188. Vander Ark, T. "PBS: Taste of College Encourages Students to Continue Classes." Getting Smart Blog. July 2012. gettingsmart.com/2012/07/pbs-taste-college-encourages-students-continue-classes/

189. See Principal Gomez's full statement at ccta.psjaisd.us/apps/pages/index.jsp?uREC_ID=132671&type=d&pREC_ID=261307.

190. Vander Ark, T. "Educate Texas: 10 Years, 135 New Schools, Lots of Lessons." Getting Smart blog. February 2014. gettingsmart. com/2014/02/educate-texas-10-years-135-new-schools-lots-lessons/

191. Allen, L. and Wolfe, R. "Back on Track to College: A Texas School District Leverages State Policy to Put Dropouts on the Path to Success." Jobs for the Future. September 2010. www.jff.org/ publications/back-track-college-texas-school-district-leverages-state-policy-put-dropouts-path

192. Tang, G. "Collective Impact—Creating a Self-Sharpening Education System." Getting Smart blog. July 2014. gettingsmart. com/2014/07/collective-impact-creating-self-sharpening-education-system/

193. Kania, J. and Kramer, M. "Collective Impact." Stanford Social Innovation Review. Winter 2011. www.ssireview.org/articles/entry/ collective_impact

194. Smith, P. "What Would Real Community Engagement Look Like?" Getting Smart blog. May 2014. gettingsmart.com/2014/05/real-community-engagement-look-like/

195. Access the full I-SEEED grant proposal at www.wkkf.org/ news-and-media/article/2014/04/wkkf-family-engagement-grantee-cohort.

196. Vander Ark, T. "Closing the Motivation Gap." Getting Smart blog. December 2013. gettingsmart.com/2013/12/closing-motivation-gap/

197. Vander Ark, T. "What Does it Mean When a College Kid from Ecuador Beats the Best?" Getting Smart blog. October 2012. gettingsmart.com/2012/10/what-does-mean-when-college-kid-from-ecuador-beats-best/

198. Robinson, K. and Harris, A. "Parental Involvement Is Overrated." New York Times. April 2014. opinionator.blogs.nytimes. com/2014/04/12/parental-involvement-is-overrated/?_php=true&_type=blogs&_r=0

199. Vander Ark, T. "Good Work: Tapping the Dark Matter." Getting Smart blog. May 2014. gettingsmart.com/2013/04/good-work-tapping-the-dark-matter/

200. Ibid.

201. Donohue, N. "What Would Real Engagement Look Like?" Getting Smart blog. July 2014. gettingsmart.com/2014/07/real-engagement-look-like-2/

202. Vander Ark, T. "Good Work: Tapping the Dark Matter." Getting Smart blog. May 2014. gettingsmart.com/2013/04/good-work-tapping-the-dark-matter/.

203. See an interview with Donohue at https://www.youtube. com/watch?v=DWCB0eWOi5c

204. Bales, S. "Framing Education Reform: A FrameWorks MessageMemo." FrameWorks Institute. January 2010. frameworksinstitute.org/toolkits/educationreform/resources/pdf/ education_message_memo.pdf.

205. Kurtz, B. Personal communication. April, 2014

206. Butler, G. "Building Innovation Partnerships." Getting Smart blog. March 2014. gettingsmart.com/2014/03/building-innovation-partnerships/

207. Vander Ark, T. "Progress in Pakistan: Must Watch 10 Min Video on EdReform." Getting Smart blog. January 2014. gettingsmart. com/2014/01/progress-pakistan-must-watch-10-min-video-edreform/

208. Download the full report on the London Challenge at www.ofsted.gov.uk/resources/london-challenge.

209. The London Challenge is highlighted in the March 2014 Massachusetts Business Alliance for Education/Brightlines report, "The New Opportunity to Lead," accessible at www.mbae.org/wp-content/ uploads/2014/03/New-Opportunity-to-Lead.pdf.

210. Shalvey, D. "Choosing Excellent Schools—Not Charter Versus District." Getting Smart blog. July 2014. gettingsmart.com/2014/07/ choosing-excellent-schools-charter-versus-district/

211. Ibid.

212. Ibid.

213. Ibid.

214. Vander Ark, T. "CEOs Want Hard-Working Decision-Making Team Players." Getting Smart blog. May 2013. gettingsmart. com/2013/05/ceos-want-hard-working-decision-making-team-players/

215. The Business Council. "CEO Survey Results." February 2013 www.thebusinesscouncil.org/assets/TCB_BCS_FEB_2013.pdf

216. Vander Ark, T. "President Signs Jobs Bill." Getting Smart blog. July 2014. gettingsmart.com/2014/07/president-signs-jobs-bill/

217. Lynch, J. "Let's Persevere With College and Career Ready." Getting Smart blog. April 2014. gettingsmart.com/2014/04/lets-persevere-college-career-ready/

218. Cahill, M. Personal communication. May, 2014.

219. See the Work-Based Learning Toolkit at toolkit.jobs2careers. org/devtools/home.

220. Foroohar, R. "The School That Will Get You a Job." Time. February 2014. time.com/7066/the-school-that-will-get-you-a-job/

221. Vander Ark, T. "Career Education: Even College Grads Should be Employable." Getting Smart blog. June 2014. gettingsmart. com/2014/06/career-education-even-college-grads-employable/

222. Hodas, S. "Fostering Innovation in Cities." Getting Smart blog. June 2014. gettingsmart.com/2014/06/fostering-innovation-cities/

223. See the full methods statement at www.frameworksinstitute. org/sfa-methods.html.

224. See Gershenfeld's presentation "Stakeholder Alignment in Complex Systems" at www.buseco.monash.edu.au/mgt/research/acrew/cutcher-slides.pdf.

225. Ibid.

226. Donnelly, K. "The Importance of Culture." Getting Smart blog. May 2014. gettingsmart.com/2014/05/importance-culture/

227. Edmondson, J. and Landsman, G. "Quality Collective Impact = Impactful Innovation." Getting Smart blog. July 2014. gettingsmart. com/2014/07/quality-collective-impact-impactful-innovation/

228. See Education Sector Report "Striving for Success: A Model of Shared Accountability" at www.educationsector.org/publications/striving-student-success-model-shared-accountability.

229. See StriveTogether Cradle to Career Network members at www.strivetogether.org/cradle-career-network.

230. Edmondson, J. and Landsman, G. "Quality Collective Impact = Impactful Innovation." Getting Smart blog. July 2014. gettingsmart. com/2014/07/quality-collective-impact-impactful-innovation/

231. See StriveTogether Theory of Action at www.strivetogether. org/sites/default/files/images/StriveTogether%20Theory%20of%20 Action_0.pdf.

232. Edmondson, J. "The Difference between Collaboration and Collective Impact." Striving for Change blog. November 2012. www. strivetogether.org/blog/2012/11/the-difference-between-collaboration-and-collective-impact/

233. Edmondson, J. and Landsman, G. "Quality Collective Impact = Impactful Innovation." Getting Smart blog. July 2014. gettingsmart. com/2014/07/quality-collective-impact-impactful-innovation/

234. Ibid.

235. Tang, G. "Collective Impact—Creating a Self-Sharpening Education System." Getting Smart blog. July 2014. gettingsmart.com/2014/07/collective-impact-creating-self-sharpening-education-system/

236. Ibid.

237. Cator, K. "Building a National Innovation Partnership." Getting Smart blog. June 2014. gettingsmart.com/2014/06/building-national-innovation-partnership/

238. Ibid.

239. Ibid.

240. Ibid.

241. Haines, K. "Why Harbormasters Are Critical to a City's Ecosystem." Getting Smart blog. July 2014. gettingsmart.com/2014/07/harbormasters-critical-citys-ecosystem/

242. Ibid.

243. All quotes and attributions in this and the following paragraph originally appeared at gettingsmart.com/2014/03/transforming-city-collaborative-approach.

244. See an update about the blended learning pilots in Oakland at www.rogersfoundation.org/system/resources/0000/0052/Oakland_Blended_Learning_Case_Study_Part_3.pdf.

245. Vander Ark, T. "Oakland: Where Social Justice Meets EdTech." Getting Smart blog. June 2014. gettingsmart.com/2014/06/oakland-social-justice-meets-edtech/

246. Greenfield, M. and Vander Ark, T. "Boosting Impact: Why Foundations Should Invest In Education Venture Funds." Getting Smart. March 2014. cdno.gettingsmart.com/wp-content/uploads/2014/03/Boosting-Impact-Final.pdf

247. Greenfield, M. "Innovation Ecosystems: The Role of Impact Investing." Getting Smart blog. June 2014. gettingsmart.com/2014/06/innovation-ecosystems-role-impact-investing/

248. See a list of the most active venture capital investors in EdTech since 2009 at www.cbinsights.com/blog/ed-tech-most-active-venture-capital-investors-2009.

249. See the full statement of ReSchool Colorado's goals at dkfoundation.org/our-work/reschool-colorado/reschool-colorado.

250. Ibid.

251. Anderson, A. "What's Next in Education? A New Education System." Getting Smart blog. May 2014. gettingsmart.com/2014/05/whats-next-education-new-education-system/

252. Vander Ark, T. "Strategic Philanthropy Is Making Foundations Less Responsive." Getting Smart blog. June 2012. gettingsmart.com/2012/06/strategic-philanthropy-is-making-foundations-less-responsive/

253. Greenfield, M. and Vander Ark, T. "Boosting Impact: Why Foundations Should Invest In Education Venture Funds." Getting Smart. March 2014. cdno.gettingsmart.com/wp-content/uploads/2014/03/Boosting-Impact-Final.pdf

254. Vander Ark, T. "Good & Bad Marriages: Philanthropic Partnerships." Getting Smart blog. August 2013. gettingsmart.com/2013/08/good-bad-marriages-philanthropic-partnerships/

255. Ibid.

256. Find tips for building grantmaking partnerships at gettingsmart.com/2014/05/6-tips-building-grantmaking-partnerships.

257. All quotes and attributions in this and the following paragraph originally appeared at bits.blogs.nytimes.com/2014/05/18/marc-andreessen-on-the-future-of-silicon-valleys-and-the-next-big-technology/?_php=true&_type=blogs&emc=edit_dlbkam_20140519&nl=business&nlid=56697007&ref=technology&_r=0.

258. Vander Ark, T. "How Government Helps and Harms Entrepreneurs." Getting Smart blog. April 2014. gettingsmart.com/2014/04/government-helps-harms-entrepreneurs/

259. Knopp, Linda. *2006 State of the Business Incubation Industry.* National Business Incubation Association. 2007.

260. Vander Ark, T. "How Government Helps and Harms Entrepreneurs." Getting Smart blog. April 2014. gettingsmart.com/2014/04/government-helps-harms-entrepreneurs/

261. Greenfield, M. and Vander Ark, T. "Boosting Impact: Why Foundations Should Invest In Education Venture Funds." Getting Smart. March 2014. cdno.gettingsmart.com/wp-content/uploads/2014/03/Boosting-Impact-Final.pdf

262. Greenfield, M. and Vander Ark, T. "Boosting Impact: Why Foundations Should Invest In Education Venture Funds." Getting Smart. March 2014. gettingsmart.com/wp-content/uploads/2014/03/Boosting-Impact-Final.pdf

263. America Abroad Media. " How Government Helps and Harms Entrepreneurs." Public Radio International. March 6, 2014. https://itunes.apple.com/us/podcast/america-abroad/id162363213?mt=2"

264. Ibid.

265. Ibid.

266. Ibid.

267. Bailey, J., Schneider, C. and Vander Ark, T. "Using Prizes & Pull Mechanisms to Boost Learning." Digital Learning Now. June 2014. digitallearningnow.com/site/uploads/2014/06/Advanced-DLN-SmartSeries-PrizePull_09June20141.pdf

268. Bailey, J., Owens, D., Schneider, C., Vander Ark, T. and Waldron, R. "Smart Series Guide to EdTech Procurement." Digital Learning Now. January 2014. digitallearningnow.com/site/uploads/2014/05/Procurement-Paper-Final-Version.pdf

269. "Pull mechanisms encourage funding." Global Health Technologies Coalition. www.ghtcoalition.org/incentives-pull.php

270. Childress, S. "It's Time: Connecting What Students Need & What Entrepreneurs Create." Getting Smart blog. July

2014. gettingsmart.com/2014/07/time-connecting-students-need-entrepreneurs-create/

271. Ibid.

272. Ibid.

273. Bailey, J., Owens, D., Schneider, C., Vander Ark, T. and Waldron, R. "Smart Series Guide to EdTech Procurement." Digital Learning Now. January 2014. digitallearningnow.com/site/uploads/2014/05/Procurement-Paper-Final-Version.pdf

274. Vander Ark, K. "Las Vegas: Downtown Project, Blended Progress." Getting Smart blog. July 2014. gettingsmart.com/2014/07/smart-cities-viva-las-vegas/

275. Vander Ark, T. "Smart Cities: Chicago Develops in 'Leaps' and Bounds." Getting Smart blog. April 2014. gettingsmart.com/2014/04/smart-cities-chicago/

276. Ibid.

277. See a full description of the grant program at www2.ed.gov/programs/racetothetop-earlylearningchallenge/2013-early-learning-challenge-flyer.pdf.

278. Bornfreund, L., McCann, C., Williams, C. and Guernsey, L. "Beyond Subprime Learning." New America. 2014. www.newamerica.net/sites/newamerica.net/files/policydocs/Beyond_Subprime_Learning_by_Bornfreund-et-al_New_America_Jul2014.pdf

279. Ibid.

280. Bailey, J., Schneider, C. and Vander Ark, T. "Funding Students, Options, and Achievement." Digital Learning Now. April 2013. digitallearningnow.com/site/uploads/2013/04/Funding-Paper-Final1.pdf

281. Bailey, J., Schneider, C. and Vander Ark, T. "Navigating the Digital Shift: Implementation Strategies for Blended and Online Learning." Digital Learning Now. 2013. digitallearningnow.com/site/uploads/2013/10/DLN-ebook-PDF.pdf

282. Chuong, C. and Mead, S. "A Policy Playbook for Personalized Learning: Ideas for State and Local Policymakers." Bellwether Education Partners. June 2014. bellwethereducation.org/sites/default/files/PolicyPlays_Final.pdf

283. Bailey, J., Schneider, C. and Vander Ark, T. "Navigating the Digital Shift: Implementation Strategies for Blended and Online Learning." Digital Learning Now. 2013. digitallearningnow.com/site/uploads/2013/10/DLN-ebook-PDF.pdf

284. See more about WGU's approach at gettingsmart.com/2014/02/next-gen-teacher-prep-wgu-now-leading-stem-provider.

285. See more about College for America's approach at collegeforamerica.org/about/entry/approach#sthash.u1N9Hx8A.dpbs.

286. Vander Ark, T. "Mind Trust Develops The Smart Cities Formula." Getting Smart blog. April 2013. gettingsmart.com/2013/04/mind-trust-develops-the-smart-cities-formula/

287. Tully, M. "The Mind Trust Continues To Be Dynamic Force for Education Reform." *Indianapolis Star*. October 10, 2012. www.indystar.com/search/mind%20trust%20single%20handedly%20changing%20tenor/

288. "Could you build a better school?" *Chicago Tribune*. June 25, 2014. www.chicagotribune.com/news/opinion/plan/ct-mind-trust-school-reform-indianapolis-0625-20140625,0,2289826.story

289. All quotes and attributions in this paragraph originally appeared at gettingsmart.com/2014/04/smart-cities-new-orleans.

290. Learn more about the benefits of flex schools at gettingsmart.com/2012/05/10-reasons-every-district-should-open-a-flex-school.

291. Read more about internships and other best practices in work-based learning at gettingsmart.com/2013/08/best-practices-in-work-based-learning.

292. See a profile of Career Path High at gettingsmart.com/2013/06/career-path-high-career-college-ready-flex.

293. New York City's efforts are profiled at gettingsmart.com/2014/07/smart-cities-new-york.

294. Vander Ark, T. "NGLC Grants Sponsor Innovative New Schools In DC & Chicago." Getting Smart blog. September 2013. gettingsmart.com/2013/09/nglc-grants-sponsor-innovative-new-schools-in-dc-chicago/

295. Revenaugh, M. Personal communication. July, 2014.

296. See more about Wiseman and the CPCUP at vpaf.umd.edu/newsletters/spring2014/cpcup.html.

297. Stone, W. "A 'Lost Generation Of Workers': The Cost of Youth Unemployment." NPR www.npr.org/2014/07/02/327058018/a-lost-generation-of-workers-the-cost-of-youth-unemployment.

298. See more about the Association for High School Innovation at www.bigpicture.org/2008/10/alternative-high-school-initiative-key-convener/#sthash.1XX9TzeM.dpuf.

299. Lockett, P. "Our Kids Can't Wait." Getting Smart blog. May 2014. gettingsmart.com/2014/05/kids-cant-wait/

300. Vander Ark, T. "Short Cycle Efficacy Trials Key to Personalized Learning." Getting Smart blog. December 2013. gettingsmart.com/2013/12/short-cycle-efficacy-trials-key-personalized-learning/

301. Schneider, C. and Vander Ark, T. "Assessing Deeper Learning: A Survey of Performance Assessment and Mastery-Tracking Tools."

Getting Smart. April 2014. cdno4.gettingsmart.com/wp-content/uploads/2014/04/FINAL-Assessing-Deeper-Learning.pdf

302. See a variety of schools' system software maps at www.christenseninstitute.org/wp-content/uploads/2014/06/School-systems-software-maps.pdf.

303. Bailey, J., Carter, S., Schneider, C. and Vander Ark, T. "Data Backpacks: Portable Records & Learner Profiles." Digital Learning Now. October 2012. digitallearningnow.com/site/uploads/2014/05/DLN-Smart-Series-Databack-Final1.pdf

304. Read more about Rocky Mount Prep and other innovative schools at gettingsmart.com/2014/05/5-ways-new-tools-schools-transforming-special-education.

305. Thomas, G. "Everyone's Welcome: An Approach to Special Education." Getting Smart blog. December 2013. gettingsmart.com/2013/12/everyones-welcome-approach-special-education/

306. Ibid.

307. Ibid.

308. Danner, J. "What Would Real Engagement Look Like?" Getting Smart blog. April 2014. gettingsmart.com/2014/04/real-engagement-look-like/

309. Ibid.

310. Vander Ark, T. "Pearson Implements Efficacy Frame & Shares it With Sector." Getting Smart blog. November 2013. gettingsmart.com/2013/11/pearson-efficacy-report/

311. See information about the framework at efficacy.pearson.com.

312. Vander Ark, T. "Hey EdTech, Meet Scientific Inquiry; You Should Get Acquainted." Getting Smart blog. June 2014. gettingsmart.com/2014/06/hey-edtech-meet-scientific-inquiry-get-acquainted/

313. Vander Ark, T. "Why We Need 4.0 Schools In Every City." Getting Smart blog. November 2013. gettingsmart.com/2013/11/need-4-0-schools-every-city/

314. Vander Ark, T. "Smart Cities Denver: Where Advocates & Partnerships Are Making an Impact." Getting Smart blog. May 2014. gettingsmart.com/2014/05/smart-cities-denver-advocates-partnerships-making-impact/

315. Piketty, T. *Capital in the Twenty-First Century*, translated by Goldhammer, A. Cambridge: Harvard. 2014. www.amazon.com/gp/product/067443000X/ref=as_li_tl?ie=UTF8&camp=1789&creative=9325&creativeASIN=067443000X&linkCode=as2&tag=slatmaga-20&linkId=TOVHFVOQZVGQ2B5X

316. Weiss, J. "Policymaking and Innovation Mindsets." Getting Smart blog. April 2014. gettingsmart.com/2014/04/policymaking-innovation-mindsets/

317. Ibid.

318. All quotes in this paragraph originally appeared at gettingsmart.com/2014/04/policymaking-innovation-mindsets.

319. Vander Ark, T. "How Government Helps and Harms Entrepreneurs." Getting Smart blog. April 2014. gettingsmart.com/2014/04/government-helps-harms-entrepreneurs/

320. "South, West Have Fastest-Growing Cities, Census Bureau Reports; Three of Top 10 are in Texas Capital Area." U. S. Census Bureau. May 22, 2014. www.census.gov/newsroom/releases/archives/population/cb14-89.html

321. "America's Top States For Business 2014." CNBC. www.cnbc.com/id/101758236

322. "Kids Count 2014 Data Book: State Trends in Child Well-Being." Annie E. Casey Foundation. July 2014. www.aecf.org/m/databook/aecf-2014kidscountdatabook-embargoed-2014.pdf

323. Ryerse, M., Schneider, C. and Vander Ark, T. "Core & More: Guiding and Personalizing College & Career Readiness." Digital Learning Now. May 2014. digitallearningnow.com/site/uploads/2014/05/FINAL-Smart-Series-Core-and-More-Guidance.pdf

324. Learn more about Collegiate Learning Assessment at www.collegiatelearningassessment.org.

325. See "America Works: Education and Tracking for Tomorrow's Jobs." National Governor's Association. 2014. www.nga.org/files/live/sites/NGA/files/pdf/2014/1402-Moodys-AmericaWorks_35f.pdf

326. Learn more about the NGLC grant program at nextgenlearning.org/press-release/communities-educators-six-regions-join-effort-develop-%E2%80%9Cbreakthrough%E2%80%9D-schools.

327. Kubach, S. Personal correspondence. July, 2014.

328. Ibid.

329. See Vander Ark, T. "What Role Should States Play in the Shift to Personalized Learning?" Getting Smart blog. November 2013. gettingsmart.com/2013/11/role-states-play-shift-personalized-learning/

330. See Rose's "12 Basic Guidelines for Campaign Strategy" at www.campaignstrategy.org/articles/12basicguidelines.pdf

331. All quotes and attributions in this and the following two paragraphs originally appeared at gettingsmart.com/2012/09/the-skys-limit-16-must-read-quotes-michael-fullans-stratosphere.

332. Read more about why connectivity is critical to boosting learning at gettingsmart.com/2014/06/connectivity-critical-33-ways-broadband-boosts-learning.

333. Arnett, T. "How policy affects K-12 innovation." Clayton Christensen Institute for Disruptive Innovation. June 2014. www.christenseninstitute.org/how-policy-affects-k-12-innovation/

334. Hernandez, A. "Creating Innovative Ecosystems." Getting Smart blog. May 2014. gettingsmart.com/2014/05/creating-innovative-ecosystems/

335. Hanushek, E., Jamison, D., Jamison, A. and Woessmann, L. "Education and Economic Growth." *Education Next* 8 no. 2. Spring 2008. educationnext.org/education-and-economic-growth/

336. Bhatia, P. "Reimagining the World-Class City." Ozy.com. www.ozy.com/fast-forward/of-slums-skyscrapers/32423.article?utm_source=dd&utm_medium=email&utm_campaign=06302014

337. Hernandez, A. "Creating Innovative Ecosystems." Getting Smart blog. May 2014. gettingsmart.com/2014/05/creating-innovative-ecosystems/

To receive your non-transferable digital edition
of this book, please visit
www.eifrigpublishing.com/getting-smart
and follow the instructions provided.